Silvia Dubois

THE SCHOMBURG LIBRARY OF
NINETEENTH-CENTURY BLACK WOMEN WRITERS

General Editor, Henry Louis Gates, Jr.

Titles are listed chronologically; collections that include works published over a span of years are listed according to the publication date of their initial work.

Silvia Dubois, a Biografy

of
the Slav Who Whipt
Her Mistres and
Gand Her Fredom

C. W. LARISON, M.D.

*Edited with a Translation
and Introduction by*
JARED C. LOBDELL

❧ ❧ ❧

❧ ❧ ❧

OXFORD UNIVERSITY PRESS
New York   Oxford

Oxford University Press

Oxford   New York   Toronto
Delhi   Bombay   Calcutta   Madras   Karachi
Petaling Jaya   Singapore   Hong Kong   Tokyo
Nairobi   Dar es Salaam   Cape Town
Melbourne   Auckland

and associated companies in
Berlin   Ibadan

Library of Congress Cataloging-in-Publication Data

Larison, Cornelius Wilson, 1837–1910.
Silvia Dubois: a biografy of the slav who whipt her
mistres and gand her fredom.
(The Schomburg library of nineteenth-century black
women writers)
1. Dubois, Silvia, 1788 or 9–1889.   2. Slaves—United States
—Biography.   3. Afro-Americans—Biography.   4. English
language—Phonetic transcriptions.   I. Lobdell, Jared, 1937–
II. Title.   III. Series.
E444.D83L37   1988   305.5'67'0924 [B]   87-12353
ISBN 0-19-505239-0
ISBN 0-19-505267-6 (set)
ISBN 0-19-506671-5 (PBK.)

2 4 6 8 10 9 7 5 3 1

Printed in the United States of America

The
Schomburg Library
of
Nineteenth-Century
Black Women Writers
is
Dedicated
in Memory
of

PAULINE AUGUSTA COLEMAN GATES

1916–1987

PUBLISHER'S NOTE

FOREWORD
In Her Own Write

Henry Louis Gates, Jr.

One muffled strain in the Silent South, a jarring chord and a
vague and uncomprehended cadenza has been and still is the
Negro. And of that muffled chord, the one mute and voiceless note has been the sadly expectant Black Woman, ...

The "other side" has not been represented by one who "lives
there." And not many can more sensibly realize and more
accurately tell the weight and the fret of the "long dull pain"
than the open-eyed but hitherto voiceless Black Woman of
America.

. . . as our Caucasian barristers are not to blame if they
cannot *quite* put themselves in the dark man's place, neither
should the dark man be wholly expected fully and adequately
to reproduce the exact Voice of the Black Woman.

—ANNA JULIA COOPER, *A Voice From the South* (1892)

The birth of the Afro-American literary tradition occurred
in 1773, when Phillis Wheatley published a book of poetry.
Despite the fact that her book garnered for her a remarkable
amount of attention, Wheatley's journey to the printer had
been a most arduous one. Sometime in 1772, a young African girl walked demurely into a room in Boston to undergo
an oral examination, the results of which would determine
the direction of her life and work. Perhaps she was shocked
upon entering the appointed room. For there, perhaps gath-

ered in a semicircle, sat eighteen of Boston's most notable citizens. Among them were John Erving, a prominent Boston merchant; the Reverend Charles Chauncy, pastor of the Tenth Congregational Church; and John Hancock, who would later gain fame for his signature on the Declaration of Independence. At the center of this group was His Excellency, Thomas Hutchinson, governor of Massachusetts, with Andrew Oliver, his lieutenant governor, close by his side.

Why had this august group been assembled? Why had it seen fit to summon this young African girl, scarcely eighteen years old, before it? This group of "the most respectable Characters in *Boston*," as it would later define itself, had assembled to question closely the African adolescent on the slender sheaf of poems that she claimed to have "written by herself." We can only speculate on the nature of the questions posed to the fledgling poet. Perhaps they asked her to identify and explain—for all to hear—exactly who were the Greek and Latin gods and poets alluded to so frequently in her work. Perhaps they asked her to conjugate a verb in Latin or even to translate randomly selected passages from the Latin, which she and her master, John Wheatley, claimed that she "had made some Progress in." Or perhaps they asked her to recite from memory key passages from the texts of John Milton and Alexander Pope, the two poets by whom the African claimed to be most directly influenced. We do not know.

We do know, however, that the African poet's responses were more than sufficient to prompt the eighteen august gentlemen to compose, sign, and publish a two-paragraph "Attestation," an open letter "To the Publick" that prefaces Phillis Wheatley's book and that reads in part:

> We whose Names are under-written, do assure the World, that the Poems specified in the following Page, were (as we

verily believe) written by Phillis, a young Negro Girl, who was but a few Years since, brought an uncultivated Barbarian from *Africa,* and has ever since been, and now is, under the Disadvantage of serving as a Slave in a Family in this Town. She has been examined by some of the best Judges, and is thought qualified to write them.

So important was this document in securing a publisher for Wheatley's poems that it forms the signal element in the prefatory matter preceding her *Poems on Various Subjects, Religious and Moral,* published in London in 1773.

Without the published "Attestation," Wheatley's publisher claimed, few would believe that an African could possibly have written poetry all by herself. As the eighteen put the matter clearly in their letter, "Numbers would be ready to suspect they were not really the Writings of Phillis." Wheatley and her master, John Wheatley, had attempted to publish a similar volume in 1772 in Boston, but Boston publishers had been incredulous. One year later, "Attestation" in hand, Phillis Wheatley and her master's son, Nathaniel Wheatley, sailed for England, where they completed arrangements for the publication of a volume of her poems with the aid of the Countess of Huntington and the Earl of Dartmouth.

This curious anecdote, surely one of the oddest oral examinations on record, is only a tiny part of a larger, and even more curious, episode in the Enlightenment. Since the beginning of the sixteenth century, Europeans had wondered aloud whether or not the African "species of men," as they were most commonly called, *could* ever create formal literature, could ever master "the arts and sciences." If they could, the argument ran, then the African variety of humanity was fundamentally related to the European variety. If not, then it seemed clear that the African was destined by nature to be a slave. This was the burden shouldered by Phillis Wheatley when she successfully defended herself and the authorship of her book against counterclaims and doubts.

Indeed, with her successful defense, Wheatley launched two traditions at once—the black American literary tradition *and* the black woman's literary tradition. If it is extraordinary that not just one but both of these traditions were founded simultaneously by a black woman—certainly an event unique in the history of literature—it is also ironic that this important fact of common, coterminous literary origins seems to have escaped most scholars.

That the progenitor of the black literary tradition was a woman means, in the most strictly literal sense, that all subsequent black writers have evolved in a matrilinear line of descent, and that each, consciously or unconsciously, has extended and revised a canon whose foundation was the poetry of a black woman. Early black writers seem to have been keenly aware of Wheatley's founding role, even if most of her white reviewers were more concerned with the implications of her race than her gender. Jupiter Hammon, for example, whose 1760 broadside "An Evening Thought. Salvation by Christ, With Penitential Cries" was the first individual poem published by a black American, acknowledged Wheatley's influence by selecting her as the subject of his second broadside, "An Address to Miss Phillis Wheatly [*sic*], Ethiopian Poetess, in Boston," which was published at Hartford in 1778. And George Moses Horton, the second Afro-American to publish a book of poetry in English (1829), brought out in 1838 an edition of his *Poems By A Slave* bound together with Wheatley's work. Indeed, for fifty-six years, between 1773 and 1829, when Horton published *The Hope of Liberty*, Wheatley was the *only* black person to have published a book of imaginative literature in English. So central was this black woman's role in the shaping of the Afro-American literary tradition that, as one historian has maintained, the history of the reception of Phillis Wheatley's poetry *is* the history of Afro-American literary criticism. Well into the nineteenth century, Wheatley and the black literary tradition were the same entity.

But Wheatley is not the only black woman writer who stands as a pioneering figure in Afro-American literature. Just as Wheatley gave birth to the genre of black poetry, Ann Plato was the first Afro-American to publish a book of essays (1841) and Harriet E. Wilson was the first black person to publish a novel in the United States (1859).

Despite this pioneering role of black women in the tradition, however, many of their contributions before this century have been all but lost or unrecognized. As Hortense Spillers observed as recently as 1983,

> With the exception of a handful of autobiographical narratives from the nineteenth century, the black woman's realities are virtually suppressed until the period of the Harlem Renaissance and later. Essentially the black woman as artist, as intellectual spokesperson for her own cultural apprenticeship, has not existed before, for anyone. At the source of [their] own symbol-making task, [the community of black women writers] confronts, therefore, a tradition of work that is quite recent, its continuities, broken and sporadic.

Until now, it has been extraordinarily difficult to establish the formal connections between early black women's writing and that of the present, precisely because our knowledge of their work has been broken and sporadic. Phillis Wheatley, for example, while certainly the most reprinted and discussed poet in the tradition, is also one of the least understood. Ann Plato's seminal work, *Essays* (which includes biographies and poems), has not been reprinted since it was published a century and a half ago. And Harriet Wilson's *Our Nig,* her compelling novel of a black woman's expanding consciousness in a racist Northern antebellum environment, never received even *one* review or comment at a time when virtually *all* works written by black people were heralded by abolitionists as salient arguments against the existence of human slavery. Many of the books reprinted in this set experienced a similar fate, the most dreadful fate for an author: that of being ignored then relegated to the obscurity of the rare book section of a university library. We can only wonder how many other texts in the black woman's tradition have been lost to this generation of readers or remain unclassified or uncatalogued and, hence, unread.

This was not always so, however. Black women writers dominated the final decade of the nineteenth century, perhaps spurred to publish by an 1886 essay entitled "The Coming American Novelist," which was published in *Lippincott's Monthly Magazine* and written by "A Lady From Philadelphia." This pseudonymous essay argued that the "Great American Novel" would be written by a black person. Her argument is so curious that it deserves to be repeated:

> When we come to formulate our demands of the Coming American Novelist, we will agree that he must be native-born. His ancestors may come from where they will, but we must give him a birthplace and have the raising of him. Still, the longer his family has been here the better he will represent us. Suppose he should have no country but ours, no traditions but those he has learned here, no longings apart from us, no future except in our future—the orphan of the world, he finds with us his home. And with all this, suppose he refuses to be fused into that grand conglomerate we call the "American type." With us, he is not of us. He is original, he has humor, he is tender, he is passive and fiery, he has been

taught what we call justice, and he has his own opinion about it. He has suffered everything a poet, a dramatist, a novelist need suffer before he comes to have his lips anointed. And with it all he is in one sense a spectator, a little out of the race. How would these conditions go towards forming an original development? In a word, suppose the coming novelist is of African origin? When one comes to consider the subject, there is no improbability in it. One thing is certain,—our great novel will not be written by the typical American.

An atypical American, indeed. Not only would the great American novel be written by an African-American, it would be written by an African-American *woman:*

> Yet farther: I have used the generic masculine pronoun because it is convenient; but Fate keeps revenge in store. It was a woman who, taking the wrongs of the African as her theme, wrote the novel that awakened the world to their reality, and why should not the coming novelist be a woman as well as an African? She—the woman of that race—has some claims on Fate which are not yet paid up.

It is these claims on fate that we seek to pay by publishing The Schomburg Library of Nineteenth-Century Black Women Writers.

This theme would be repeated by several black women authors, most notably by Anna Julia Cooper, a prototypical black feminist whose 1892 *A Voice From the South* can be considered to be one of the original texts of the black feminist movement. It was Cooper who first analyzed the fallacy of referring to "the Black man" when speaking of black people and who argued that just as white men cannot speak through the consciousness of black men, neither can black *men* "fully and adequately . . . reproduce the exact Voice of the Black Woman." Gender and race, she argues, cannot be conflated, except in the instance of a black woman's voice, and it is this voice which must be uttered and to which we must listen. As Cooper puts the matter so compellingly:

> It is not the intelligent woman vs. the ignorant woman; nor the white woman vs. the black, the brown, and the red,—it is not even the cause of woman vs. man. Nay, 'tis woman's strongest vindication for speaking that *the world needs to hear her voice*. It would be subversive of every human interest that the cry of one-half the human family be stifled. Woman in stepping from the pedestal of statue-like inactivity in the domestic shrine, and daring to think and move and speak,— to undertake to help shape, mold, and direct the thought of her age, is merely completing the circle of the world's vision. Hers is every interest that has lacked an interpreter and a defender. Her cause is linked with that of every agony that has been dumb—every wrong that needs a voice.
>
> It is no fault of man's that he has not been able to see truth from her standpoint. It does credit both to his head and heart that no greater mistakes have been committed or even wrongs perpetrated while she sat making tatting and snipping paper flowers. Man's own innate chivalry and the mutual interdependence of their interests have insured his treating her cause, in the main at least, as his own. And he is pardonably surprised and even a little chagrined, perhaps, to find his legislation not considered "perfectly lovely" in every respect. But in any case his work is only impoverished by her remaining dumb. The world has had to limp along with the wobbling gait and one-sided hesitancy of a man with one eye. Suddenly the bandage is removed from the other eye and the whole body is filled with light. It sees a circle where before it saw a segment. The darkened eye restored, every member rejoices with it.

The myopic sight of the darkened eye can only be restored when the full range of the black woman's voice, with its own special timbres and shadings, remains mute no longer.

Similarly, Victoria Earle Matthews, an author of short stories and essays, and a cofounder in 1896 of the National Association of Colored Women, wrote in her stunning essay, "The Value of Race Literature" (1895), that "when the literature of our race is developed, it will of necessity be different in all essential points of greatness, true heroism and real Christianity from what we may at the present time, for convenience, call American literature." Matthews argued that this great tradition of Afro-American literature would be the textual outlet "for the unnaturally suppressed inner lives which our people have been compelled to lead." Once these "unnaturally suppressed inner lives" of black people are unveiled, no "grander diffusion of mental light" will shine more brightly, she concludes, than that of the articulate Afro-American woman:

> And now comes the question, What part shall we women play in the Race Literature of the future? . . . within the compass of one small journal ["Woman's Era"] we have struck out a new line of departure—a journal, a record of Race interests gathered from all parts of the United States, carefully selected, moistened, winnowed and garnered by the ablest intellects of educated colored women, shrinking at no lofty theme, shirking no serious duty, aiming at every possible excellence, and determined to do their part in the future uplifting of the race.
>
> If twenty women, by their concentrated efforts in one literary movement, can meet with such success as has engendered, planned out, and so successfully consummated this convention, what much more glorious results, what wider spread success, what grander diffusion of mental light will not come forth at the bidding of the enlarged hosts of women writers, already called into being by the stimulus of your efforts?
>
> And here let me speak one word for my journalistic sisters

who have already entered the broad arena of journalism. Before the "Woman's Era" had come into existence, no one except themselves can appreciate the bitter experience and sore disappointments under which they have at all times been compelled to pursue their chosen vocations.

If their brothers of the press have had their difficulties to contend with, I am here as a sister journalist to state, from the fullness of knowledge, that their task has been an easy one compared with that of the colored woman in journalism.

Woman's part in Race Literature, as in Race building, is the most important part and has been so in all ages. . . . All through the most remote epochs she has done her share in literature. . . .

One of the most important aspects of this set is the republication of the salient texts from 1890 to 1910, which literary historians could well call "The Black Woman's Era." In addition to Mary Helen Washington's definitive edition of Cooper's *A Voice From the South*, we have reprinted two novels by Amelia Johnson, Frances Harper's *Iola Leroy*, two novels by Emma Dunham Kelley, Alice Dunbar-Nelson's two impressive collections of short stories, and Pauline Hopkins's three serialized novels as well as her monumental novel, *Contending Forces*—all published between 1890 and 1910. Indeed, black women published more works of fiction in these two decades than black men had published in the previous half century. Nevertheless, this great achievement has been ignored.

Moreover, the writings of nineteenth-century Afro-American women in general have remained buried in obscurity, accessible only in research libraries or in overpriced and poorly edited reprints. Many of these books have never been reprinted at all; in some instances only one or two copies are extant. In these works of fiction, poetry, autobiography, biography, essays, and journalism resides the mind of the nineteenth-century Afro-American woman. Until these works are made readily available to teachers and their students, a significant segment of the black tradition will remain silent.

Oxford University Press, in collaboration with the Schomburg Center for Research in Black Culture, is publishing thirty volumes of these compelling works, each of which contains an introduction by an expert in the field. The set includes such rare texts as Johnson's *The Hazeley Family* and *Clarence and Corinne*, Plato's *Essays,* the most complete edition of Phillis Wheatley's poems and letters, Emma Dunham Kelley's pioneering novel *Megda,* several previously unpublished stories and a novel by Alice Dunbar-Nelson, and the first collected volumes of Pauline Hopkins's three serialized novels and Frances Harper's poetry. We also present four volumes of poetry by such women as Mary Eliza Tucker Lambert, Adah Menken, Josephine Heard, and Maggie Johnson. Numerous slave and spiritual narratives, a newly discovered novel—*Four Girls at Cottage City*—by Emma Dunham Kelley (-Hawkins), and the first American edition of *Wonderful Adventures of Mrs. Seacole in Many Lands* are also among the texts included.

In addition to resurrecting the works of black women authors, it is our hope that this set will facilitate the resurrection of the Afro-American woman's literary tradition itself by unearthing its nineteenth-century roots. In the works of Nella Larsen and Jessie Fauset, Zora Neale Hurston and Ann Petry, Lorraine Hansberry and Gwendolyn Brooks, Paule Marshall and Toni Cade Bambara, Audre Lorde and Rita Dove, Toni Morrison and Alice Walker, Gloria Naylor and Jamaica Kincaid, these roots have branched luxuriantly. The eighteenth- and nineteenth-century authors whose works are presented in this set founded and nurtured the black women's literary tradition, which must be revived, explicated, analyzed, and debated before we can understand more completely the formal shaping of this tradition within a tradition, a coded literary universe through which, regrettably, we are only just beginning to navigate our way. As Anna Cooper said nearly one hundred years ago, we have been blinded by the loss of sight in one eye and have therefore been unable to detect the full *shape* of the Afro-American literary tradition.

Literary works configure into a tradition not because of some mystical collective unconscious determined by the biology of race or gender, but because writers read other writers and *ground* their representations of experience in models of language provided largely by other writers to whom they feel akin. It is through this mode of literary revision, amply evident in the *texts* themselves—in formal echoes, recast metaphors, even in parody—that a "tradition" emerges and defines itself.

This is formal bonding, and it is only through formal bonding that we can know a literary tradition. The collective publication of these works by black women now, for the first time, makes it possible for scholars and critics, male and female, black and white, to *demonstrate* that black women writers read, and revised, other black women writers. To demonstrate this set of formal literary relations is to demonstrate that sexuality, race, and gender are both the condition and the basis of *tradition*—but tradition as found in discrete acts of language use.

A word is in order about the history of this set. For the past decade, I have taught a course, first at Yale and then at Cornell, entitled "Black Women and Their Fictions," a course that I inherited from Toni Morrison, who developed it in the mid-1970s for Yale's Program in Afro-American Studies. Although the course was inspired by the remarkable accomplishments of black women novelists since 1970, I gradually extended its beginning date to the late nineteenth century, studying Frances Harper's *Iola Leroy* and Anna Julia Cooper's *A Voice From the South,* both published in 1892. With the discovery of Harriet E. Wilson's seminal novel, *Our Nig* (1859), and Jean Yellin's authentication of Harriet Jacobs's brilliant slave narrative, *Incidents in the Life of a Slave Girl* (1861), a survey course spanning over a century and a quarter emerged.

But the discovery of *Our Nig,* as well as the interest in nineteenth-century black women's writing that this discovery generated, convinced me that even the most curious and diligent scholars knew very little of the extensive history of the creative writings of Afro-American women before 1900. Indeed, most scholars of Afro-American literature had never even read most of the books published by black women, simply because these books—of poetry, novels, short stories, essays, and autobiography—were mostly accessible only in rare book sections of university libraries. For reasons unclear to me even today, few of these marvelous renderings of the Afro-American woman's consciousness were reprinted in the late 1960s and early 1970s, when so many other texts of the Afro-American literary tradition were resurrected from the dark and silent graveyard of the out-of-print and were reissued in facsimile editions aimed at the hungry readership for canonical texts in the nascent field of black studies.

So, with the help of several superb research assistants—including David Curtis, Nicola Shilliam, Wendy Jones, Sam Otter, Janadas Devan, Suvir Kaul, Cynthia Bond, Elizabeth Alexander, and Adele Alexander—and with the expert advice

Foreword

of scholars such as William Robinson, William Andrews, Mary Helen Washington, Maryemma Graham, Jean Yellin, Houston A. Baker, Jr., Richard Yarborough, Hazel Carby, Joan R. Sherman, Frances Foster, and William French, dozens of bibliographies were used to compile a list of books written or narrated by black women mostly before 1910. Without the assistance provided through this shared experience of scholarship, the scholar's true legacy, this project could not have been conceived. As the list grew, I was struck by how very many of these titles that I, for example, had never even heard of, let alone read, such as Ann Plato's *Essays*, Louisa Picquet's slave narrative, or Amelia Johnson's two novels, *Clarence and Corinne* and *The Hazeley Family*. Through our research with the Black Periodical Fiction and Poetry Project (funded by NEH and the Ford Foundation), I also realized that several novels by black women, including three works of fiction by Pauline Hopkins, had been serialized in black periodicals, but had never been collected and published as books. Nor had the several books of poetry published by black women, such as the prolific Frances E. W. Harper, been collected and edited. When I discovered still another "lost" novel by an Afro-American woman (*Four Girls at Cottage City*, published in 1898 by Emma Dunham Kelley-Hawkins), I decided to attempt to edit a collection of reprints of these works and to publish them as a "library" of black women's writings, in part so that I could read them myself.

Convincing university and trade publishers to undertake this project proved to be a difficult task. Despite the commercial success of *Our Nig* and of the several reprint series of women's works (such as Virago, the Beacon Black Women Writers Series, and Rutgers' American Women Writers Series), several presses rejected the project as "too large," "too limited," or as "commercially unviable." Only two publishers recognized the viability and the import of the project and, of these, Oxford's commitment to publish the titles simultaneously as a set made the press's offer irresistible.

While attempting to locate original copies of these exceedingly rare books, I discovered that most of the texts were housed at the Schomburg Center for Research in Black Culture, a branch of The New York Public Library, under the direction of Howard Dodson. Dodson's infectious enthusiasm for the project and his generous collaboration, as well as that of his stellar staff (especially Diana Lachatanere, Sharon Howard, Ellis Haizip, Richard Newman, and Betty Gubert), led to a joint publishing initiative that produced this set as part of the Schomburg's major fund-raising campaign. Without Dodson's foresight and generosity of spirit, the set would not have materialized. Without William P. Sisler's masterful editorship at Oxford and his staff's careful attention to detail, the set would have remained just another grand idea that tends to languish in a scholar's file cabinet.

I would also like to thank Dr. Michael Winston and Dr. Thomas C. Battle, Vice-President of Academic Affairs and the Director of the Moorland-Spingarn Research Center (respectively) at Howard University, for their unending encouragement, support, and collaboration in this project, and Esme E. Bhan at Howard for her meticulous research and bibliographical skills. In addition, I would like to acknowledge the aid of the staff at the libraries of Duke University, Cornell University (especially Tom Weissinger and Donald Eddy), the Boston Public Library, the Western Reserve Historical Society, the Library of Congress, and Yale University. Linda Robbins, Marion Osmun, Sarah Flanagan, and Gerard Case, all members of the staff at Oxford, were extraordinarily effective at coordinating, editing, and producing the various segments of each text in the set. Candy Ruck, Nina de Tar, and Phillis Molock expertly typed reams of correspondence and manuscripts connected to the project.

I would also like to express my gratitude to my colleagues who edited and introduced the individual titles in the set. Without their attention to detail, their willingness to meet strict deadlines, and their sheer enthusiasm for this project, the set could not have been published. But finally and ultimately, I would hope that the publication of the set would help to generate even more scholarly interest in the black women authors whose work is presented here. Struggling against the seemingly insurmountable barriers of racism *and* sexism, while often raising families and fulfilling full-time professional obligations, these women managed nevertheless to record their thoughts and feelings and to *testify* to all who dare read them that the will to harness the power of collective endurance and survival is the will to write.

The Schomburg Library of Nineteenth-Century Black Women Writers is dedicated in memory of Pauline Augusta Coleman Gates, who died in the spring of 1987. It was she who inspired in me the love of learning and the love of literature. I have encountered in the books of this set no will more determined, no courage more noble, no mind more sublime, no self more celebratory of the achievements of all Afro-American women, and indeed of life itself, than her own.

A NOTE FROM
THE SCHOMBURG CENTER

Howard Dodson

The Schomburg Center for Research in Black Culture, The New York Public Library, is pleased to join with Dr. Henry Louis Gates and Oxford University Press in presenting The Schomburg Library of Nineteenth-Century Black Women Writers. This thirty-volume set includes the work of a generation of black women whose writing has only been available previously in rare book collections. The materials reprinted in twenty-four of the thirty volumes are drawn from the unique holdings of the Schomburg Center.

A research unit of The New York Public Library, the Schomburg Center has been in the forefront of those institutions dedicated to collecting, preserving, and providing access to the records of the black past. In the course of its two generations of acquisition and conservation activity, the Center has amassed collections totaling more than 5 million items. They include over 100,000 bound volumes, 85,000 reels and sets of microforms, 300 manuscript collections containing some 3.5 million items, 300,000 photographs and extensive holdings of prints, sound recordings, film and videotape, newspapers, artworks, artifacts, and other book and nonbook materials. Together they vividly document the history and cultural heritages of people of African descent worldwide.

Though established some sixty-two years ago, the Center's book collections date from the sixteenth century. Its oldest item, an Ethiopian Coptic Tunic, dates from the eighth or ninth century. Rare materials, however, are most available for the nineteenth-century African-American experience. It is from these holdings that the majority of the titles selected for inclusion in this set are drawn.

The nineteenth century was a formative period in African-American literary and cultural history. Prior to the Civil War, the majority of black Americans living in the United States were held in bondage. Law and practice forbade teaching them to read or write. Even after the war, many of the impediments to learning and literary productivity remained. Nevertheless, black men and women of the nineteenth century persevered in both areas. Moreover, more African-Americans than we yet realize turned their observations, feelings, social viewpoints, and creative impulses into published works. In time, this nineteenth-century printed record included poetry, short stories, histories, novels, autobiographies, social criticism, and theology, as well as economic and philosophical treatises. Unfortunately, much of this body of literature remained, until very recently, relatively inaccessible to twentieth-century scholars, teachers, creative artists, and others interested in black life. Prior to the late 1960s, most Americans (black as well as white) had never heard of these nineteenth-century authors, much less read their works.

The civil rights and black power movements created unprecedented interest in the thought, behavior, and achievements of black people. Publishers responded by revising traditional texts, introducing the American public to a new generation of African-American writers, publishing a variety of thematic anthologies, and reprinting a plethora of "classic texts" in African-American history, literature, and art. The reprints usually appeared as individual titles or in a series of bound volumes or microform formats.

The Schomburg Center, which has a long history of supporting publishing that deals with the history and culture of Africans in diaspora, became an active participant in many of the reprint revivals of the 1960s. Since hard copies of original printed works are the preferred formats for producing facsimile reproductions, publishers frequently turned to the Schomburg Center for copies of these original titles. In addition to providing such material, Schomburg Center staff members offered advice and consultation, wrote introductions, and occasionally entered into formal copublishing arrangements in some projects.

Most of the nineteenth-century titles reprinted during the 1960s, however, were by and about black men. A few black women were included in the longer series, but works by lesser known black women were generally overlooked. The Schomburg Library of Nineteenth-Century Black Women Writers is both a corrective to these previous omissions and an important contribution to Afro-American literary history in its own right. Through this collection of volumes, the thoughts, perspectives, and creative abilities of nineteenth-century African-American women, as captured in books and pamphlets published in large part before 1910, are again being made available to the general public. The Schomburg Center is pleased to be a part of this historic endeavor.

I would like to thank Professor Gates for initiating this project. Thanks are due both to him and Mr. William P. Sisler of Oxford University Press for giving the Schomburg Center an opportunity to play such a prominent role in the set. Thanks are also due to my colleagues at The New York Public Library and the Schomburg Center, especially Dr. Vartan Gregorian, Richard De Gennaro, Paul Fasana, Betsy

Pinover, Richard Newman, Diana Lachatanere, Glenderlyn Johnson, and Harold Anderson for their assistance and support. I can think of no better way of demonstrating than in this set the role the Schomburg Center plays in assuring that the black heritage will be available for future generations.

CONTENTS

SILVIA DUBOIS,

BORN MARCH 5th, 1768.

Silvia Dubois

INTRODUCTION

Jared C. Lobdell

This book may be mostly history or it may be mostly folklore, but it is in any case well worth reading. It is a colloquy—an extended interview—with a long foreword by the interviewer and two appendices, one of them mine, and it is the product of a meeting between two "originals" of the sort that seem to have been commoner in the last century than in this.

Cornelius Wilson Larison, who conducted the interview (or interviews, since there are also three short exchanges preserved in the first appendix), was a physician, sometime professor at Bucknell (then the University of Lewisburg), founder of his own school (the Academy of Science and Art at Ringoes, New Jersey), and, above all, pioneer in spelling reform. To this last we owe, first, the existence of the Reminiscences of Sylvia Dubois, and second, the fact that (up until 1980, at least) virtually no one read them—they being printed in Dr. Larison's singular phonetic alphabet.

The colloquy took place on January 27, 1883, on Sourland Mountain, near the border between Hunterdon and Somerset counties in New Jersey; it was printed by Dr. Larison in December 1883, along with bits and pieces of the interviews on November 1, November 20, and December 20, 1883, and Dr. Larison's own remarks. The original version was reprinted photographically by the Negro Universities Press in 1969 and a version in normalized spelling was published by the Princeton History Project in the *Princeton Recollector*, vol. V, no. 4 (Winter 1980). This book is an edited and annotated version of the original text, a facsimile reprint of which appears at the end of the volume. My normalization of Dr. Larison's spelling—including that of Sylvia's name—differs from the *Recollector* version in a number of instances, and I have not taken Sylvia's dating of events (including her birth) on faith.

Indeed, dating represents the chief editorial problem. While we know that Dr. Larison was born in 1837 and died in 1910, it is far from clear when Sylvia Dubois was born: her death, as it happens, can be dated within a few months.[1] Although Dr. Larison attempted to verify Sylvia's putative birth date—March 5, 1768—his verification will not stand up to further inquiry. In the paragraphs following (from original, pp. 83–87), I have interspersed his search for "verification" with my own comments on what he wrote.

> To verify the statements above made respecting Sylvia's age [that she was born two days after Richard Compton, who was born March 3, 1768], I visited Mr. Gomo to consult the ancient record of the Compton family. I soon learned that Mrs. Gomo was a niece of Richard Compton—that she was the daughter of Richard Compton's sister Deborah, who was born January 5, 1793. This lady, Deborah Compton, had married Vanlieu, by whom she had Mrs. Gomo. After Vanlieu's death she married D. Danbury. After Danbury's death, she lived with her daughter, Mrs. Gomo, to whom she used to tell that her brother Richard and Sylvia Dubois were about of an age.

Thus far no particular problems with the trail, though second-hand hearsay evidence is not much to go on.

From second-hand hearsay the account jumps farther afield, to third-hand hearsay:

> Mrs. Gomo, now an old lady [in her sixties, actually] informs me that several old folks used to tell her, when a girl, that

her Uncle Richard and Sylvia Dubois were about of the same age, that they had seen both Richard and Sylvia nurse the same mother at the same time, and that her Uncle Richard used to tell that his mother used to say that he was two days older than Sylvia. [Of course, third-hand evidence is not the same as no evidence.]

It happened that the old Bible in the possession of Mrs. Gomo did not contain a full record of the Compton family, that the record here made dated no farther back than the birth of Deborah Compton, which occurred, as above stated, January 5, 1793. But Mrs. Gomo informed me that the old Bible, having the ancient record for which I was searching, was in possession of her daughter, Mrs. John Elbertson, living about two miles east of Rock Mills. Upon visiting Mrs. Elbertson, and stating the purpose of my visit, she kindly produced the old book and welcomed me to the hospitalities of her comfortable home. [Now, finally, the hunt is winding to a close.]

In this record I found, among others, the following statement: Richard Compton, born March 3, 1768; Deborah Compton born January 5, 1793. Hence we learn that, were Richard Compton still living, he would be almost 115 years old. Then, if tradition is true, and in this case it is corroborated in so many ways that I cannot doubt it, Sylvia Dubois will be 115 years old upon the 5th day of March, 1883.

The good doctor has hunted home—but let us now examine that evidence and look at contradictory evidence a little later on.

First, if the entry is correct, there was a Richard Compton born March 3, 1768. This is not as useful a piece of information as it might be, since Richard was a common name in the Compton family and since Dr. Larison does not say whether the bible provided evidence that this Richard was indeed Deborah's uncle. Second, though the doctor speaks of corroboration, it is not possible that the entry which was the original source for Sylvia's age should be used to corroborate that age. The two pieces of evidence are the entry and the tradition that Sylvia was born two days later. At this point neither is corroborated.

Curiously, Dr. Larison goes on to discuss Sylvia and her family in terms that would seem to contradict his own conclusions. "Sylvia is in good health and good condition of mind. Her memory is excellent and she is as much interested in the affairs of life as is the most of people at thirty-five. She looks as if she might live many years yet." If indeed she was 115, this is scarcely credible. But there is more.

"Unto Sylvia have been born six children: Moses, Judith, Charlotte, Dorcas, Elizabeth, and Rachel. Rachel lives in Princeton. Lizzie owns and resides upon the lot described in this article: with her now lives her aged mother. She is a large and stout woman and looks as if she might live to be as old as her mother. She is well-proportioned and very active." Up to this point we can have no quarrel with Dr. Larison, though it is worth noting that he lists Lizzie next to last here while describing her elsewhere as the youngest (the position here being correct). But he continues the description in a way that distinctly contradicts his final paragraph below.

"It is said that it is not easy to find, even among the 'bullies,' a man that is a match for her in a hand to hand conflict or in a fist fight." Note the present tense here—*is* not easy to find, *is* a match for her. "Perhaps she is as near like her mother in build, prowess, and endurance, as a daughter can be: she seems mild, complacent, and courteous, but rumor says that she has taken part in many a prize fight, that she has never been particular whether the champion who was to meet her was male or female, and that she has seldom if ever come out of a contest second best. It is also told that she has sometimes gone a long distance to meet the champion who dared to challenge her or to provoke her ire." I am quoting this here, at length, for two reasons: in the original text it is a digression best left out, and it is a kind of evidence of age that Dr. Larison, while providing it, seems to have overlooked.

"Lizzie Dubois is far famed as a fortune teller. To hear her descant upon the events of his life, many a young fellow wends his way to the humble hut of this sable lady, and, elated with the information gained, drops his piece of silver into Lizzie's hand, hastes away to watch secretly the unfolding of every mystery. Nor is her stock of lore barren of witchery. From afar, the votaries of witchcraft go to Lizzie in quest of knowledge respecting stolen goods and other things that are supposed to be known only to those who are in communication with the spirits of the nether abodes." This passage, it will be noted, suggests a considerable age, though it is not inconsistent with her being in her forties or fifties.

However, Dr. Larison writes, "Lizzie is about 78 years of age, but she is so well preserved that she would pass for a negress of forty. Her chances to live to be 120 years old are very good." At this point, one might ask the doctor, in the vernacular, to come off it. No one's chances of living to 120 are very good, and if someone who is supposed to be 78 looks about 40, then the chances are she is closer to 40 than to 78. And if she is frequently engaged in fist fights, the chances become even better—especially if she is frequently engaged in successful fist fights.

Dr. Larison's own account is thus open to question on two

sets of grounds. First, there is no corroboration for the combined tradition and bible birth date that led to the original determination of Sylvia's age. Second, the descriptions of Sylvia and Lizzie make them sound more like (say) 85 and 45 (or at the outside 95 and 55) than 115 and 78.

Indeed, it would appear that the very tradition itself is suspicious: the birth of a black baby and a white baby at about (or exactly) the same time, both of them nursed by the black mother, is a common motif in folklore and literature— Thomas à Becket Driscoll and Valet de Chambre in *Pudd'n-head Wilson*, or William Green Hill and Wilkes Booth Lincoln in *Miss Minerva and William Green Hill*, for example. Quite possibly the motif derives originally from that of the willing animal foster-brother.[2] Be that as it may, and even though life may have imitated art in this case, the folkloristic quality of the relationship between Richard Compton and Sylvia Dubois should raise a warning flag.

But, it might be argued, she was ten years old when Monmouth was fought, and that, too, would make her birthdate fall in late 1767 or early 1768. This, however, is not entirely independent evidence, since the same person who told her that Richard Compton was born in 1768 could well have told her that the Battle of Monmouth was fought in 1778. It would be better to take a date and age unlikely to be contaminated by later information, and of such dates the narrative provides us with two. Sylvia was five years old when her master went to live in Flagtown, and fourteen years old when he went to live in Great Bend on the Susquehanna. (She was two when her master suretied her mother, and we may be able to use this date also, but this is not something she would remember.)

Now when did her master move to Flagtown and when to

Great Bend? Flagtown is a hamlet in Hillsborough, Somerset County, New Jersey, and Great Bend (or Willingborough) a town then in Luzerne but now in Susquehanna County, Pennsylvania. Her master lived in both places at least twice, but we should be able to disentangle his life history sufficiently to place both moves within a few months of the time they took place, and thus to date Sylvia's birth within a year.

Sylvia's master was Dominicus ("Minna") Dubois, though she calls him Minical in her reminiscence. He was born at Harlingen, Somerset County, New Jersey, March 5, 1756, the third son of Abraham Dubois (1725–92).[3] The oldest—and richest—son was Abraham (1751–1807), and the second son was Nicholas (1753–1825).[4] Abraham was a jeweler, a West Indies merchant, and a land speculator; Nicholas was the stay-at-home; and Minna was the wanderer, though partly in his brother Abraham's service. Of Minna's younger years there are conflicting stories: Sylvia, for example, records that he "had been captured while fighting on the water, somewhere near New York" (the full passage is given on p. 56), while Minna's grandson recalls that his grandfather "was a wild youth, ran away, shipped and went to France. This was just before the Revolution. In the war that was then going on between France and England, my grandfather Dubois joined the French navy. The vessel to which he belonged was captured by the English, and he and the other prisoners were taken to England and kept as prisoners in the mountains of Wales, until the war was over."[5]

Several details of this statement cannot be true for several reasons. For one, Minna Dubois was a private and then a sergeant in Captain Vroom's company, Second Battalion, New Jersey militia, before June 6, 1777, and then under Captain Coonrad Ten Eyck.[6] For another, he was recorded as a single

man with a horse resident in Hillsborough Township, Somerset County, in 1779.[7] But he was not registered there in
1780, and since New Jersey militia service could be taken at
sea, he might well have been captured (perhaps, as Sylvia
says, near New York) in 1780 and held to the end of the
war.

Minna married, first, Marie Pittenger in 1779. She died
April 3, 1786, leaving an infant son Abraham, born that
year.[8] He married, second, Elizabeth Scudder in 1793, who
outlived him.[9] They had a daughter Jane, born 1810.[10] The
gap between marriage to Marie Pittenger in 1779 and the
birth of Abraham in 1786 would support an argument that
Minna went to sea in 1779/80, returning in 1783/84. He
seems to have left virtually no traces in Hillsborough after
1779, though his brother Nicholas certainly did.[11] One piece
of evidence for Minna's total absence is that when Minna's
father died on November 5, 1792, intestate, the administra-
tors of his estate were Nicholas Dubois and John Baird, both
of Hillsborough, and not Minna Dubois.[12]

In fact, there is evidence that Minna Dubois went out to
Great Bend on his brother's behalf in 1791, was thereafter
commissioned a justice of the peace there, and then returned
to New Jersey by 1794.[13] He was not a resident of Great
Bend in 1800, and the tavern he subsequently kept was kept
by someone else in 1801.[14] In 1804 he almost certainly was
a resident of Great Bend, when he was a partner in the Great
Bend and Cohecton Turnpike (connecting with the Newburgh
and Cohecton Turnpike at Cohecton).[15] Letters from Abraham, Minna's brother, to Minna, dealing with the location
of the turnpike, are printed in Appendix II.

If Minna returned to Hillsborough (and presumably Flagtown) at the time of his marriage, in 1793/94, and returned

to Great Bend in 1803/4, and if Sylvia went to live with him
on the farm at Flagtown when she was five, and trekked to
Great Bend when she was fourteen, then she was born in
1788/89. So much for her being 115 years old in 1883.

For 1788/89 there is confirmatory evidence. Manuscript
schedules of the 1830 and 1850 censuses, though erroneous
in part, can be brought to bear on the question. In 1830,
when Sylvia was living with her grandfather, Harry Put,
near Rock Mills, her age is given as between 36 and 55 (that
is, born after 1774/75 and before 1794/95), and her grandfather's age at between 55 and 100.[16] The 1850 Census has
her name wrong—"Savilla"—and makes her 45, which is too
young. On the other hand, it also gives the ages of her
daughters, Elizabeth and Rachel, as 26 and 23, which are
almost certainly correct if we assume the accuracy both of the
1830 census on Sylvia's age and of Dr. Larison's description
of "Lizzie" in 1883.[17] Since these were her youngest children
(of six), she could not reasonably have been 45, even if we
had no other evidence—which, of course, we do.

One other piece of evidence may be worth noting here.
Her mother was Dorcas Compton, slave originally to Richard
Compton, who bought her time of Richard Compton, but
who was thereafter slave to Minna Dubois, then to William
Baird, then to Miles Smith.[18] This same Miles Smith, on
November 12, 1821, manumitted his slave Henry Compton,
almost surely the son of Dorcas Compton and therefore the
brother (or half brother) of Sylvia Dubois.[19] From the
evidence of the manumission, Henry was not born after
1800, and was born before Dorcas became slave to Miles
Smith, which was no later than 1803.[20] One supposes that
Henry, since he bore the surname Compton, was born during
one of the times when Dorcas was temporarily free—presum-

ably between William Baird and Miles Smith. This, though it cannot be used for dating purposes, fits in with the early 1790s for the time when Dorcas traded masters from Minna Dubois to William Baird. All this suggests that Sylvia was born in 1788/89 and went to Great Bend about 1803.

We have fewer clues yet on when she returned. Her mother had moved from Flagtown to New Brunswick (which was where Miles Smith manumitted Henry Compton, and indeed where Miles Smith lived most of his life). The fact that Dorcas Compton had not been living in New Brunswick when Sylvia left Flagtown might suggest that Sylvia's departure was in 1802 rather than 1803, but it tells us very little about the date of her return. Sylvia rafted down the Delaware with a family named Brink, but the name was not uncommon, and I have been unable to trace the family. Evidence on the length of her stay at Great Bend will have to come from Great Bend; and what evidence there is turns out to be mostly negative.

Her master was a grand jury man at Wilkes-Barre, which means that she is referring to a time before the erection of Susquehanna County out of Luzerne, in 1812.[21] She does not mention the birth of his daughter in 1810, and surely she would not have knocked her mistress down if she had been obviously pregnant, which gives a kind of *terminus a quem* of 1809. Sylvia's eldest child was a year and a half old when she left, which, given what can be determined from 1830 and 1850 Census schedules, suggests a date in or about 1807/8.[22] If we assume that her years in Great Bend were 1803 to 1808, we should not be far off.

But if she was so inaccurate on her own age, how accurate can her reminiscences be, seventy-five or eighty years after the events (at least so far as the events in Great Bend are concerned)? Just how much of this is history and how much is folklore? In one sense, of course, it is, as a document, social history all the way through: but if we seek to use it for clues as to what actually happened in Great Bend in the first decade of the nineteenth century, we face a more difficult version of the question.

A single example of the difficulties should suffice here (others being mentioned in the notes to the text). Sylvia records that "There was a great many niggers around the neighborhood of Great Bend, and sometimes we'd meet at one master's house, and sometimes at another's" and goes on to say "I never tired of frolics—not I—nor at General Training, neither" (see note 22, pp. 84–85). But the standard history of Susquehanna County records that in 1801 there were but three slaves in Great Bend.[23] The numbers could have grown rapidly, of course—or Sylvia's reminiscences of frolics could belong to her time of freedom in New Jersey— or both. The references to General Training, on the other hand, would seem to belong to the time of her freedom, since Great Bend was, in fact, frontier country in the early 1800s, and General Training presumably more serious there and then that it was in New Jersey fifteen or twenty years later. But her reminiscences *could* be correct. And this is the sort of problem we encounter throughout if we look at her reminiscences as data for the history of the early nineteenth century.

But if we look at them as data for the social history of the later nineteenth century, we have far fewer problems—and, incidentally, much more fun. Note, for example, that it was the "damned Democrats" who burned down her house—of course. Her entire account of the people of Sourland Mountain is interesting for social historians and sociologists of

Introduction

backwoods cultures, and I would not willingly forego even those remarks that tell us less of the culture and more of Sylvia herself. "They're a set of damned turtles: they carry all they've got on their backs." Or, "The whites are just as good as the niggers, and both are as bad as the devil can make 'em."[24] Or, "every devil of 'em is for himself and the devil's for 'em all."

Indeed, though Dr. Larison's shorthand occasionally flagged—leading him to attribute to Sylvia statements in his own unmistakable style—by and large the cadences of her speech come through splendidly. "The men of the age of my master looked brave. They were tall and commanding and stout of limb, and graceful and handy" (eighteenth century cadences, these). Or, "By and by it began to get too heavy—and then it got down, and then we got down, and then I knew there'd be a time" (her story of the keg of brandy). Or, "when the time came, the jig was out" (not, as we might expect, "up").

This last phrase suggests another area wherein Sylvia's words are of interest—as words. Because Dr. Larison printed her remarks phonetically, we can be sure, for example, that she spoke of the "Markis" de Lafayette, and I have left it so (as it also is, by the way, in Horatio Alger's 1867 *Ragged Dick*).[25] She uses the form "they'm" for "they am" at the beginning of the colloquy, the word "sniptious" (in the Appendix), "kinty-koy" (which *sounds* like an Africanism though it is not), and the expression "main-a-poche" (which has recently come to my attention as a dialectal Marylandism for "delirium tremens," from which Sylvia distinguishes it).[26] There is an echo of the caller's language in her description of the dancing when she was young, and there are other echoes of early usage—"kick their tripes out" for example.[27]

In short, her reminiscences are something like a gold mine for the historian of language.

And for the historian of food and drink as well. We learn how to make apple brandy and peach brandy, how to make nigger butter, and what people ate at Hillsborough (ca. 1793–1803) and Great Bend (ca. 1803–8). Taverns run throughout her reminiscences: she was born in a tavern kept by Richard Compton; her master kept a tavern at Great Bend; and she inherited her grandfather's tavern at Rock Mills. But I believe her tavern reminiscences all date from the time at Great Bend; that part of this book deals with Pennsylvania, though admittedly a part of Pennsylvania far removed from the rest of the state.

The question whether "oral history" is usable as historical evidence in the same way documents and written accounts are usable has engaged the attention of African historians in particular. The point to be determined is *why* events are remembered—because they are significant, because they uphold an individual's position in the community, because they are good stories, because they are a "mythic" retelling of the past.[28] "As oral traditions become interpretations of the past rather than descriptions of observed events, they become more and more susceptible of manipulation."[29] And as time goes on they become more and more "mythic" and less and less historical.[30]

With this in mind, we can look at Sylvia's reminiscences and categorize them, or at least make a first attempt at categorizing. The "reminiscences" of Princeton and Monmouth assert Sylvia's position in the community. They are not lies: they are foundation myths, the kind of "remembering with advantages" that makes Agincourt still a magic name. The incident of the keg of brandy at Great Bend is purely and simply a good (and obviously often-told) story—like the Beech Woods and the beating by Sylvia's mistress. The making of brandy and the food are remembered because they were significant to Sylvia. Whenever the reminiscence has mythic overtones or seems designed to give Sylvia status, we may reasonably beware of taking it as straight history. As with—for example—Sylvia's age.

Originally the book was entitled *Silvia Dubois, (Now 116 Yers Old.) A Biografy of the Slav Who Whipt Her Mistres and Gand Her Fredom,* which is wrong on at least two and a half counts. She was not 116 but about 94, the book is not a biography, and when she whipped her mistress (if she did) she may or may not have been a slave.[31] It is entirely possible that the doctor took too much of what she said at face value. Although—as we have noted—he did try to check her age, he did not do much other checking. It may be worthwhile here to consider just what kind of man Dr. Larison was; after all, it is through him that Sylvia's personality and her history was presented to us.

What manner of man was this Cornelius Wilson Larison? He was, in a word, a crank (in another word, perhaps, a polymath), a man of wide (though largely self-taught) learning, a spelling reformer, an educator; a hardworking man, imperious, florid of style, Victorian in attitudes, but quirky enough, and interested enough in local history, to have preserved for us Sylvia Dubois *as she presented herself to him.* But was this the "real" Sylvia Dubois?

On the credit side, for Dr. Larison as a reporter of local history, is the fact that he was approaching the history from inside, so to speak. He was born, of Danish descent, in Delaware Township, New Jersey, on January 10, 1837, the son of Benjamin (1805–92) and Hannah Holcombe Larison

(1808–69). As a boy in school he "always recited alone and when he met a new word he had difficulty in pronouncing it until the master told him. He did not like to guess and he refused to learn the pronunciation of syllables and words that were not pronounced as printed. The master would then get out the dunce cap. . . ."[32] The master was frequently gouged, bitten, and kicked by his unruly pupils—including Cornelius, who on one notable occasion was both beaten and choked by the master.[33] In other words, he grew up in somewhat the same world of casual back-country violence that was part of Sylvia's heritage.

He also grew up stubborn, and that stubbornness he carried into his career as a schoolmaster: When a student ("Sarah, a colored lass about five feet, six inches tall, and broad and strong") gave him trouble in class, after being warned, he took up a cut branch of a peach tree, "grabbed her top-knot, pushed her head over the desk and applied the young tree to her back and shoulders. Her calico dress split under the force of the blows."[34] He beat her till she was limp, whereupon she was "coerced but not subdued," and the same scene was played out time and again until (eventually) "Sarah was complacent and devoted to her studies."[35] In short, the master's stubbornness was the equal of hers; the unlovely details serve to emphasize both our distance from 1859 and the stubborn and wilful nature of both contestants.

But if stubborn and opinionated, he had an enquiring mind. He had attended the University of Lewisburg (now Bucknell University) before his schoolmastership. Afterward (from 1861 to 1863) he attended Geneva Medical College (then the medical division of Hobart College, which subsequently moved to Syracuse, where it became the Syracuse University College of Medicine); he received his M.D. in

January 1863.[36] Thereafter he married, moved to the house
at Ringoes where he lived the rest of his life, teaching,
doctoring, promoting spelling reform, and—in the year 1883—
preserving the memory of Sylvia Dubois for posterity.

This was not his only endeavor at preservation. He published (all but one in his own "reformed" spelling) *The Tenting
School* (1883), *The Larison Family* (1888), *The Class Abroad*
(1888), *The Fisher Family of Amwell* (1892), *Reminiscences of
a Teacher* (1898), and a number of historical pamphlets. Two
of the books, *The Tenting School* and *The Class Abroad*, are
detailed descriptions of field trips taken by Dr. Larison and
his students and deserve republication for their picture of
New Jersey in the late 1870s and early 1880s.[37] Only *The
Class Abroad* (actually *The Clas Abroad*) would have to be
translated into ordinary spelling.

Not that I am any great admirer of the doctor's style, either
in those books or here in Sylvia's reminiscences. I would
gladly do without much of the description of the sleighride
to "Cedar Summit"—"meandering amid huge rocks, thickets
of cedars, umbrageous forests" and so on—not to mention
such polysyllabic ponderosity as "the prolificness of her mind
in this direction is transcendant" or "her words grew more
bulky and a little sulphurous" and his simple pedantries like
"rotes" for words or mockeries like "mansion" for Sylvia's
hut. But his language is part of the social history of his times,
and though I have omitted his preface (most of which deals
with his orthography), using his "Gleanings" in its place,
and have in a few places abridged his remarks (which still
appear in full in the original version), as well as rearranged
the order of sections of his text, I have not felt free to alter
his words or to change their order within his sentences.[38]
One part of that text, at least, should be as valuable to social

historians as Sylvia's own reminiscences, though far from being as pleasant in style. I refer to his account of Put's Tavern. Here is where the interplay in attitudes is most noticeable, and it is partly because of the doctor's disapproval of Put's Tavern that he recorded the scene at all. I wish he had recorded more.

What we have here throughout is the material for social history, particularly for that part of social history dealing with slave life and the life of the uneducated free black in the middle-states part of the north, from the end of the eighteenth century to as late as 1883. We also have, incidentally, material for the history of the tavern at Great Bend, for the history of Put's Tavern, and for the history of language. But we can never be quite sure of the degree to which Sylvia is telling her interlocutor what she thought he wanted to hear, and we should remember that he had heard her stories before. His questions may have been aimed at getting from her only those particular tales (or even expressions) he wanted to hear.

Nonetheless, they are usable for history, if we are careful—besides being a snapshot of attitudes in 1883. I have allowed Sylvia to use the word "nigger" as Dr. Larison took it down, and I have kept his description of the "Negro laugh" though my readers may find it as obnoxious as I do. In his "scientific" labeling of "Negro" characteristics he is as much a child of his age as in everything else, but I think his spirit, for all his stubbornness, was that of a scientist. As Sylvia said, "Most of folks think that niggers ain't no account, but if you think what I tell you is worth publishing, I will be glad if you do it. 'T won't do me no good, but maybe 't will somebody else."

And it will. Above all else, above all questions whether

this is history or folklore, and if history then what kind, the reminiscences of Sylvia Dubois are good reading. I have tried to annotate them as lightly as seemed consistent with the canons of historical scholarship, with the need to provide background information on the obscure history of an obscure area—and with the fact that I have been living with this project for many years. I do not want to leave questions in the readers' minds, but I do not want to spoil the fun.

Sylvia, by the way, survived her interview by six years, independent to the last: her will was proved in Flemington on May 7, 1889.[39] She had outlived her master by more than 65 years—he died at Great Bend on March 14, 1824— and her mistress by more than 40.[40] And though she was not a centenarian when Dr. Larison interviewed her, it would appear that, most likely, she made her century after all.

NOTES

1. The standard account of Dr. Larison's life is Harry B. Weiss, *Country Doctor: Cornelius Wilson Larison 1837–1910, Physician, Farmer, Educator of Hunterdon County, New Jersey* (Trenton, N.J., 1953). The evidence for the date of Sylvia's death is given in note 39. The last mention of her in life is in the Flemington (N.J.) *Gazette-Advertiser*, March 23, 1888, and the *Hunterdon County Democrat*, April 10, 1888, both being denials of her death in the Blizzard of '88.

2. See Thompson b. B 311.1 (Stith Thompson, *Motif-Index of Folk-Literature*, vol. VI, Index (Bloomington and London, 2d printing, 1966), p. 101 for reference. Obviously the black-white foster brother relationship is a child of slavery, and the most recent folk example I can call to mind, as the text suggests, is that in Frances Boyd Calhoun, *Miss Minerva and William Green Hill*

(Chicago, 1909, repr. Knoxville, 1976), p. 11: "an' Wilkes Booth Lincoln, him an' me's twins, we was borned the same day only I's borned to my mama an' he's born to his'n an' Doctor Jenkins fetched me an' Doctor Shacklefoot fetched him." I quote that as an authentic folk voice: William Green Hill (1900–64) was a real child, and Mrs. Calhoun reported real conversations, though not necessarily attributing the remarks to those who made them. In any case, a black ex-slave's reference to a white foster brother cannot be taken at face value.

3. *Genealogical Magazine of New Jersey*, vol. XXXIII (1958), p. 68 ("Bible Records: Dubois Family"). He was baptized April 28, 1756 (ibid., vol. XVIII, p. 41, "Records of the Harlingen Dutch Reformed Church"). See also William R. Heidgerd, *Descendants of Chretien Du Bois of Wicres, France*, Part II (New Paltz, N.Y., 1969), p. 144. On his father's dates see ibid., I (New Paltz, 1968), p. 66.

4. Abraham's wealth in 1779 and 1780 is given in Kenn Stryker-Rodda, "New Jersey Rateables" in *Genealogical Magazine of New Jersey*, vol. LIII (1978), p. 72. Some records of his later career are in the Abraham Dubois Papers in the Historical Society of Pennsylvania at Philadelphia (West Indies papers 1792–1809) and in his Letter Book at the Eleutherian Mills Library at Greenfield, Delaware (of which the portion for 1805–7 covers financial interests during his life). On the career of Nicholas Dubois see footnote 11, below. The birth and death dates are from Heidgerd, *Descendants*, II, p. 144.

5. Printed in Appendix II from Emily C. Blackman, *History of Susquehanna County* (Philadelphia, 1873), p. 66.

6. James P. Snell, *History of Hunterdon and Somerset Counties, New Jersey* (Philadelphia, 1881), pp. 91 (for the date of Vroom's promotion from Captain), 92. (Also, William Stryker, *A List of the Officers and Men of New Jersey in the Revolutionary War* [Trenton, 1872], p. 464)

7. Stryker-Rodda, "N.J. Rateables," LIII, p. 72.

8. Heidgerd, *Descendants*, II, p. 144.

9. Ibid. See also the Joseph Dubois reminiscence in Appendix II. Elizabeth Scudder Dubois is the Sister Betsey of Abraham Dubois's letters (also in Appendix II), and the mistress of Sylvia's reminiscence.

10. See the Joseph Dubois reminiscence and Heidgerd, *Descendants*, II, p. 144.

11. Nicholas Dubois, the stay-at-home, was Overseer of the Poor for Hillsborough Township in 1779, 1784–88, and 1790–99. See Robert Moevs, ed., *Hillsborough Township: The First Years, 1746– 1825, Earmarks and Town Meetings* (Neshanic, N.J., 1975), pp. 18, 24–28, 30–37, 39, 41. He was Overseer of the Roads in 1789 (ibid., p. 29) and Supervisor of the Highways 1792–99 (ibid., pp. 32–37, 39, 41). In 1800 he was Poundkeeper (ibid., p. 43). Of higher offices he was Judge of Election in 1797 (p. 37) and Commissioner of Appeal in 1803–4 (pp. 50–51) and again 1807– 14 (pp. 58, 60, 63, 65, 67, 71, 73, 75). He was Moderator of the Regular Town Meeting in 1795, 1799, 1819, 1822, 1823, and 1825, and of Special Town Meetings in 1811 (2) and 1817 (ibid., pp. 35, 41, 86, 92, 94, 100, 69–70, 83). He was Township Committeeman in 1804, 1807, 1809–19, and 1822–23 (pp. 51, 58, 63, 65, 67, 71, 73, 75, 77, 79, 81, 84, 86, 92, 94). Finally, he was Chosen Freeholder in 1798–99, 1802, 1809–14, and 1819 (pp. 39, 41, 47, 63, 65, 67, 71, 73, 75, 86) and had been Justice for the County in 1784, 1789, and 1795–98 *(Minutes of the Meetings of the Justices and Chosen Freeholders for the County of Somerset 1772– 1822* (Somerville, 1977), pp. 45, 79, 105, 120–21, 136).

12. New Jersey Wills, Somerset County, B 34, p. 101, File 89812, quoted in Heidgerd, *Descendants*, Part I, p. 66.

13. Specifically, Minna Dubois purchased, on September 21, 1791, 601 acres, south of the river, on both sides of the mouth and the Salt Lick, from Benaiah Strong (Blackman, *History of Susquehanna County*, p. 53). This was not the only land he bought, as in November 1795 he sold land north of the river, above the ferry, to Jonathan Newman (ibid., p. 63). Presumably he did not need to be resident in Great Bend to sell the land, but he should certainly have

gone there to buy it. Evidence that he stayed there comes from
Robert J. Taylor, ed., *The Susquehannah Company Papers*, vol. X
(Ithaca, 1971), pp. 347—48, where there is a reference to his having
held a commission as Justice of the Peace, but having been absent
for at least two years (as of 1796) by reason of his having returned
to New Jersey.

14. R. V. Jackson, ed., *Pennsylvania 1800 Census* (Bountiful,
Utah, 1972), s. n. Luzerne County. The innkeepers in 1801 were
David Summers, Robert Corbett, James Parmeter, and Sylvanus
Hatch (Blackman, p. 72).

15. He is described as being "of Luzerne County" in the Act
dated March 29, 1804 (Rhamanthus M. Stocker, *Centennial History
of Susquehanna County, Pennsylvania* [Philadelphia, 1887], p. 46)
and since no one would generally choose to travel from New Jersey
to Great Bend in the winter, he probably came by fall 1803.

16. U.S. Federal Census (MS), 1830, for Amwell Township,
Hunterdon County, New Jersey (copy at Hunterdon County Historical Society, Flemington, N.J.).

17. U.S. Federal Census (MS), 1850, for Amwell Township,
Hunterdon County, New Jersey (copy at Hunterdon County Historical Society, Flemington, N.J.).

18. This assumes that Sylvia's reminiscence (pp. 53—55) is to be
trusted here, which is not certain. On the other hand, she distinguishes between her father's master, John Baird, and her mother's
master, William Baird, and we know that her mother did belong
to Richard Compton (from her name), Minna Dubois (Sylvia's
name), and presumably Miles Smith (see below and Appendix II)

19. Appendix II, Manumission of Henry Compton, November
12, 1821.

20. Appendix II, Testimonial of Miles Smith, June 13, 1825.

21. Susquehanna County was erected by Act of the Legislature
in 1810, moneys for the county segregated by Act of the Legislature
in 1811, and the organization of the county completed in 1812.
Actually, the first Susquehanna grand jury was dismissed by the
Court of General Sessions in Montrose, January 25, 1813, so it is

only presumed that it began its session in 1812. See Stocker, *Centennial History*, pp. 63 (on the acts of the Legislature), 72 (on the grand jury).

22. From the Census schedules, not much: I have been unable to trace any of her children certainly except the youngest two (b. 1823/24 and 1826/27). But none of the "possibles" in any way contradicts the 1807 suggested date.

23. Blackman, *History of Susquehanna County*, p. 72.

24. The use of the apostrophe in " 'em" is, of course, technically incorrect, as "em" is merely the seventeenth century form of "hem"—a Middle English variant of "them"—but I see no point in being so much a precisian as to annoy the reader by printing "em" without the apostrophe. Nevertheless, it should be remembered that this usage did not denote a lack of education or breeding.

25. See Horatio Alger, *Ragged Dick* (New York, 1962; orig. 1867), p. 156: " 'I'll cut you off with a shillin', you young dog,' as the Markis says to his nephew in the play at the Old Bowery."

26. "Main-a-poche": this is a dialectical Marylandism for *delirium tremens* according to a 1977/78 feature story in the *Washington Post*, which I foolishly neglected to preserve and have been unable to locate at any time since.

27. "Tripes": *Oxford English Dictionary* (s.v. *tripe*) has two examples of this usage: to mean, as we would say, "gut" or, as *OED* says, "paunch or belly." One is from Skelton, *Philip Sparrow* (1529), the other from Beresford, *Miseries of Human Life* (1806/7), both rhyming with "gripes." There is no reference in the *Dictionary of American English*.

28. See, in particular, Joseph C. Miller, "The Dynamics of Oral Tradition in Africa" in Bernardo Bernardi, et al. (eds.), *Antropologia e storia* (Milan, 1978), pp. 75–102. More briefly, see Robert Harms, "Oral Tradition and Ethnicity" in *Journal of Interdisciplinary History*, vol. X (1979), pp. 61–85, esp. pp. 64–65.

29. Harms, "Oral Tradition," p. 64.

30. See Steven Feierman, *The Shambaa Kingdom* (Madison, 1974), pp. 64–65.

31. See A. Leon Higginbotham, Jr., *In the Matter of Color* (New York, 1978), pp. 267–310, esp. pp. 299–305. If Minna went surety for Dorcas Compton when Sylvia was two (1791, before he went to Great Bend the first time), then Sylvia was born a slave. She became *his* slave in 1794 (by our reckoning). She was born after 1780, and therefore would have been freed automatically in Pennsylvania at the age of 28 (1817 by our reckoning), but apparently only if she had been born there. Because she was brought into Pennsylvania by a resident, she should have been registered within six months of arrival (by early 1804). I have found no record of her registration, nor is it clear whether Minna Dubois was confident she would have remained a slave after 1817 even if she had been registered. She may well have been a free woman after 1804 in Pennsylvania—though not, without her papers, in New Jersey.

32. Taken from Larison's own reminiscences in Weiss, *Country Doctor*, p. 29.

33. Ibid., p. 30.

34. Ibid., p. 45.

35. Ibid., p. 46.

36. Ibid., pp. 42–44 (Lewisburg), pp. 54–55 (Geneva).

37. Ibid., pp. 217–30, for a bibliography of Larison's works.

38. I have removed a slightly dithyrambic passage on a 116-year-old woman's having her photograph taken (on November 30, 1883), since she was not 116, or even 100.

39. Sylvia Dubois, Will (proved May 7, 1889), in the Surrogate's Office, Flemington (Hunterdon County), N.J.

40. Heidgerd, *Descendants*, II, p. 144. See also Joseph Dubois in Appendix II, where, however, his grandfather's age is wrongly given as 70; he was 68.

FOREWORD

Cornelius W. Larison

[From Original, pp. 100–13]

About twenty-one years ago, the practice of medicine brought me into acquaintance with many of the most aged people living in the southern part of Hunterdon and Somerset Counties, and the northern part of Mercer. Since that time, it has been my fortune to maintain an acquaintance with nearly all the old folks for many miles around. As I have always had an ear for history, and especially a deep interest in all that relates to the history of my native county, and of the people who dwell here, I have ever listened to, and often made notes of, the stories that the aged have told me. Hence I have slowly accumulated a store of facts, such as every lover of history cannot well forget—even if he wanted to.

Of these facts, some relate to the fairest phases of life—to heroic patriotism, to high-souled philanthropy,[1] to untiring devotion to the Christian cause, to filial affection, and the like; some, to the darkest dreariest phases of human life—to scenes of revelry, acts of debauchery, to squalid poverty, to abject degeneracy, and to heinous crimes. But facts are facts, and it has taken each and all of these and thousands that are yet untold to form the lives of the citizens of our county— the doings of the people among whom we live—and no history of our county can be complete, nor of much value as

Editorial notes provided by Jared C. Lobdell.

a record of the lives of a people, that does not chronicle at the same time the doings of the great and the small, the rich and the poor, the proud and the humble, the exalted and the abject, the virtuous and the vicious, the frugal and the squalid. Too often, what is called history is but the record of the fairest facts of a single famous individual, or of a favored few, which look well upon paper and are pleasing to the ear, but which only represent the scintillations of society, or of some favored individual, entirely ignoring the doings of the masses, and shunning with disdain the deeds, the patience, and the sufferings of the poor. Too often we forget that it takes the peasant as well as the priest and the president to make society, form the constituency of a state. Too often we forget that the degenerate and the abject are indispensable parts to society—that they have rights and privileges —and that they are but the counterparts of the best of the citizens of a commonwealth.

On this occasion it is my business to record the acts and sayings of one who has not been illustrious for philanthropic deeds. But a study of this record—of these acts and sayings— is worthy, and will repay anyone who wishes to know the results of a life of dissoluteness, who wishes to see what unbridled passions lead to, who wishes to know how abject and squalid a person can be, and yet live not far from the fairest phases of civilized life.

That my readers may better comprehend the life of the heroine of this tale, I will give a brief sketch of an ancient mountain tavern, once famous for ill fame. This house, tradition says, stood upon the north side of the road that extends westward from the Rock Mills, near its intersection with the road that extends from Wertsville to Hopewell. It was the property of a manumitted Negro and was called Put's Tavern—afterwards, Put's Old Tavern, a property that Sylvia Dubois inherited from her grandfather, Harry Compton.

The founder of this house, and for many years its proprietor, was the character who figures in the colloquy in this book as Harry Compton, the fifer of note in the army of the Revolution. Harry was a slave to General Rufus Putnam, who sold him to Captain Ryner Staats, who sold him to Richard Compton, from whom he bought his time and became free.[2] As General Rufus Putnam was his first master, and more distinguished than either of the other two masters, Harry was often called after his first master, Harry Putnam; indeed, this name he preferred. Accordingly, when he became the proprietor of a hotel, and a man of note as a mountain tavern keeper, for short they called him Harry Put, and the house that he kept was usually called Put's Tavern.

Harry Putnam's house, although far famed and much frequented, especially by sporting characters, was never licensed. In early times, the selling of whisky and other intoxicating liquors as a beverage was allowed to almost everyone—unless, by so doing, the vendor became very offensive. In the place in which Harry's house was built, even an extravagance in the sale of liquor or in the demonstrations consequent upon the use of it, was less likely to be complained of than to be encouraged. Consequently, in peace and prosperity, he managed his business, accumulated wealth, and became renowned. His house, far removed from the gaze of the cultured and the pious, became the scene of cock fights, fox chases, hustling matches, prize fights, etc., etc. Indeed, Put's Tavern became famous as a place of resort for all such as indulged in such games or liked to be present where such things transpired. It was the center for the dissolute. From afar, renowned gamesters came—and tradition says, many were the pounds, shillings, and pence they carried off with them, and many were the young men and young women ruined in that house.

At Put's House, color was but little regarded. Blacks and whites alike partook in the pastimes or the business of the occasion. That the blacks were regarded equal with the whites there may be some doubt, but that the blacks were as good as the whites there is no question. But be these things as they may, they pretended to associate upon terms of equality—too much so for the well being of their posterity.

Twenty years ago I was physician to several old gamesters, the maladies of whom were incurred by frequenting this celebrated house of ill fame and the consequent intercourse with such as congregated there. Although the mishaps leading to disease occurred during boyhood or early manhood, the *materes morbi* were never eradicated, and these old offenders of Nature's laws, as they grew older, constantly needed the care of a medical adviser. Although they were wont to curse the day they learned to foend[3] and deplored the shame and misery which their offences had brought them, yet often, while I was engaged in preparing medicine for them, they used to delight in telling me of the grand old times they used to have in their young days, at Put's Old Tavern. Not one of these numerous bits of history is fit to be recorded in this narrative; everyone of them was revolting to people of culture; most of them would shock the modesty of a Hottentot; and many of them would blanch the cheek and chill the blood of the most dissolute. They were scenes perpetrated by intellectual but lewd men, of the basest passions, fired by whisky and hilarity, in an atmosphere entirely free from decency or shame. Thus let loose, in company with their peers, their passions worked out such things as could be done only by the most daring, the most lustful, and the most wanton. To those who know only a fragment of the history of this ancient house, it is not a wonder that there are so many shades of color in the population of the neighborhood of Cedar Summit, nor that in those of lighter shades there is so much tendency to vice and crime.

Harry Put had an instinctive desire to be free. Being industrious, frugal, and honorable, he managed to buy his time of his master, Richard Compton. Charcoal being much in demand in those times, he turned his attention to the burning of coalpits and at the business accumulated a little money. With his earnings he purchased a site and erected a house. His social qualities, and the supply of liquor always on hand, made his house a popular place of resort. Soon he found it necessary to enlarge—so rapidly did his patronage increase—and finally he found it necessary to rebuild.

The new house, tradition says, was somewhat pretentious. It consisted of four large rooms upon the first floor, and a half story, suitably divided into rooms, above. Along the entire front was a porch, and the windows and doors were ample. Nearby stood the sheds and other necessary outbuildings, the whole surrounded by a virgin forest that extended for miles in every direction.

It is hardly to be supposed that Harry Put, a slave whose spirit prompted him to make the sacrifices necessary to purchase his freedom, had a vicious tendency. It is easier to believe that he was an industrious, easy-going, flexible, far-seeing Negro, who, unschooled in ethics and freshly liberated from bondage, had not a just appreciation of freedom and morality, and withal a strong greed for gain and a desire to be popular. Thus constituted, he became a fit tool for such as desired to frequent a house far removed from the gaze of the law-abiding and the pious, that, while there, their passions could be unbridled, their acts unseen by the virtuous, and their deeds unknown except to the basest of men.

The guests that visited Put's House were not all from the mountain, nor yet from the adjacent valleys. Far from it— from Trenton they came, and from Princeton, and New Brunswick, and New York, and Philadelphia, and even from cities farther away. The news of a cock fight, an old gamester says, usually spread through a community and reached the ears of gamblers, in olden times, faster than the stink of a skunk traverses the air of a valley. The same old wit used to say, the ear of a gamester is as sharp to hear the report of a cock fight as the nose of a vulture is to scent a dead horse.

So, whenever the air of the mountain became polluted with the concoction of a cock fight, every gamester that sniffed the air for a hundred miles around winded the game and, with his wench or his drab, set out for the mountain. As a consequence, a speckled host assembled. The Negro of the mountain was there, and there too was the Negro of the valleys round about. The mountain bandit was there, and there too were the banditti of the adjacent valleys and of the nearer cities. And there too was every gambler who dwelt within a radius of many a mile, who could walk or ride, that could possibly leave home. The Negress in rags and the drab in brocade and in satin, the Negro with his patched coat, the city bandit in his beaver suit, the farmer-gamester in his linsy-woolsy, the mechanic in satinette, drinking and talking, laughing and shouting, intermingled as though every element of distinction had been removed, and the business of life was only hilarity.

I recall a statement made many years ago by a very worthy

patient, respecting a cock fight that he witnessed at this place, that occurred in his boyhood. The story—or that part of it which I venture to tell—runs thus: "When about eighteen years old, I was sent by my father to see a certain man respecting a certain business. When I arrived at his house I was informed that he was not at home—that he had gone to Put's Old Tavern to attend a cock fight. Accordingly I directed my way thitherward, and when near the house, I saw a great concourse of people, of all colors, of all sizes, and of both sex. They were in the wood, a little way from the house. Some were well dressed, some were superbly dressed, some were badly dressed, and some were hardly dressed at all. They were intermittently mixed—the ragged and the dandy. Here a wench with hardly enough patches to keep the flies off stood talking to a man dressed in costly broadcloth; there a thick-lipped Negro, ragged and dirty and drunk, stood talking with women dressed in brocade and decked with the most gaudy jewels. Here a group boisterous in making bets—there a bunch hilarious with fun and rum— yonder a ring formed around two bullies, one a white man, the other black, fighting for no other reason than to see which could whip. While, in this group and in that, were white men and Negroes, white women and wenches, with scratched faces and swollen eyes—the results of combats that had grown out of jealousy, whiskey, or the intrigues of shrewd men who liked to see fights.

"The wood was vocal with Negro laugh—'yah! yah! yah! yah!' and 'wah! wah! wah! wah!'—and with shouts of mirth and merriment, of indecent songs, and of boisterous profanity. A more appalling and a more disgusting scene I never witnessed. I was upon a horse; I did not dismount. I inquired for, and found, the man I was sent to see, transacted my business, reined my horse toward the road, and left the wood in utter disgust."

Of all the incidents respecting Put's House that have come to my ears the above is the mildest. But the above is only a part of the story; the rest is too dark to be told.

That the house was better kept after it descended into the hands of our heroine, or that the guests that frequented it were of a higher order, is much to be doubted. However, its popularity waned and its patrons were those of less note. As the demand for timber increased, the wood upon the side and the top of the mountain was cut away; the sun shone in upon places that hitherto were dark; the land in places was tilled; civilization and virtue encroached upon the environs of the scene of the dissolute. Put's Tavern became a thing of opprobrium and in the year 1840 it was burned to ashes. Such is the history of the house that was the arena, tradition says, of the vilest deeds that were ever perpetrated in Hunterdon County.

Sylvia much complained of the loss of property incurred by the conflagration. All that she had was in this building: beds, chairs, books, culinary apparatus, and whatever else is necessary to an outfit to keep a mountain tavern. The conflagration occurred during her absence. She states that she is satisfied that the house was plundered before it was fired. In evidence of this, she states that several articles of furniture and several books—one a bible containing the family record— were found scattered over the mountain, some in one house, some in another. But it seems she was never able to reclaim one of these things.

In Sylvia's day, Put's Tavern was regarded only as a cake and beer house. But that other drinks could often be got there, there seems to be an abundance of evidence. Indeed, on one occasion, it is said, the house was visited by an officer of the law and the proprietor, free of charge, enjoyed a ride to the county seat.

In her day, Sylvia was somewhat famous as a breeder of hogs. For this business, the great unfenced mountain forest was very favorable. Her herd was often very large and her stock very noted. Often, to improve his breed, a farmer would go a long way to Sylvia's herd, to buy a hog. Nor did he expect to purchase her stock at a low figure. She well knew the value of hogs and always got a fair price.

After the burning of Put's Tavern, I am told that Sylvia erected another house and dwelt upon the land that she had inherited. This house, it is said, was built of cedars. The architecture was primitive. The poles of which it was made were cut about as long as a rail, and arranged somewhat after the pattern followed in building the frame of a wigwam. These poles were covered with cedar brush and the like, arranged somewhat after the manner of fixing straw in thatching a roof.

What the furniture of this house was I have failed to learn. But that it was ample, and that the edifice was spacious and comfortable, there can be no doubt. Nor can it be doubted that Sylvia was ever selfish or inhospitable. Even her sow and pigs, it is said, shared with her the comforts of her mansion. Nor did she compel her chickens to go to an outbuilding, or a tree, to roost, but, considerate and conservative, she made each one feel at home beneath her hospitable roof.

Thus, at peace with beast and fowl, Sylvia, for a while, spent her days. But perpetual and unsullied happiness has not been bequeathed to any mortal. During her absence some vile incendiary fired her domicile and Sylvia again was houseless. Advanced in years, penniless and dismayed, she accepted an invitation to abide with her daughter, and with her daughter she still lives.

[From Original, pp. 16–34, 37–39]

The twenty-seventh of January 1883 dawned frosty and dreary. The mercury pointed to twenty degrees above zero. The sky was overcast and soon the weather appeared threatening. Hills and dales, mountains and valleys, uplands and leas, were covered with snow; and, save the numerous bold areas of woods and the spreading boughs of leafless orchards, the prospect was quite arctic.

The chilly air caused the cattle to remain in their stalls or to snuggle together upon the lee side of buildings. The poultry refused to descend from their roost. The sparrow hovering its little frost-bitten feet uttered its sharp chirp in a plaintive way. While the snow bird, in quest of weed seed, busily hopped over the frozen crust or diligently flitted among the dead branches of ambrosia, scarcely taking the time to utter his shrill notes—tehee dee dee dee—so eager was he to find food for his morning meal and then to hasten to his sheltered haunt.

But the sleighing was good and the cares of busy life forced many a cotter from his home to brave the frigid air of the chilly morning. Horses stepped quick, light and free, and the jingle of sleighbells echoed from the four corners of the horizon. But the furry muffs covering the heads and faces of the well-robed passengers told well that no one left his home that morning to sleigh-ride for pleasure.

It was Saturday, and as the duties of the schoolroom did not demand our labor for the day, we turned our attention to the abject and the aged. Accordingly, about 7 o'clock A.M., we adjusted our wrappings, mounted the sleigh, and directed our way to Cedar Summit, the most elevated portion of the Sourland Mountain. Rapidly we sped along. And, as we reached the brow of the mountain, for a moment we paused to survey the landscape. Toward the west, north, and east, the view was unobstructed, and the prospect was grand.

Elevated 400 feet above the Redshale Valley, we scanned the basin of the Raritan from the source of the stream to its exit into the sea. The bold mountains that skirt it on the north rose gently up and seemed to slope so gradually toward the north that they seemed knolls and hills. The plain, though rolling and ridged, seemed entirely level. Everywhere was snow. Indeed, the dreary sameness of the snowy fleece was only relieved by sparse areas of woodlands and the long line of peering fences. Even the distant villages could hardly be descried, so completely were they enveloped in the fleece of snow. But nearer by, from the chimney of many a farmhouse ascended the sooty smoke in curling festoons.

Onward we hastened, over a road that meandered now amid an umbrageous forest, now amid rocky areas overgrown with cedars, now amid the small rocky fields of the mountain farmer. Everywhere the feathery boughs of the cedars that skirted the way were pendant with snow—a beautiful spectacle. The branches of the great oaks maintained their light somber gray, adding dreariness to the winter scene. The oval backs of the huge rocks lifted a mound of snow, like the houses of the Esquimaux.[4] The mountaineers' huts, far removed from the road, away back near some spring or upon the brink of some plashing rill, exhibited no signs of life, save the sooty column of curling smoke that lazily ascended amid the forest boughs.[5]

From the main road to each mountaineer's hut, or to the

sparse groups of squalid settlements, footpaths or narrrow byways extend back, sometimes for miles, meandering amid huge rocks, thickets of cedars, umbrageous forests, through marshes and swamps, and over streams that are not everywhere forded. These byways are best known to the mountaineers. Their stock of geographic knowledge consists mainly in an acquaintance of these winding ways. And while each mountainer in the darkest night follows each and any one of these byways with as much certainty and as much dexterity as a cat traverses a beam in the night or her meandering path through a gloomy hay-mow, a person not skilled in the ways of the mountainers would at midday be not more successful in his journeying here than in the labyrinth of Egypt or of Corinth. Accordingly, when we had arrived at the corner at which the road extends eastward to Rock Mills, to lead our way to the hut of Sylvia Dubois, we employed one who professed to be acquainted with these meandering paths.[6]

To me, the site at which we left the main road to go in to Sylvia's mansion looked no more like a road than did any other half rod of ground upon the same side of the road for the last half mile. But faith in our guide induced us to follow him implicitly wherever he led. The way was very crooked, perhaps not a single rod of the path extended in the same direction. Not could we see far ahead of us, sometimes not a rod. But on we moved, around huge rocks, between large trees, over large stones, through narrow and dangerous pass ways, now amid a thicket of cedars, or a growth of brambles, or a copse of bushes, or a sparse forest of umbrageous oaks and hickories. Sometimes the road was rutty, sometimes sidling, sometimes up a sharp knoll, sometimes down a steep bank—never level, sometimes stony, and always dangerous. But by and by a vista appeared. We were on a slight eminence.

Opening up before us was an area of land cleared of trees, bushes, and brambles, fenced and farmed. It is the property of Elizabeth, the youngest daughter of Sylvia Dubois.[7] Upon it her modest mansion rises, a hut ten feet square, built of logs, roofed with boards, unadorned with porch, piazza, colonade, or veranda. Primitive simplicity enters into every phase of its architecture. It contains not an element that is not absolutely needed. Nearby stands the scraggling branches of a dead apple tree, and beneath it is the shelter of the faithful dog. Around the area is a fence built in the most economic way—in some places it is made of crutches with one pole, in some places with crutches and two poles, in some places there are two stakes and a rider, in other places it is made of rails so arranged that one end rests upon the ground while the other is elevated by means of stakes fixed across another inclining rail.

Peering above the snow, here and there, were stalks of maize, cabbage, bean vines, pea brush, and other evidences that the enclosed area, during the spring, summer, and autumnal months, had been tilled and had yielded a sparse supply to the tenants of the soil.

When from the eminence we had surveyed the hut and its environs, we descended to the fence that enclosed the lot, fastened and blanketed our horses, and advanced toward the habitation.

The door is double, consisting of an upper and a nether part. The upper part stood ajar, and in the center of the opening appeared the full round face of a large buxom Negress—the owner and proprietor of the mansion which we visited and the youngest daughter of Sylvia Dubois, the lady of whom we had heard so much talk. Our visit was a surprise. Yet with marked complaisance and that hospitality that characterizes the fearless mountainer, we were invited in and bade to be seated by the stove.

The room was not well lighted. And as I was sitting down I noticed, sitting upon a chair, a dusky form closely snuggled up in the narrow space between the stove and the wall. As my eyes became accommodated to the degree of lightness of the room, I saw that this dusky form was the elderly lady that we desired to see—that she had fixed herself in the warmest part of the room and that she was asleep.

I scanned her closely. Though sitting, her sleep was as tranquil as that of a babe. Her head, tied up with a handkerchief, after the usual manner of colored ladies, was bowed forward, so that the chin rested upon her fleshy chest. Her hands were folded upon her lap. Her feet were extended beneath the stove. Her countenance was severe but serene.

Her apparel was not Parisian, yet it was reasonably whole and not dirty. There seemed to be enough of it and adjusted entirely in accordance with the genius of the African race. Indeed, the spectacle was such that it elicited the expression (thought, not made), "Well! you are at home in the enjoyment of life, just as you would have it."

Cautiously, but critically, I surveyed the room and the furniture. The logs composing the wall were not entirely straight, and the interspaces between them in some places were large. At one time these interspaces had been filled with mud—and then, no doubt, the house was comparatively warm. But now, in many places, by frost and rain and by bug and mouse, the mud has crumbled and fallen out, and the openings admit alike the light and the wind. Within reach of my chair I could pass my hand between the logs until it was entirely out of doors; and in some places I could see through a crevice two feet long; in others I could pass my fingers along an open space between the logs from ten to fifteen inches. Through these open spaces, the wind was passing at a rapid rate.

The inner surface of the wall was not even. Each log showed its barky contour, and each interspace its clay ledge or its open space. Calcimine and white wash did not appear, and wallpaper with gilded border was wanting. The ceiling is wanting. In its stead is the bare roof, or the splintery surface of some rails that extend from wall to wall, for the support of such things as are in the way if lying upon the floor.

In erecting the edifice, the logs in the southern facade had been laid up to the height of four and a half feet, with an open space near the center to serve as a door. The next layer of logs extend entirely around, forming the plates for the roof and the lintel of the door. From these log-plates ascend, at a sharp inclination to the ridge-pole, the rafters, which in some places are covered with shingles, in others with boards or bark.

Upon either side of the door, from the log-plate that caps the front wall to its counterpart upon the back wall, extend oak rails, with the flat splintery side downwards. This forms, upon either side of the door, a small loft, upon which are piled bundles of clothes, bed-clothes and bedding, and I know not what else. To get upon these lofts there are neither steps nor ladder, and yet they are handy. Standing upon the floor, a tall person can reach almost to any part of them, and take down, or put away anything desired. I noticed that the chairs that were not in use had been placed upon one of these lofts, out of the way.

So low is the lintel that, in the act of entering the door, a person is obliged to stoop; and when rising up, after entering, were he not careful to be in the open space between the lofts, he would bang his head against the rail floor. Although this was my first visit, I was fortunate enough, upon entering, to be in the right position. But I was not a little surprised as I looked around and found that while my feet and legs and the lower part of my body were downstairs, my shoulders, arms, and head were upstairs. However, the surprise did not unfit me for surveying the lofts, their arrangements, and their contents. Perhaps I would have surveyed these apartments and their contents longer and more critically, but when well engaged in viewing these things, the thought occurred: What may they be doing below—may my nether parts not be in some danger or at the least may they not demand my attention? Accordingly I stooped down, accepted a proffered chair, and seated myself in a space that seemed to be the most out of the way, and began, as foresaid, a critical survey of the environs of my position.

The floor seemed to be made of boards and split wood, laid upon the ground, and perhaps pounded upon, until nearly level. I saw no puddles of standing water, and yet the floor was not entirely dry. The interspaces between the floor-boards would easily have allowed me to ascertain the quality of the soil upon which the house is built. Although these interspaces were tolerably well filled with clay, yet the floor somewhat reminded me of the appearance of a corduroy road.

The logs out of which this house is built served a term of years in the wall of an older house. The primitive house which was an earlier mansion on this lot was built a long while ago. In the course of time the ends of the logs of that house rotted off and the edifice became unsafe. Thereupon, one afternoon about eighteen years ago, Elizabeth convoked her neighbors, in the capacity of a frolic, as such gatherings are here called, to reconstruct her mansion. According to her plan, they took down the old building, notched the logs back a suitable distance from the end, and piled them up in such a way that out of the usable material of the old house they constructed the present edifice. We are told that the old house was somewhat larger on the ground, somewhat higher, and in every way more stylish than the present mansion.

The household furniture—so far as I could see—consisted of an old time cook stove, a dinner pot, a water pail, six chairs, a small cupboard, and some bed-clothes that appeared to have been long in use and not well protected from dirt.

The cook stove is one of that pattern which was in use from thirty to forty years ago. It was made for burning wood. It is now much the worse for wear. There is yet remaining of what it once was a part of each fire-door and a considerable [number] of the top plates. But the fire is well aired; it has an abundance of draft from every side. It stands close up in the southwest corner, in a diagonal manner, in such a way that the pipe-end is toward the corner and the fire-end toward the center of the house. The smoke finds exit through two joints of pipe that extend from the stove almost to the roof. From the roof upward extends a kind of chimney, made of a piece of sheet-iron bent almost into a cylinder, with fantastic scallops around the top—whether the work of an artisan or the result of the disintegrating influence of rust I do not know. Although the space between the pipe and the chimney is large, somehow the sparks and the smoke—that is, some of them—follow this interrupted flue up and out of the house.

Although I saw, out of doors, no pile of wood from which they could draw, and I think I saw not a single stick, the stove was well fed, the sparks rushing up the interrupted smoke-way furiously. And, although my back was a little cold, my shins and knees were about as hot as I have ever had them, and my eyes were as filled with smoke as they have ever been, not excepting the times during which I have been attending a fire in a smokehouse.

The dinner-pot was ample and appeared to have seen service. Of course, it was upon the stove, the water in it boiling furiously, but from it I failed to detect any odor of seething pottage—beef or mutton, pork or chicken.

The chairs were bottomed with rush, and they were in good repair.

Along the wall, upon the west side of the room, stood a box or cupboard, about three feet long, eighteen inches wide, and two and a half feet high, painted and armed with doors. Upon it was a tin kerosene lamp that burned without a chimney, and judging from the crust of soot and lamp-black upon the rail ceiling directly above the place it occupied, it smoked well, even if it failed to light the room.

These were the only articles of furniture that I saw. That there were others, excepting such as may have been in the cupboard, is hardly possible.

During the time I was making the survey, there was not silence. All the while we conversed. Our talk ran sociably and our host was as complacent as a French belle.

At length we announced that we had come to interview the aged lady, Mrs. Sylvia Dubois. Hereupon her daughter aroused her mother, told her that parties had called to see her, and introduced us to our heroine. Our greetings were not very formal, nor much prolonged. But while exchanging salutes, our host, for a moment freed from entertaining us, adjusted things about the room, made ineffable apologies respecting the appearance of the apartment, and extended to us such politeness and such attention as made us feel that we were welcome guests.

I had seen Sylvia on a former occasion and knew something of her idiosyncrasies. Indeed, I had, during a former interview, heard her relate many of the most important instances of her life. So what follows, in this colloquy, to some extent I had heard her relate before and was at this time drawn out by a series of prepared questions, in the order in which it is here stated, so that to the reader it would be somewhat coherent.

Sylvia is large of stature. In her palmy days she has been not less than 5 feet 10 inches high. She informs me that she usually weighed more than 200 pounds. She is well-proportioned, of a nervo-lymphatic temperament, and is still capable of great endurance. Years ago, she was known to be the strongest person in the settlement, and the one who had the greatest endurance. She was industrious and was usually in great request during the housecleaning and soapmaking season of the year. Everybody wanted Sylvia to help clean house and to help make soap. She was so strong she could lift anything that needed to be moved and could carry anything that had to be toted, and she was so willing to use her strength that her popularity was ineffable. So Sylvia went everywhere and everybody knew her—especially the children, who, as a rule, were wonderfully afraid of her.

According to her own account, to children she was not very wooing. On the contrary, she used to take delight in telling them goblin stories and in making them afraid of her. She used to tell them that she would kidnap them, and that she would swallow them alive; and it is said, to children she looked as if she might do such things.

Usually, children kept out of her way. Usually, when they saw her coming, they sought refuge in the company of older folks—in some secluded place—in a foot-race. As a joke, she tells a story respecting an occurrence in the boyhood of a certain individual now well advanced in years. He, a little more bold than the average boy of ten years, on one occasion ventured to be a little saucy to her, and for the time kept out of her way. But a few days after, while he was busy playing in a garden, around which was a high picket fence, Sylvia entered the gate about the time the lad saw her. To try his mettle she exclaimed, "Now I'll have you, sir!" Up he bounced. Every limb was in motion. The high pale fence was a trifling barrier—one awful yell he gave, and then through the raspberry briars and over the fence he went like a cat, and howling lustily as he ran, disappeared from view by creeping under an old barrack.

Her love of freedom is boundless. To be free is the all-important thing with Sylvia. Bondage, or even restraint, is near akin to death for Sylvia. Freedom is the goal—freedom of speech, freedom of labor, freedom of the passions, freedom of the appetite—unrestrained in all things. To enjoy this she would go to any extremes, even to the extremes of living upon the charity of her acquaintances in the hut in which we found her—away from civilization and culture, with but little to eat, with less to wear, and the poorest kind of shelter. Thus she gains the object of her desire. And she is indeed free—every passion is free, every desire is gratified. Less restraint I never saw in any person, nor indeed could there be.

Sylvia, in her own way, was not a little religious, and was well used to speaking the name of the Supreme Being; and, what is more remarkable in a woman, she seemed to be so familiar with all those words expressive of the attributes of God. Indeed, I have seldom known a clergyman, even when an excellent Hebrew and Greek scholar, to be more familiar with these terms than Sylvia, nor more in the habit of using them. And yet, between Sylvia and a clergyman, there seemed to be a marked difference in the way in which each used them. For, while the clergyman uses these terms mainly in speaking of the goodness and omnipotence of God and in invoking His blessing, Sylvia seemed to use them in an interjectional or an adjectival way, to embellish her language and to give force to her expressions. And, of all that I have ever listened to, I have not heard anyone handle these terms more rhetorically, or yet more in accordance with the principles of elocution. And, as it will detract very greatly from the merits of her discourse in case I omit this part of her language, I beg my readers the privilege of leaving the words in her phrases, just as she uttered them, as much as is bearable.

While Sylvia's familiarity with the titles with which Jehovah is wont to be addressed is exceedingly great, her knowledge of that other being called the Devil is by no means limited. If his character has ever been better portrayed by any other person, or if he has ever been addressed by or known by any other terms than those she used, it has not come to my knowledge. Indeed, it seemed that every title, appellation, and epithet that had ever been used in reference to his Satanic Majesty, she handled with particular freedom and ease. Indeed, the prolificness of her mind in this direction is transcendant. For where rotes with the most exquisite prefixes and suffixes fail to serve her purpose, she extemporaneously and without hesitation coins an overflow of self-explaining compounds that seem to fully meet the demand even of her own extreme cases.

Nor is she barren of ideas respecting those imaginary beings

called by the learned Fairies, Nymphs, Sprites, Elfs, Demons, and the like. To her, every grot and corner, every
wood and swamp, hill and meadow, is inhabited by these
imaginary beings, who are ceaselessly plying their arts in
interfering with human affairs—working to this person wealth
and happiness, to that one poverty and woe.

NOTES

1. I have not determined what doctrine is implicit in the adjective
"high-souled," though it sounds theosophical or Rosicrucian. The
Recollector version prints "high-sold" for the original "hi-sold," but
I think my reconstruction more likely.

2. Ryner Staats was a Lieutenant and then Captain in the Second
Battalion of New Jersey militia, wounded at Germantown October
4, 1777. (William Stryker, *A List of the Officers and Men of New
Jersey in the Revolutionary War* [Trenton, 1872], p. 412.) There is
no evidence for his contact with Rufus Putnam, so I suspect "mythic"
remembering and that the Putnam involved was Seth Putnam of
Somerset County—but perhaps not. After the Revolutionary War
(the relevant period for mythmaking), Rufus Putnam was better
known than cousin Israel.

3. "foend": I have no answer on this. It *could* be a dialectal
version of "foin" ("thrust at, stab, pierce, prick" *OED*), or it could
be a nineteenth-century medical Latinism (the "oe" spelling in
general is characteristic of G. A. Koch, *Gradus ad Parnassum*,
Leipzig, 1878).

4. In the original, *Esquimos*, which suggests the older spelling
used here.

5. Note "mountainers" rather than "mountaineers" as we might
expect.

6. In later years Dr. Larison's daughter, Mame Larison Blackwell, tried to find the site of Sylvia's cabin. Helen Legler described
one such attempt, in the *Princeton Recollector*, vol. V, no. 4 (Winter
1980), p. 18:

The daughter mentioned by Dr. Larison in his first recorded visit to Silvia was my friend, Mrs. Mame Larison
Blackwell. Years ago, when I bought an old farm house near
Reaville, I was referred to her for information. It was the
homestead of a family related to her mother's people, so I
got a great deal of her own family's history as well.

In those days my mother was living with me, and it was
our pleasure to drive along the old roads to get acquainted
with our new environment. We often stopped to ask Mrs.
Blackwell to join us, and she was always willing—and ready,
after removing her apron and putting on a little jeweled pin.

Many were the stories she'd told us about "Old Sil," and
she asked if we could go to the mountain to see if she could
find the site of her cabin. We passed a rock which she called
"Knitting Betty," and stopped where she thought we might
be close to the spot she remembered. I thought, of course,
that the ruins would be at the edge of the road, but not at
all! She plunged into the woods, with me close behind her,
and behind rocks, through briars, over fallen tree trunks, we
were soon out of sight of the road and the car—and my very
worried mother. I was even more worried, having heard that
the mountain was alive with copperheads.

Mrs. Blackwell, in her late 'seventies, wore full long skirts,
which she necessarily looped over her arm as we plodded on,
exposing her ankles to whatever fangs lay in wait. I doubt
that my blue jeans would have been much protection to mine.

Our search was inconclusive. She felt we were near the
spot, possibly even on it, but there were no identifiable scraps
among the general woodland litter. We also failed to see any
copperheads, and if they saw us, they were probably as afraid
of us as I was afraid of them.

7. The 1850 Census gives Rachel as the youngest daughter (see
Introduction, p. 11), which agrees with the order of listing in Dr.
Larison's discussion of Sylvia's age, but not with his statement here.

THE REMINISCENCES
OF SYLVIA DUBOIS

INTERVIEW WITH CORNELIUS W.
LARISON, JANUARY 27, 1883

[From Original, pp. 34–37]

The old lady did not awake from her slumber quickly. Nor
did she quickly comprehend that she had visitors. But, as
aged folks usually do, she awoke slowly—a part of her at a
time, as it were. At first, she moved her hands and arms,
then her feet and legs, then rubbed her face, then she moved
her body upon the chair, and in the course of some minutes,
she began to realize that she had guests, and that she must
entertain them. Thereupon, adjusting her clothes, and quickly
turning her head toward me, she ejaculated:

"Who are these?"

To this interrogation her daughter replied: "Why, mommy!
Dr. Larison, his daughter, and Miss Prall. They want to see
you—they want to talk with you."

Quickly and sternly she replied: "Want to see me! I don't
know why they should want to see me, such an old thing as
I am—pretty near dead now, and God knows I ought to have
been dead long ago."

Hereupon, I began to inquire about her health. She informed me that she was well—and that she was always well
except sometimes she suffered "colds." She said that she had
never had a spell of severe sickness and did not intend to

Editorial notes provided by Jared C. Lobdell.

have, that "t'aint no use to be sick. Folks don't feel well when they'm sick; they feel best when they'm well."

"Just so, Sylvia," I replied, "but it seems that folks can't always be well—sickness will come sometimes."

To this comment the old lady hastily replied: "They wouldn't be sick half so much if they'd behave 'em selves, and stay at home and eat plain vittles. They want to run all over, and be into all kind of nigger shines, and stuff 'emselves with all kinds of things; and their guts won't stand it. Then they get sick; and like enough send for a doctor—and when he comes, if they're not pretty careful, they'll have a hell of a time; for he's sure to go right for the guts, first pass; never knew one of 'em to miss. A big dose of calomel and jalap to begin business, and then the war is begun.[1] These doctors, they've got no mercy on you, 'specially if you're black. Ah! I've seen 'em, many a time, but, they never come after me, I never gave 'em a chance—not the first time."

When I had grown quiet from a fit of laughter, provoked by the old woman's style, as much as from the matter spoken, I told her that I had come to talk with her—to learn what I could respecting her great age, her course of life, the history of her family, the customs of the people who lived a century or more ago, her present welfare and her future prospects.

With this statement Sylvia seemed pleased, and announced that she was ready and willing to inform me respecting matters as far as she was able. At once, she assumed an attitude, and an air that showed she was "all attention" and ready to talk. I had provided myself with paper and pencil to take down in shorthand her language as it fell from her mouth. Respecting this, I informed her, and requested the privilege that I might print and publish anything that she told me. To this request she replied:

"Most of folks think that niggers ain't no account, but if you think what I tell you is worth publishing, I will be glad if you do it. 'T won't do me no good, but maybe 't will somebody else. I've lived a good while, and have seen a good deal, and if I should tell you all I've seen, it would make the hair stand up all over your head."

[From Original, pp. 40–83]

I began my interrogations by saying "I expect you have always been pretty well acquainted with the people living on this mountain." To this remark she quickly replied: "Yes, and I tell you that they are the worst set of folks that has ever lived; they lie and steal, and cheat, and rob, and murder, too. Why, a person is in danger of his life up here and he can't keep nothing. They'd steal the bread out of a blind nigger's mouth, and then murder him if he told of it. That's the way it goes up here—they're worse than the devil himself.

"But," I replied, "there must be some good ones among them." To this she ejaculated, "No, there ain't, not one. They're all bad and some are worse. You never seen such folks; they're the damnedest that ever lived."

"Well, then, how do they live?"

"Live? Why, they don't live, they only stay, and hardly that. A good many of them don't stay long in the same place, neither. They're a set of damned turtles: they carry all they've got on their backs—and that ain't much, neither—and then they're ready to get up and get out any time, and you catch 'em if you want to."

"Well, if they're so bad, do any of them live together, or does each one live alone?" I inquired.

To this she replied, "Live together? I guess they do, too

many of 'em. Why, in some of them shanties there are a dozen or more, whites, and blacks, and all colors, and nothing to eat and nothing to wear, and no wood to burn. And what can they do? They have to steal."

"And then there is no distinction of color up here?"

"No, not a bit. The niggers and whites all live together. The whites are just as good as the niggers, and both are as bad as the devil can make 'em."

"Well, then, do the negroes marry the whites?"

"When they want to, but they don't do much marrying up here—they don't have to—and then it's no use. It's too much trouble."

"Well, then, how about the children? Are there any?"

"Yes, a plenty of 'em, and all colors—black and white and yellow and any other color that you have ever seen, but blue. There ain't no blue ones yet."

"Well, if their parents are not married, how do they bring up the children?"

"Bring 'em up? They don't bring 'em up. Why, as soon as they are born, every devil of 'em is for himself, and the devil's for 'em all. That's how that goes. And I tell you, they have a blamed hard time of it, too."

"And then how do they name the children?"

"Name 'em? Why, they name 'em after their daddies, to be sure—if they know who they are. But that don't make any odds, 'cause, before they are grown up, half of 'em don't know their own young ones from anybody's else's, and the other half of 'em wouldn't own 'em if they did. And the young ones ain't no better—they often swear they had no daddies. You see, just as soon as they get big enough, they travel out to get something to eat, and if the feed is pretty good, maybe they'll stay—never get back. And if they come

back, they find so many more in the nest, they can't stay if
they want to. Why, none of 'em that's good for anything ever
stays here. They go away when they are small and get work
and stay. You'll find folks born on this mountain living in
Princeton, New Brunswick, in Trenton, in New York, and
the devil knows where all. And if they are driving team for
some big bugs, or are waiters in some great hotel, they'll
never own they were born on this mountain, not a bit of it.
They know better. But if one turns out to be a poor devil,
and gets into some bad scrape—that fellow is sure to come
back to the mountain. That's the way they keep the ranks
full—full of the scoundrels that can't stay anywhere else.
That's the way it goes with the folks here."

"Have you always lived on this mountain, Sylvia?"

"No, I was born on this mountain in an old tavern that
used to stand near the Rock Mills; it stood upon the land
now owned by Richard Scott. The old hotel was owned and
kept by Richard Compton; it was torn down a long while ago
and now you can't tell the spot on which it stood.[2] My parents
were slaves, and when my master moved down to Neshanic,
I went along with them; and when my master went to Great
Bend, on the Susquehanna, I went with him there.[3] Afterwards I lived in New Brunswick, and in Princeton, and in
other places. I came back to the mountain because I inherited
a house and a lot of land at my father's death. That's what
brought me back to the mountain."

"Who was your father?"

"My father was Cuffy Baird, a slave to John Baird. He
was a fifer in the Battle of Princeton. He used to be a fifer
for the minutemen in the days of the Revolution."

"Who was your mother?"

"My mother was Dorcas Compton, a slave to Richard

Compton, the proprietor of the hotel at Rock Mills. When I was two years old, my mother bought her time of Richard Compton, Minical Dubois going her security for the payment of the money. As my mother failed to make payment at the time appointed, she became the property of Minical Dubois. With this failure to make payment, Dubois was greatly disappointed and much displeased, as he did not wish to fall heir to my mother and her children, as slaves to him. So he treated mother badly—oftentimes cruelly. On one occasion, when her babe was but three days old, he whipped her with an ox-goad, because she didn't hold a hog while he yoked it. It was in March; the ground was wet and slippery, and the hog proved too strong for her under the circumstances. From the exposure and the whipping she became severely sick with puerperal fever. But after a long while she recovered.

"Under the slave laws of New Jersey, when the slave thought the master too severe, and the slave and the master did not get along harmoniously, the slave had a right to hunt a new master. Accordingly my mother Dorcas went in quest of a new master, and as Mr. William Baird used to send things for her and her children to eat when Dubois neglected or refused to furnish enough to satisfy their craving stomachs, she asked him to buy her.[+] This he did. And she liked him well, but she was ambitious to be free. Accordingly, she bought her time of Baird, but failed to make payment, and returned to him his slave.

"She was then sold to Miles Smith, who was a kind master and a good man. But she was ambitious to be free—so of Smith she bought her time and went away to work and to live with strangers. But as she failed to make payment at the appointed time, she was taken back a slave and spent the remainder of her days with him, and was buried about 45 years ago upon his homestead.

"Of course, I remained a slave to Minical Dubois. He did not treat me cruelly. I tried to please him and he tried to please me and we got along together pretty well—except sometimes I would be a little refractory, and then he would give me a severe flogging. When I was about five years old, he moved upon a farm near the village of Flagtown.[5] While there I had good times—a plenty to eat, a plenty of clothes, and a plenty of fun—only my mistress was terribly passionate and terribly cross to me. I did not like her and she did not like me, so she used to beat me badly. On one occasion, I did something that did not suit her. As usual she scolded me. Then I was saucy. Hereupon she whipped me until she marked me so badly I will never lose the scars. You can see the scars here upon my head today, and I will never lose them if I live another hundred years.

"When I was about ten years old, the Battle of Monmouth occurred. I remember very well when my master come home from that battle. Cherries were ripe and we were gathering harvest. He was an officer, but I do not know his rank.[6] He told great stories about the battle, and of the bravery of the New Jersey Militia, and about the conduct of General Washington. He said they whipped the British badly, but it was a desperate fight. He told us that the battle occurred on the hottest day he ever saw; he said he came near perishing from the excess of heat and from thirst, and that a great many did die for the want of water."

"I also remember when my father and others returned from the battles of Trenton and Princeton—but I was younger then and only remember that it was winter, and that they complained that they had suffered much from cold and exposure.[7]

"Before the Battle of Princeton, my master had been a prisoner of war. He had been captured while fighting on the water, somewhere near New York. I used to hear him tell how he and several others were crowded into a very small room in the hold of a vessel—the trap door securely fastened down and the supply of fresh air so completely shut off that almost all who were imprisoned died in a few hours. In this place they were kept two days. Dubois, by breathing with his mouth in close contact with a nail hole, held out until he was removed. Two or three others were fortunate enough to find some other defects in the woodwork, through which a scanty supply of air came.[8]

"When I was in my fourteenth year, my master moved from Flagtown to his farm along the Susquehanna River.[9] This farm is the land on which the village called Great Bend has been built. When we moved upon the farm, there was but one other house in the settlement for the distance of several miles. These two houses were built of logs. The one upon my master's farm had been kept as a tavern, and when he moved into it he kept it as a tavern. The place was known as Great Bend. It was an important stopping place for travelers on their way to the Lake Countries and to other places westward. Also, it was a place much visited by boatmen going down and up the river. Here, too, came great numbers of hunters and drovers. In fact, even in these days Great Bend was an important place.

"In moving to Great Bend, we went in two wagons. We took with us two cows; these I drove all the way there. After we crossed the Delaware at Easton, the road extended through a great forest, with only here and there a cleared patch and a small log hut. Even the taverns were only log huts—sometimes with but one room downstairs and one upstairs. Then there would be two or three beds in the room upstairs, and one in the room downstairs.

"The great forest was called the Beech Woods. It was so big that we was six days in going through it. Sometimes we would go a half day without passing a house or meeting a person. The woods was full of bears, panthers, wildcats, and the like. About these I had heard a great many wild stories. So I made sure to keep my cows pretty close to the wagons.[10]

"Usually we stopped over night at a hotel. But, as the houses were small, often it would happen that others had stopped before we arrived, and the lodging rooms would all be occupied. Then we would sleep in our wagons, or in the outbuildings. In those days travelers had to get along the best way they could.

"As my master saw that the site upon which he lived was favorable to business, during the third summer after our arrival he erected a large new frame house—the first house, not built of logs, in Great Bend.[11] Then he began to do a large business and became a very prominent man there, as he was while he lived in New Jersey.[12]

"Already several people had moved to the neighborhood, had erected log houses, cleared the lands, and begun to cultivate fields and raise stock. Very soon, in the village, storehouses and mills were built.[13] Indeed, Great Bend began to be the center of a large and thriving settlement.

"At this time hunters used to come to this point to trade—to sell deer meat, bear meat, wild turkeys, and the like, and to exchange the skins of wild animals for such commodities as they wished. At our tavern they used to stay, and they were a jolly set of fellows. I liked to see them come; there was fun then.

"There was a ferry across the Susquehanna at Great Bend. The boat upon our side was owned by my master; the one upon the other side was owned by Captain Hatch.[14] I soon learned to manage the boat as well as any one could, and often used to ferry teams across alone. The folks who were acquainted with me used to prefer me to take them across, even when the ferrymen were about. But Captain Hatch did not like me. I used to steal his customers. When I landed my boat upon his side, if anybody was there that wanted to come over to the Bend, before he knew it I would hurry them into my boat and push off from the shore, and leave him swearing. You see, the money I got for fetching back a load was mine, and I stole many a load from old Hatch; I always did, every time I could.

"Along with the ferry boat always were one or two skiffs. These we took along to have in readiness in case of accident. When the load was heavy, or when it was windy, two or more ferrymen were required. At such times, I would help them across, but I always come back alone in a skiff. In this way I got so that I could handle the skiff first rate, and was very fond of using it. Oftentimes I used to take single passengers over the ferry in a skiff; sometimes two or more at once. This I liked, and they used to pay me well to do it. I had a good name for managing the skiff—they used to say that in using the skiff I could beat any man on the Susquehanna—and I always did beat all that raced with me.

"Oftentimes when the ferrymen were at dinner, someone would come to the ferry to cross. They would holloa to let us know that someone wanted to cross. Then there would be a race. I'd skip out and down to the wharf so soon that I'd have 'em loaded and pushed off before anyone else could get there—and then I'd get the fee. I tell you, if they did not chuck knife and fork and run at once, 't was no use—they couldn't run with me—the fee was gone. I've got many a shilling that way, and many a good drink too."

I asked, "Was your master willing that you should cheat the ferryman out of his fees in that way?"

She replied, "He did not care; he thought I was smart for doing it. And sometimes, if I had not been in the habit of hurrying things up in this way, people would have waited at the ferry by the hour—but you see, they didn't have to wait when I was about, and this is why they liked me, and why my master liked me too."

"Well, Sylvia, what kind of times did you have while at Great Bend?"

"What kind of times? Why, first rate times. There were plenty of frolics, and I used to go and dance all night—folks could dance then. Why, there were some of the best dancers up there that I ever saw. Folks knew how to dance in those days."

"Then you think that the young folks of this neighborhood don't know how to dance?"

"I know they don't. I've seen 'em try and they can't dance a bit. They've got no step."

"Have you seen anybody try to dance very lately?"

"Yes, last winter they made a party over here at one of the neighbors, and they invited me over and I went. They had a fiddle and they tried to dance—but they couldn't—not a damned one of 'em."

"Well, what was the matter?"

"What was the matter? Why, they had no step. You can't

dance unless you have the step, and they were as awkward as
the devil; and then they were so damned clumsy. Why, if
they went to cross their legs, they'd fall down."

"Then you think that to dance well it is necessary to cross
the legs?"

"Sometimes it is—nobody can dance much without crossing
the legs. But they couldn't do it—they'd get tangled in the
rigging and capsize. Why, they cantered over the floor like
so many he-goats."

"Well, did you show them how to dance?"

"Well, yes, I took a step or two, but I couldn't do it as I
used to when I was young. They thought I did well, but they
don't know—they've never seen good dancing. Why, when I
was young, I'd cross my feet ninety-nine times in a minute
and never miss the time, strike heel or toe with equal ease,
and go through the figures as nimble as a witch. But now
they're so clumsy that when one takes a foot off the floor,
somebody has to hold him up while he shakes it. And then
when they reel they push and crowd like a yoke of young
steers, and they bang each other until they are in danger of
their lives."

"Yes, Sylvia, the art of dancing has fallen into decline,
and I am sorry for it. The young folks of this generation are
not only clumsy and awkward, but they are bad figures. There
is nothing in their sports to develop a good form, and as a
consequence this generation is characterized by bad development—weak bodies with ugly faces, and poor minds."

Hereupon Sylvia began to say, "But they think they're
great things and very handsome. But they ain't. They're poor
scrawny mortals—make no appearance and can't do nothing.
Why, the men of the age of my master looked brave. They
were tall and commanding and stout of limb, and graceful

and handy; they had good faces, great high foreheads, and large bright eyes and broad mouths with good teeth. They stood up straight and walked with freedom and ease. I tell you, in those old times there were good-looking men—brave looking men, they were all so. General Washington was, and Lafayette was, and my master was, and all the great men that I ever saw were, and they were all good dancers and danced whenever they had a chance. They used to say that General Washington was the most beautiful dancer in America—that he could even beat the Markis de Lafayette.[15]

"The big yankees from York State and New England used to come to our house, and they were fine looking men—all of 'em were. And they were very tall and very straight and very dignified; and their wives were well formed and beautiful, and very dignified women.[16] And they were all very polite—had the best of manners—were the most accomplished folks I ever saw. And they were all good dancers—the best of dancers—and they never got tired of dancing. Even the old men and old women danced—and they were just as good figures as you ever saw, and very graceful."

"I see, Sylvia, that you had good times when at the Great Bend."

"Guess we had! When my master moved into his new house, we had a big time. All the grand folks were there, and I tell you, things were lively.[17] We had a plenty of brandy, and they used it too—a big time, I tell you. Ay! Ay! The biggest kind of a time."

"Did you use any brandy?"

"Well, I did, but not till towards night; I had too much to do. I had to see to the rest; I knew where everything was, and I had to help them get them. But I looked out for myself. There was one keg of brandy that I knew was made very good, for I helped make it. We used to make our own brandy, and I always helped my master make it, and knew just as well how to do it as anybody.

"I left this keg till it was the last thing to be moved. Then, when I and a certain fellow began to move it, we concluded that we would see if it had kept well. We had no cup, so we drawed it out in an earthen pot, and then he drank, and then I drank—till we drank all we could. But still there was some left in the pot, and we couldn't get it back in the keg, for we had no funnel. We didn't want to throw it away; that looked too wasteful. So we concluded we'd drink it up, so he drank and I drank, till it was gone. This made us pretty full, but we started with the keg. By and by it began to get too heavy— and then it got down, and then we got down, and then I knew there'd be a time, because I knew if my master saw me, I'd get a hell of a licking. And some of the rest knew that too. And they didn't want to see me licked, so they got me up and helped me off towards the house to put me to bed.

"I used to be subject to the cramps, and sometimes I used to have it very bad—so that my mistress used to give me medicine for it; and once, a little while before, I was so bad with it that she thought I was going to die with it. Well, I thought now I had better have the cramp, and then maybe I wouldn't get licked. So I began to have pain—and soon it got pretty bad—worse than I'd ever had it before. Anyhow, I made more fuss than I ever had before and yelled a good deal louder.

"Pretty soon they called missy, and she was awfully frightened; she thought I would die for sure; she said she'd never seen me so weak with it before. So she had me carried and placed upon the trundle bed in her own room and attended to me nicely. She gave me some medicine which she thought helped me amazingly; but before the medicine could do any good, the rum stopped all my yelling and grunting too. In fct, I was so drunk that I couldn't see, hear, nor feel. For a while I thought I was dead, but by and by the brandy began to wear off and I began to see. I cautiously squirmed to see whether anybody was about, and there sat missy, fanning me. I cautiously opened my eyes just the least bit, to see how she looked. She looked very pitiful—I was too drunk to laugh, but 'My God,' thought I, 'if you only knew what I am doing, you'd throw that fan away and give me hell.'

"At night, my master came to bed very late. When he came in to undress, I was making believe that I was asleep. I didn't dare to get well too soon. At once, mistress began to tell him how sick I was, and how near I came to dying, but I didn't fool him. He looked at me a little and then went to bed. He said, 'Paugh! She's only drunk—she's been drinking with the men. Go to sleep— she'll be all right in the morning.' And so I was, too, but that cured me of drinking."

"Then you never drank after that?"

"I never got drunk after that. Sometimes when others have been drinking, I have taken a dram too. But I didn't get drunk—I never do. I know my measure and I take no more."

"Did your mistress ever find out that you were deceiving her when you were drunk?"

"I guess not. If she had, she'd ha' killed me—if she could. But I have laughed about it a great many times. I spoiled her fun for that night—she had to leave her company and take care of me—it was pretty hard for her, for she had a great deal of big company there that night, and she was hell for company."

"Well, your mistress was always kind to you, wasn't she?"

"Kind to me? Why, she was the very devil himself. Why, she'd level me with anything she could get hold of—club, stick of wood, tongs, fire-shovel, knife, axe, hatchet, anything that was handiest—and then she was so damned quick about it too. I tell you, if I intended to sauce her, I made sure to be off always."

"Well, did she ever hit you?"

"Yes, often. Once she knocked me till I was so stiff that she thought I was dead. Once after that, because I was a little saucy, she leveled me with the fire-shovel and broke my pate. She thought I was dead then, but I wasn't."

"Broke your pate?"

"Yes, broke my skull. You can put your fingers here, in the place where the break was, in the side of my head, yet. She smashed it right in—she didn't do things to the halves."

(Hereupon I examined Sylvia's head and found that at some time long ago the skull had been broken and depressed for a space not less than three inches, that the deepest fragment had not been elevated as surgeons now do, and that in consequence there is to this day a depression in which I can bury a large part of the index finger.)

"Well, Sylvia, what did your master say about such as was done by your mistress?"

"Say? Why, he knew how passionate she was. He saw her kick me in the stomach one day so badly that he interfered. I was not grown up then; I was too young to stand such. He didn't tell her so when I was by, but I have heard him tell her when they thought I was not listening that she was too severe—that such work would not do—she'd kill me next."

"Well, did his remonstrating with her make her any better?"

"Not a bit—made her worse. Just put the devil in her. And then, just as soon as he was out of the way, if I was a little saucy, or a little neglectful, I'd catch hell again. But I fixed her. I paid her up for all her spunk. I made up my mind that when I grew up I would do it, and when I had a good chance, when some of her grand company was around, I fixed her."

"Well, what did you do?"

"I knocked her down and blamed near killed her."

"Well, where and how did that happen?"

"It happened in the barroom. There was some grand folks stopping there, and she wanted things to look pretty stylish, and so she set me to scrubbing up the barroom. I felt a little glum and didn't do it to suit her. She scolded me about it and I sauced her. She struck me with her hand. Thinks I, it's a good time now to dress you out, and damned if I won't do it. I set down my tools and squared for a fight. The first whack, I struck her a hell of a blow with my fist. I didn't knock her entirely through the panels of the door, but her landing against the door made a terrible smash, and I hurt her so badly that all were frightened out of their wits, and I didn't know myself but that I'd killed the old devil."

"Were there anyone in the barroom then?"

"It was full of folks. Some of them were Jersey folks who were going from the Lake Countries home to visit their friends. Some were drovers on their way to the west. And some were hunters and boatmen staying a while to rest." [18]

"What did they do when they saw you knock your mistress down?"

"Do? Why they were going to take her part, of course. But I just sat down the slop bucket and straightened up, and

smacked my fists at 'em, and told 'em to wade in if they dared
and I'd thrash every devil of 'em, and there wasn't a damned
a one that dared to come."

"Well, what next?"

"Then I got out and pretty quick too. I knew it wouldn't
do to stay there, so I went down to Chenang Point and there
went to work." [19]

"Where was your master during this fracas?"

"He? He was gone to tend court at Wilkes-Barre.[20] He
was a grand jury man and had to be gone a good many days.
He often served as grand jury man, and then he was always
gone a week or two. Things would have gone better if he
had been home."

"When he came home what did he do?"

"He sent for me to come back."

"Did you go?"

"Of course I did; I had to go. I was a slave, and if I didn't
go, he would have brought me, and in a hurry too. In those
days the masters made the niggers mind, and when he spoke
I knew I must obey.

"Them old masters, when they got mad, had no mercy on
a nigger—they'd cut a nigger all up in a hurry—cut 'em all
up into strings, just leave the life, that's all. I've seen 'em do
it, many a time."

"Well, what did your master say when you came back?"

"He didn't scold me much. He told me that as my mistress
and I got along so badly, if I would take my child and go to
New Jersey and stay there, he would give me free. I told
him I would go. It was late at night; he wrote me a pass,
gave it to me, and early the next morning I set out for
Flagtown, New Jersey." [21]

"It seems that you got along with your master much better
than you did with your mistress?"

"Yes, I got along with him first rate. He was a good man and a great man too; all the grand folks liked Minical Dubois. When the great men had their meetings, Minical Dubois was always invited to be with 'em, and he always went, too. He was away from home a great deal; he had a great deal of business and he was known all over the country. I liked my master and everybody liked him.

"He never whipped me unless he was sure that I deserved it. He used to let me go to frolics and balls and to have good times away from home, with other black folks, whenever I wanted to. He was a good man and a good master. But when he told me I must come home from a ball at a certain time, when the time came, the jig was out. I knew I must go; it wouldn't do to disappoint Minical Dubois.

"Did parties often occur?"

"Yes, and I always went, too. Old Minical would always let me go, because I was a good negress and always tried to please him. I had good times when he was around, and he always done things right. But you mustn't get him mad.

"In the long nights of winter, we often had frolics, almost every week. We'd hardly get over one frolic when we'd begin to fix for another. Then there was the holidays—Christmas, and New Year, and Easter, and the Fourth of July, and General Training. But the biggest of 'em all was General Training. That was the biggest day for the nigger—I tell you that was the biggest day. The niggers were all out to General Training—little and big, old and young; and then they'd have some rum—always had rum at general trainings—and then you'd hear 'em laugh a mile. And when they got into a fight, you'd hear 'em yell more than five miles."

"Did the niggers yell when they fought?"

"The cowards did, worse than anything you ever heard— worse than anything but a cowardly nigger."

"Where did you hold your frolics?"

"There was a great many niggers around the neighborhood of Great Bend, and sometimes we'd meet at one master's house, and sometimes at another's. We was sure to have a fiddle, and a frolic, and a first rate time; but none of 'em had a better time than myself—I liked frolics. I could dance all night and feel as jolly as a witch all next day. I never tired of frolics—not I—nor at General Training, neither."[22]

"Did you say your master used to make his own brandy?"

"Yes, he often made it—always made his peach brandy. Anyone can make peach brandy—the best that was ever drunk. You just burn about four pounds of dried peaches until you can rub them to powder in your hands; you must burn 'em in a pot that has a very tight cover on. Then rub 'em fine in your hands, or, if some pieces are too hard for that, pound 'em fine with a hammer. Then put this powder of burnt peaches into a barrel of new apple whiskey, and in four weeks, if you shake the barrel every day, you will have a barrel of peach brandy good enough for anybody.

"You make apple brandy in almost the same way. You burn about four pounds of apples dried with the skins on. Make them into powder, and put 'em in a barrel of new apple whiskey, and shake the barrel every day for four weeks. In four weeks you have a barrel of apple brandy better than any you ever saw. A little of that will make a fellow talk and won't burn his guts out, neither. Folks used to drink brandy right along—drank it every day—drank a plenty of it, and didn't get the main-a-poche nor the delirium tremens, neither.[23] Why, the brandy used to be good—tasted good and was pleasant to drink; you can't get none such now, not a bit of it. A drink of brandy now burns like fire—burns all the way down—goes through the guts worse than a sheet of red-hot sand paper."

"How did you go to Flagtown?"

"On foot, to be sure. I came right down through the Beech Woods, all alone, excepting my young one in my arms. Sometimes I didn't see a person for half a day; sometimes I didn't get half enough to eat, and never had any bed to sleep in; I just slept anywhere. My baby was about a year and a half old, and I had to carry it all the way. The wood was full of panthers, bears, wildcats, and wolves; I often saw 'em in the daytime, and always heard 'em howling in the night. O! that old panther—when he howled it made the hair stand up all over my head.

"At Easton, I went on board of a raft to go down the Delaware. A man by the name of Brink had his wife and family on board of a raft, bound for Philadelphia. I went on board to help the wife, for my passage. They were nice folks and I had a good time; I left the raft not far from Trenton, but I do not know exactly where—there was no town at the place at which I got off the raft.

"Then I proceeded directly to Flagtown, to see my mother. I did not find her there—she had moved to New Brunswick. On my way, a man called to me, asking me 'Whose nigger are you?' I replied 'I'm no man's nigger—I belong to God I belong to no man.'

"He then said 'Where are you going?' I replied "That's none of your business. I'm free. I go where I please.'

"He came toward me. I sat down my young one, showed him my fist, and looked at him; and I guess he saw 't was no use. He moseyed off, telling me that he would have me arrested as soon as he could find a magistrate.

"You see that in those days the negroes were all slaves, and they were sent nowhere, nor allowed to go anywhere without a pass; and when anyone met a negro who was not with his master, he had a right to demand of him whose negro he was; and if the negro did not show his pass, or did not give good evidence whose he was, he was arrested at once and kept until his master came for him, paid whatever charges were made, and took him away. You see, in those days anybody had authority to arrest vagrant negroes. They got paid for arresting them and charges for their keeping till their master redeemed them. But he didn't arrest me—not a bit.

"When I got to New Brunswick, I found my mother. Soon after I went to work, and remained in New Brunswick several years. From New Brunswick I went to Princeton to work for Victor Tulane. I remained in his family a long while; I worked for him when Paul Tulane was a child; I worked there when he was born. Victor Tulane was a great man and a good man, and he used his servants well. And Paul was a nice boy and Madam Tulane was a good woman; and I liked 'em all, and all the servants liked 'em.[24]

"After a long while, I visited my grandfather, Harry Compton, who lived at the forks of the road, near this place. He was then an old man; they say he was more than a hundred years old, and I guess he was. But he was yet quite active; he wanted me to stay with him and take of him and I stayed; and at his death I inherited his property.[25] I lived on the old homestead until a few years ago, when them damned Democrats set fire to my house, and burned up my home and all that I had. Since that time I have lived at this place, with my youngest daughter."

"Well, Sylvia, you have lived a long while and have suffered a great many hardships, and I expect that you are tired of living."

"No, I ain't. I'd like to live another hundred years yet— and I don't know but I will, too. My teeth are good, and if I can get enough to eat, I don't know why I should die.

There's no use in dying—you ain't good for anything after you are dead."

"Well, Sylvia, I expect you are well acquainted with this mountain, and with all the folks that live on it."

"Yes, I know every foot of it, every hole and corner of it, every place where anybody lives or ever has lived. And I know the folks, too; and some of 'em are pretty bad ones, too; in fact, they are all bad, and some of them are worse. What the devil will ever do with them when he has to take 'em, I don't know. Surely he don't want 'em and wouldn't have 'em if he could help it. The only reason that some of these folks up here don't die sooner than they do is, the devil won't have them. He just puts off taking them because he knows what a time he'll have when he gets 'em. Why, some of them are starved to death long enough before they die, but they can't die—there's no place for them to go after they are dead. They ain't fit to go to heaven, and the devil won't have 'em, and so they have to stay here. Why, this mountain is worse than hell itself. Why, if some of these folks don't behave better after they go into the infernal regions than they do while here, the devil will have a time of it. He'll never manage 'em; he'll have to call a congress and have an amendment fixed to the constitution. A brimstone fire won't do; it will never faze 'em; it don't here. I've seen it tried and it don't do at all—only make 'em worse.

"Well, Sylvia, you tell a pretty hard story about your neighbors."

"Tell a hard story! I tell the truth, and I could tell more of it. Why, you don't know 'em. There is more folks killed up here than anybody knows of, and you know somebody is killed up here every year. And nobody is ever hanged for it and it gets worse and worse. If they kill anybody up here, they just take the murderers off to Flemington and keep them in jail awhile till they have a trial, and then they turn 'em out to come back here, and then they are worse than they were before. They just kill anybody then.

"And they steal! Why, you wouldn't believe how much they steal. They don't steal much of one another, because that wouldn't do. If they were caught at that, they'd get killed damned soon, and then they ain't got much to be stoled. But they go off from the mountain, down into the valleys, and there they steal anything they can find—sheep and chickens, and grain, and meat, and clothes—and anything else that they can eat or wear. And nobody can find anything that has been stolen by the folks up here, for when anything is to be stolen, they all know about it, and they all lie for each other, and they all know where it is to be hid, and they all help to keep folks from finding it, so it does no good to hunt up here for stolen goods. And then they know so damned well how to hide things, too. They don't hide what they steal in their houses until all the houses have been searched; when they steal anything they hide it in some hole that nobody but mountainers know of, or else under some rocks, or under some wood, where nobody but the mountainers would think of looking. That is the way they do business up here, and if you tell 'em of it, they'll kill you—damned if they won't."

"And Sylvia, you have lived right here, in the midst of them, for fifty years, without falling into their ways?"[26]

"Yes, and longer too. I know 'em; I've been to 'em—but they never troubled me much. They know it wouldn't do. They know I'd give 'em that." (So saying, she brought her right fist into her left hand until the smack could be heard fifty yards.)

"Well, Sylvia, what do you think ought to be done with these bad folks?"

"Ought to be done with 'em? Why, some of 'em ought to be hanged right up by the neck; and some of 'em ought to be tied up and licked nearly to death—tied right up to a post and licked till within an inch of the life. That's what ought to be done with 'em—that's the way I'd serve 'em. I'd take 'em up to Flemington, and lick 'em till they'd never want to be licked again."

"Have you ever been to Flemington, Sylvia?"

"Been to that damned Flemington? Yes, I've been there, and it is the damnedest place in the world."

""Why, Sylvia, what had you got against Flemington?"

"I've got enough against it. You can't get anything there without money. Nobody is considered anything there unless he has money. Nobody will tell you anything unless you give 'em money. If you ask a lawyer anything, he won't tell you a bit until he gets your money. You can't get justice there unless you have some money—and you can't get it then, because, if another person has more money than you have, they'll all of 'em—every damned lawyer, the judge, and the jury—go for him, and a poor body has no show at all. I know 'em—I've been to 'em—they're a bad set."

"Have you been to the lawyers at Flemington, Sylvia?"

"Yes, I have—but it didn't do any good. These damned S———s have been trying to get my property away from me for many years, and I wanted to consult a lawyer to get him to put these devils through, but I couldn't. Not a damned lawyer would take my case, because I had no money. They said they could not talk without money. They couldn't do anything for me unless I paid 'em some money."

"Why didn't you pay them some money?"

"Pay 'em? I couldn't—I hadn't a cent to my name."

"Well, Sylvia, how did you feel when they told you that they could do nothing for you without you gave them some money?"

"Feel? I felt like kicking their damned tripes out. They think they are so damned big because they are dressed up a little, and they are too damned proud to be decent. If they'd come over on the mountain, we'd show 'em; we'd skin every devil of 'em—I'd do it myself, old as I am. I'd just like to put my fist against their eyes." (So saying, she brought the fist against the hand until it smacked aloud.)

"Were you ever at Flemington when you were not consulting lawyers?"

"Yes, often. I used to go whenever there was any doings there; whenever there was General Training, and whenever the big men had their meetings there. All the niggers used to go to Flemington on those big days; and then they'd get licked—good God, how they'd get licked! Why, they'd tie 'em right up and lick 'em to death—cut 'em into pieces—cut 'em all into string."

"Did you ever see them whip the negroes?"

"See 'em? Yes, I have—see 'em lick a dozen of 'em at a time. Tie 'em right up to a post, and give 'em hell, right on the bare back—fetch the blood every time, and they'd holler. Good God, they'd howl till you could hear 'em a mile; and then, when they'd cut the back all in slits, they'd put salt in the gashes, and then they'd howl. Lord God, no panther in the Beech Woods ever made half so much noise. That's the way they fixed the nigger in old times, them damned Flemingtoners—they think they are so damned big."

"What did the negroes do, that they whipped them so badly?"

"Why, of course they'd get some whiskey, and then they'd get into a kinty-koy, and make a noise perhaps.[27] They'd get into a row or a fight, and then somebody would get hurt, and then the one that got hurt would complain to the authorities, and then the constables would be after the niggers—and when they caught 'em, they'd tie 'em right up without judge or jury, and pull off the shirt, and put it right on the bare hide. My God, how they licked 'em—cut the hide all in gashes. That's the way they used to fix the old slaves—give 'em a holiday to have a little sport, and then if they had any fun, lick 'em till they'd have a sore back till the next holiday come."

"Well, Sylvia, would they want to go to the next holiday?"

"Yes, the niggers always wanted to go, back sore or well—never knew one to miss when his master tole him he could go. Then he'd be sure to get licked worse than he was before, because some niggers couldn't have a holiday without getting into a fight—then he'd be sure to get tied up and licked."

"Were you at Flemington when the little negro was hanged for murdering his mistress?"[28]

"Yes, and that was the damnedest time I ever saw. The niggers quarreled and fought and pounded each other, and bit each other's ears off, and then pounded each other's noses down, bunged each other's eyes, and some got blamed near killed. And then them damned Flemingtoners got after 'em, and they tied 'em up, and licked 'em without mercy—cut 'em all in strings—just left the life, no more. That was a great time. I'll never forget that."

"Well, Sylvia, did the negroes not deserve to be whipped sometimes?"

"Yes, sometimes—most always, I expect. They had to lick 'em; there was no other way; they had to make 'em mind.

The niggers that behaved well never got licked, but some wouldn't behave. They'd always get into a row, or steal something, and then they'd be sure to get licked."

"Sylvia, they say that you are very old, over a hundred years old. Do you know how old you are?"

"Not exactly—can't tell exactly. They didn't used to keep a record of the birth of niggers; they hardly kept a record of the birth of white children; none but the grand folks kept a record of the birth of their children—they didn't no more keep the date of a young nigger than they did of a calf or a colt; the young niggers were born in the Fall or in the Spring, in the Summer or in the Winter, in cabbage time or when cherries were ripe, when they were planting corn or when they were husking corn, and that's all the way they talked about a nigger's age."

"But, Sylvia, is there no way to tell approximately when you were born?"

"To be sure, there is, and that's what makes folks say that I am a hundred and fifteen years old. They tell this by the record of the birth of Richard Compton. My mother and many other old folks used to tell me that, when my mother was a slave to Richard Compton, there was born to him a son, whom they called Richard after his father. When this son Richard was two days old, I was born; so there is but two days difference between the date of Richard Compton's birth and my birth.[29]

"In an old Bible which is now in the possession of Mr. Richard Gomo who lives near Rock Mills, is the record of the Compton family. By referring to this record they tell how old I am—I can't read, but I expect they tell me right. I know that I am older than anybody else around here—older than their parents were; and in most cases I knew their great-grandparents.

"I remember that while we were small children, I and Richard Compton were about of a size, and that we used to play together. My mother and his mother used to tell me that we both nursed the same breast, alternately, the same day. As we were so near the same age, when his mother wished to go away to visit, or upon business, Richard was left in the care of my mother; and while his mother was away, he used to nurse my mother with me. Once, Mrs. Compton and one of the neighbors was gone to the city a whole week; and while gone, Richard was left in charge of my mother. Then she used to take us both upon her lap, and while he was nursing one breast, I was nursing the other. They used to say that this was the reason Richard and I got along so well together. As long as he lived, he always claimed to be about my age, and we always visited, and we used to talk over the circumstance that we used to be together when we were babies, and when we were children, and that we had always visited, and always intended to visit.[30]

"A great many old folks used to tell me that they had seen me nurse my mother at the same time that Richard Compton was nursing her; and that he and I were about the same in age. As we lived at a tavern, I expect folks saw us more, and that more folks noticed us than would have done so in a less public place."[31]

[From Original, pp. 87–91]

"Sylvia, you have an unusually strong frame, and you have lived to an exceedingly great age; you must have been very properly fed in childhood, or else these things could not be. Upon what did they used to feed you, that you have grown so large and so strong?"

"They gave us Indian dumplings, samp porrage, corn bread, potatoes, pork, beef, mush, and milk, and nigger butter; and we didn't get a bellyful of these sometimes—I've often gone to bed hungry, but 't was no use to complain— you had your measure and you got no more. That's the way they fed young niggers in old times, but they made 'em grow."

"Tell me how the dumplings, porrage, corn bread, and nigger butter were made."

"To make Indian dumplings, scald the Indian meal, work it into a ball, and then boil until done in the liquor that meat—pork or beef—has been boiled in. These were eaten without any dip, butter, or sauce.

"To make samp porrage: boil equal parts of beef and pork together until done; remove the meat and stir into the liquor in which the meat was boiled course Indian meal, and boil until done."

"Corn bread was made by mixing equal measures of Indian meal and rye meal together, and baking it in an oven.

"Nigger butter was made by mixing two parts of lard with one part of molasses. This nigger butter was what we had to use on our bread; and we did well if we didn't have to spread it deuced thin. The bread was so hard that it needed greasing; and this was all that we had to grease it with—we had no gravy.

"We used to have pies occasionally. Sometimes they were made out of sweet apples, sometimes out of sour ones without any sugar or molasses—didn't feed niggers sugar and molasses much in those days. The white folks didn't get much of 'em—their pies were almost as sour as ours, and there was very little sugar in their coffee, and the sugar that they used was as black as my hide.

"We never drank coffee or tea. Sometimes we got some cider. The white folks only drank tea and coffee on Sunday, or when they had company.

"They used to boil or roast our potatoes with the skins on, and then we didn't take the skins off—we ate 'em skins and all. And the white folks ate theirs just so; but they had gravy or butter to put on theirs. The white folks didn't eat wheat bread, only on Sunday or when they had company. They ate rye bread; they didn't cultivate much wheat—'t wouldn't grow—never had more than enough to make pie-crust and cakes out of. They ate a great deal of mush and samp porrage, and Indian cakes, and these were good enough if you had a plenty of good milk and butter and gravy to eat with 'em.

"I expect folks nowadays think that this was hard fare, but 't was good enough when we had enough of it. But sometimes we didn't get a bellyful—that went a little hard. If the folks nowadays would live as we used to, they'd be a good deal stronger, more healthy, and wouldn't die so soon. They eat too many dainties—too much sugar, too many sweet puddings and pies, too much rich cake and too much fresh bread; and they drink too much coffee and tea; and they don't dress warm enough—that calico ain't the thing for health. We used to wear woollen underclothes, and our skirts were always made of linsey-woolsey. Our stockings were woollen and our shoes were made of good thick leather, so heavy that you could kick a man's tripe out with 'em.

"This is the way we used to dress, and it was a good way, too. The old masters knew how to take care of their niggers.

"We had good beds to sleep in; the ticks were filled with

straw, and we had plenty of woollen blankets and coverlets, as they used to call 'em. The fires were all made of wood, and usually they were big. The fire places usually extended entirely acrost one end of the kitchen—15 to 20 feet wide, with large stone jambs that made 'em three or more feet deep, provided with a chimney that two or three could climb up and stand in, side by side. In the back part of this huge fireplace a large back-log—as much as two or three could carry—was placed, and upon the handirons another log called a fore-stick, as much as a man could carry, was placed; and then between this back-log and fore-stick was piled smaller wood, until it made a fire that would scare the young folks of this generation out of their wits. This big fire not only warmed, but it also lighted the room. As a rule, the niggers had no other light, and no other fire than this—they had to stay in the kitchen—this was their part of the house, and here they had good times, too. The white folks were in another part of the house, where the fireplace was not quite so big. Sometimes the white folks had stoves, and then they lighted their room with tallow candles. There was no kerosene then, nor any coal; they didn't know how to use such things."

NOTES

1. Calomel and jalap: Calomel is mercurous chloride, "a heavy white tasteless compound used as a purgative" and jalap is the purgative root of *Exogonium jalapa*, or a drug made from it. (*Dictionary of American English* (Chicago, 1942), s. vv). See *Century Magazine*, Aug. 1888, pp. 551–52, "He done his lev'lest best; not only bleeding but calomel and jalap."

2. The following item from *Somerset County: 250 Years* (Somer-

ville, 1938), p. 61, may be of interest. "One of the 'notorious women' of the 1700s in Somerset County was Mrs. Richard Compton. . . . All she did to gain this notoriety apparently was to keep 'ginger cake and spruce' beer in her house near Somerville Academy." Mrs. Compton, the item informs us, was universally known as Aunt Yauncy. This would not appear to have been the same tavern, but, if the reference is based on folk memory, one cannot tell for sure. The tavern-*keeper* is presumably the same.

3. Neshanic (in the "northwest declivity of Neshanic Mountain") is in fact a couple of miles west of Flagtown (James P. Snell, *History of Hunterdon and Somerset Counties, New Jersey* (Philadelphia, 1881), p. 786), but Sylvia uses them interchangeably.

4. This suggests that Dorcas Compton had other children at the time she was owned by Minna Dubois, but if so, why were they not (like Sylvia) left with him? Since they evidently were not, the passage raises questions. When one considers Sylvia's own recollections of Minna Dubois, it raises even more questions. I am, after consideration, inclined to reject it as representing Sylvia's confused recollections of her mother's confused recollections.

5. If this passage is accurate, then Sylvia's mistress was married to her master at the time of the move—and thus (given a marriage date of 1793) Sylvia could not have been born before 1787/88. Since Minna had returned from Great Bend to New Jersey in 1793/94, she could not have been born after 1789.

6. This passage, so far as it concerns Sylvia, is "remembering with advantages"— not to say invention. Moreover, her master never rose higher than sergeant, even if he was in the battle.

7. Likewise invention so far as Sylvia's presence is concerned.

8. My friend Jesse Lemisch, who knows more about sailors in (and just before) the Revolution than any one else alive, tells me he has found no references to Dominicus Dubois in any of the documents he has studied over the past quarter-century. If we conflate Sylvia's account (heard presumably before 1808 and recollected 1883) with that of Joseph Dubois (heard presumably after 1820 and recollected 1873), we might fairly conclude that Minna went to sea

as a militiaman around 1780, was captured in a fashion in some way connected with the French (or else escaped in some way connected with them), and returned home around 1783/84.

9. That is, he owned the farm and then moved to it, if her recollection is correct. The house (or cabin) *had been kept* as a tavern, and he continued to keep it so. But the history of the inns at Great Bend is confused. Horatio Strong had one in 1796 (Rhamanthus M. Stocker, *Centennial History of Susquehanna County, Pennsylvania* [Philadelphia, 1887], p. 530), and Minna Dubois bought his land of Benajah Strong—but Benajah was not one of the tavern-keepers in 1801 (p. 546).

10. Compare William Stuart, *Sketches of the Life of William Stuart* (Bridgeport, Conn., 1854, repr. New Milford, Conn., 1932), pp. 19–23 (printed in Appendix II).

11. She was thus in Great Bend at least till 1806 (if Minna Dubois returned there early in 1803) or 1807 (if he came in or after the summer of 1803).

12. But in New Jersey he was *not* prominent, which suggests that her early (pre-1803) recollections of New Jersey are melded with the (post-1803) recollections of Great Bend.

13. Mills were built as early as 1792 (Stocker, *Centennial History* p. 532)—and the Strong tavern, bought by Oliver Trowbridge, had a framed addition (p. 530): since this is listed as being in Great Bend Township (north bank) rather than Hallstead Borough (south bank) in 1887 (pp. 528, 546), Sylvia may not be accurate here.

14. Sylvanus Hatch was commissioned Ensign in the Pennsylvania Militia in 1796 (*Pennsylvania Archives*, 9th series, vol. II [Harrisburg, 1931].) The "Captain" was presumably a courtesy title. Joseph Dubois has provided us with a description of the ferries (Appendix II).

15. One doubts if Sylvia ever saw General Washington. The Marquis de Lafayette, on the other hand, did visit (and dance in) New Brunswick on September 24, 1824 (Marian Klamkin, *The Return of La Fayette 1824–1825* (New York, 1975), p. 75.)

16. Compare Stuart's descriptions of taverns (Appendix II).

17. Presumably the members of the Turnpike Company, grand jury men, long-time residents, local dignitaries, and perhaps even Tench Francis, who owned 13,158 acres in 1801 (Emily C. Blackman, *History of Susquehanna County* [Philadelphia, 1873], p. 72). Apparently, however, not all parties chose Minna's tavern over the competition. From Blackman, *History of Susquehanna County*, p. 76, comes this reminiscence.

Mr. Joseph Backus, now of Bridgewater, says of himself in 1809:—

"Being then a lad of seventeen, I was wending my way from the land of steady habits, in company with Captain Gifford, who was on his way hither to visit his friends, who had previously emigrated to this then uncultivated wilderness. Having reached Great Bend, crossed the river, and stopped to feed at Du Bois's Hotel, while we were waiting for the team to feed, a company from Bridgewater came out there for the purpose of trading with Mr. Bowes, the merchant—quite a common occurrence in those days, there being then only one small mercantile establishment where Montrose now stands, kept by Isaac Post, on the very spot where Koon now keeps. I believe he also kept public house, and I think that that and one other house were the only tenements where Montrose now stands. This company proved to be some of the very friends the captain was coming to visit, so you can imagine the pleasure of meeting; and they manifested it by postponing their return, crossed the river to Hatch's, took dinner, spent the afternoon right merrily, and were ready to start home about sundown; a bitter cold night, snow about three feet deep."

18. Not such a distinguished company as "there were some grand folks stopping there" would suggest.

19. That is, Chenango, N.Y. Note that "down" is downriver—in this case, north.

20. If he was in Wilkes-Barre, as we noted in the Introduction, it was before 1812. Also, and perhaps more interesting, it was not in June 1807, when he was in Princeton (see letter of Abraham Dubois, October 7, 1807, in Appendix II). A list of grand jury

men at Wilkes-Barre would be helpful here: I have not found one.

21. Presumably to see her mother, who was therefore (presumably) still in Flagtown when Sylvia left in 1803 (or 1802?).

22. On this see the discussion in the Introduction, p. 13. It is worth noting that the first General Training in the county was held at Parkevale on the Meshoppen in 1806 (as were trainings in 1807 and 1808). Stocker, *Centennial History*, p. 213. This is the other end of the county from Great Bend.

It is, of course, possible that Sylvia attended General Training in Parkevale, but it is not likely. On the other hand, consider a contemporary description of General Training in Somerset County (by contemporary I mean in the first quarter of the nineteenth century). This is from Andrew D. Mellick, Jr. (ed. Hubert G. Schmidt), *Lesser Crossroads* (New Brunswick, 1948), pp. 376–77.

> Another great day for the Bedminster colored people, always celebrated by Dick and Nance, was "general training," usually occurring in the middle of June. Then it was that Dick took the big wagon and put on its tow and linen wagon cover, tying up the sides so that from within an unobstructed view could be had of the martial array. Nance and the children were placed on chairs in front, and behind was a barrel of root beer of Dick's own manufacture and a corn basket full of large round ginger cakes—they called them bolivars—baked by Nance the day before. In addition there was a plentiful supply of new-mown grass from the bleach patch in the garden, which was always mowed at that time, to keep the beer cool and to give the horses a bite during the day. Dick, in his Sunday clothes and displaying a most conspicuous nosegay, would then seat himself on the foreboard, seize the reins, and with the stalk of a long whip against his shoulder and the lash hanging behind would set off with his happy family and join the procession of teams that from early morning had been slowly moving up the long hill in the direction of Pluckamin.
>
> On reaching the grounds, the horses were taken out and

tied to a fence, and the business and pleasures of the day commenced. As long as the barrel and basket held out, beer was to be had for two cents a glass and cakes for a penny a piece. Between customers the sable merchants had plenty of friendly visitors, the children meanwhile playing about the wagon or sitting quietly in round-eyed wonder at all the glories of the day. With the approach of night Dick "geared" his horses and drove slowly home, his spirits lightened by the pleasures he had experienced and his pockets full-weighted with big copper pennies. He would now have pocket money for all his needs for months to come, and some to drop in the black bag each Sunday morning at church when the deacon passed it in the gallery, which Dick always did with a most reverential bow.

23. The reference to "main-a-poche" is omitted in the *Recollector*. See note 26 to the Introduction.

24. Paul Tulane will reappear in note 6 to Appendix I.

25. As Dorcas Compton, Harry's daughter and Sylvia's mother, was a slave, she could not inherit real property—could not indeed hold valid title to real property. Hence Harry would have to devise it to Sylvia if he wanted it to remain in the family, even if Dorcas Compton were still alive—which, given Sylvia's inexactitude with dates is not clear. Harry was alive in 1830, dead by 1840 (when the tavern burned), and Dorcas died (on Sylvia's showing) ca. 1838. On the rights of slaves to hold property see Henry S. Cooley, *Slavery in New Jersey* (Baltimore, 1896), pp. 53–54.

26. More than fifty years, as she was resident in Amwell in 1830, with Harry Put, and probably more than 55 (see note 28).

27. "Kinty-koy": not in fact an Africanism but Algonquian "kin-ticoy" (var. kenticoy), a ceremonial dance or festival (*DAE*, vol. III [Chicago, 1942], p. 1364).

28. James Guise was hanged in Flemington for the murder of his mistress in 1828 (Snell, *History*, p. 105). He was the second and last slave to be executed for murder in Hunterdon County.

29. See the Introduction. I have been unable to check the relevant

family bible, but I have noted that a Richard Compton was in the Hunterdon County militia in 1792 (Hiram E. Deats, "The Hunterdon Militia 1792," in *Genealogical Magazine of New Jersey*, vol. IX (1934), p. 49), and that a Richard Compton was Overseer of Roads in Hillsborough (Somerset County) in 1784–87 (Robert Moevs, ed., *Hillsborough Township: The First Years, 1746–1825, Earmarks and Town Meetings* [Neshanic, N.J., 1975], pp. 24–27). Since Overseer of Roads was a position ordinarily held by a younger man, but *not* one under 18, one is troubled by the putative 1768 birthdate. If the senior Richard Compton is meant, the position is insufficiently high—if the junior, highly improbable. But it may of course be a different Richard Compton.

30. Note that the latter part of this statement could be true even if the former is not.

31. The tavern, from Sylvia's description, was in Hillsborough Township, Somerset County—hence the Hillsborough Richard Compton must be connected even if the Hunterdon Richard Compton is not.

APPENDIX I:
Further Reminiscences

INTERVIEWS ON NOVEMBER 1, 1883,
NOVEMBER 20, 1883, AND
DECEMBER 20, 1883

[From Original, pp. 92–98]

Eleven months have elapsed since the writing of the preceding pages, and still Sylvia Dubois lives—hale, hearty, witty, and as pious as ever. The flash of her eye still is like a gleam of a falcon. Her gait is firm, her voice clear, her hearing acute, her vision excellent. She eats well, drinks well, and smokes better. Her memory is excellent, and she takes as much interest in passing events as would one of forty years. She enjoys a joke as well as ever, and tells one with exceeding grace. He laugh is as indicative of merriment as that of a wench of eighteen. Indeed, Sylvia is alive yet.

Sylvia's good spirits do much toward prolonging her days. Her matter-of-fact way of viewing life prevents worry and keeps the machinery of her system from friction. That which wears out the machinery of the human frame more than any other one thing (I had almost said more than all else combined) is worry. From this Sylvia is ever free: she has that firm reliance upon Providence that entirely prevents any anxiety about the future. To find one better bottomed upon the Calvinistic faith is not easy: she says she grew up among the Old School Presbyterians, that she saw their ways were good and that she adopted them—that is, those of their ways

Editorial notes provided by Jared C. Lobdell.

that suit her.[1] She says, if one will only do right, Providence will provide for him. " 'Tain't no use to worry—it only makes things worse. Let come what will, you've got to bear it—'tain't no use to flinch. Providence knows best—He sends to you whatever He wants you to have, and you've got to take it and make the best of it. I've always got along somehow, and I always will—but sometimes it's pretty damned hard sledding, I tell you."

Sylvia never fidgets. When she sits, her hands rest in her lap, and she is as motionless as a statue. When she stands, she is as firm as a tree. When she walks, her gait is precise and adroit. While talking, she gesticulates not a little, but in the maneuvering of her hands, there is much grace and marked propriety. She is a hearty laugher, but her laugh is agreeable, and not very Africanic—entirely free from that labial Guinea-Negro laugh, wah! wah! wah! wah! or that palatal laugh so peculiar to the Negro, yah! yah! yah! yah! In the act of laughing, her whole frame is in motion, so much so that one might think she'd shake the soles from her shoes.

With all her vivacity, she shows decline. During her last year, she has grown old rapidly—has become emaciated and somewhat bowed. Farther, her mind shows decline, and her conversation indicates that she is verging toward the end of life: she talks much of death and of dying and seems willing to die. In the course of conversation she remarked "None of us have a lease of life, but I know I am old, and according to the way it has been with everybody else, I see I must die. I may die very suddenly—when none are expecting it—such old folks sometimes die very suddenly, but there's no telling about that."

Upon the first of November last, I called at the humble mansion in which Sylvia resides, to inquire after her health, her wants, etc., etc. It was evening and the shades of night had well nigh prevented me from following my way, so to make matters sure, I was escorted over the rocky winding path by a guide. After several stumbles, and scratches by cedar bushes, in the distance appeared a faint light. To this, I saw our guide was aiming. It was the lamp that illuminates the hut of our heroine: soon we arrived at the door, was welcomed in, entered, and stated the reason of our errand. The old lady sat in her accustomed place—in the niche between the stove and the west wall. Beside her I placed a proffered chair and began conversation. She distinctly remembered my visit upon the 27th of January 1883 and much that we talked about, faulted me for not having come to see her sooner, and inquired after the welfare of those who were with me during my last visit.

Upon inquiry, she informed me that she had enjoyed good health—that was strong and still could walk a long way—that she had just returned from Harlingen, a distance of four and a half miles. To be certain as to the manner of returning from Harlingen, I asked her:

"Who brought you from Harlingen?"

To this, in her peculiar style, she replied:

"Brought myself—nobody brought me!"

"What! Did you walk home from Harlingen this afternoon?"

"To be sure I did. How else would I get here?"

"What! A woman one hundred and sixteen years old, walk four and a half miles in an afternoon?" [2]

"Yes. There's no other way—I had to walk."

"How long were you upon the way?"

"About two hours, I guess—we came slow—had a good deal to carry—and I can't walk fast any more."

"Are you not very tired?"

"No, I ain't much tired—I'm a little tired, to be sure, and a little hungry."

Her daughter with whom Sylvia lives seemed to be gathering her winter store, and in the little hut were more pieces of furniture and boxes than I had seen before. A table, a barrel or two, and a pile of cheese-boxes, were crowded in the back part of the room, and the space in the loft seemed very full. Indeed, the little house seemed so full that there was hardly sitting room or standing room.

Elizabeth, as usual, was lavish with apology. Her house was not in order—it needed repairing—she'd had a carpenter to view it to see what could be done—mammy's dress was old and ragged and needed washing—the fire was poor: she'd not yet got her winter wood, and her stove had almost given out—and I know not what there was for which she did not apologize.

To make arrangements for the photograph of our heroine, upon the 20th of November I again called at her daughter's home. I found Sylvia in her accustomed niche, with her head and face very much swollen and very much muffled with rags and poultices. She had suffered a severe quinsy, and had not yet fully recovered her health. She was feeble and needed supporting treatment. Accordingly, I prescribed for her, and advised her daughter how to manage her poultices, etc., etc. While I was fixing her medicine, Sylvia remarked:

"I didn't used to get quinsy, nor any other kind of sore throat, but now I'm old and my teeth are out, and the wind blows right down my throat, and I take cold. Why, sometimes it blows clear down to my stomach, and further, too—why, it blows clear through me. When I had teeth, it didn't used to do so."

Arrangements were made with Sylvia to sit for her pho-tograph as soon as she was well enough to ride to the Artist's Gallery. Upon telling her that a carriage would be ready to take her at any time, she replied,

"I want you to inform me in time for me to fix myself and get on some decent clothes. Them folks at Lambertville are a proud set, and I don't want to go down there looking just anyhow. I want to look pretty sniptious."[3]

I replied, "I see, Sylvia, you are somewhat proud in your ways."

"I always was proud and liked to appear decent, and I always did appear decent when I could, but I never dressed beyond my means—I wouldn't do that."

[From Original, pp. 114–24]

Upon the nineteenth of December occurred a severe storm, and during it the snow fell to the depth of seven inches. To everyone it seemed that winter had begun with extreme vigor, and the thoughtful began to meditate respecting the prepa-rations they had made for the bleak days and the frigid nights of these trying winter months. Our thoughts were not entirely confined to our own condition, nor to the preparations that we had made for ourselves alone. Among the destitute that occurred to our mind was that aged lady, the heroine of this volume, Sylvia Dubois, who dwells with her faithful daughter Lizzie in that little old hut near the top of the mountain. To visit her, to encourage her, and to learn her needs, was quickly determined upon, and the morning of the twentieth of December, 1883, was the time appointed to pay our respects to her aged ladyship.

The sleighing was good, the air salubrious, and the scenery

inviting. Although the sky was overcast, the day was delightful. It much resembled those quiet cloudy days that I used to
see so often follow a heavy snowstorm in northern New York
and in Canada.

Not willing to enjoy the sleighing alone, nor the treat of
visiting the home of these aged mountaineers, on my way,
about nine in the morning, I called upon two of my patients,
Mrs. Rebecca Prall and Miss Eliza Prall, whom I invited to
share with me the events of the day. Soon we were ascending
the slope of the mountain. The prospect was delightful—a
cheerful winter scene. High up the hill, upon a favorable
spot, we stopped to view. The snow-clad plain beneath us
stretched away so gently that we could detect neither ridge
nor meadow, neither the course of the roads nor the meandering streams. The villages that were but a few miles away
could hardly be distinguished, while those which were but
little farther off could not be descried—so completely were
all things covered with the new-fallen snow. Toward the
northeast, the plain seemed interminable—stretched away
without hill or vale until the snowy expanse seemed bounded
by the eastern sky. But, over against us, fifteen miles away,
rose up the graceful form of Long Ridge, which lifts its
graceful crests and its bold summits to relieve the view and
beautify the landscape.

Soon we reached the crest of Cedar Summit. The scenery
here was especially delightful. The cedars covered with snow
seemed things of art, while the huge round rocks with snowy
backs, looked like the pictures of houses in Arctic scenes.
Through the winding way we wended our course, amid a
forest mostly of cedar, until at once a mountain vista came to
view, and we looked eastward, far out over a delightful plain
that stretches away until it is bounded by the sea. But soon

the vista was past, and again we wound around huge rocks and through thickets of cedars, until—there! what is that? That squalid hut built of logs and roofed with boards, windowless and chimneyless, and is fast yielding to decay?

That? Why, that's the mansion—the home of Lizzie Dubois. That's the house you've longed to see.

We dismounted from the sleigh, but ere we reached the house, Joe, the faithful dog, gave a few shrill barks, and out came the hostess to see what was disturbing the quiet of their secluded home. She met us with a smile, and bade us go in. We entered, were seated near a very warm stove, found Sylvia in her accustomed place—between the stove and the west wall—began to chat, and the time passed pleasantly. Directly, we inquired after the health of our host and her aged mother, and after their supplies for the winter. We were informed that they were destitute—that they were in want of many things, but especially they were in want of wood. They had employed some hands to cut their winter wood, but so far they had failed to find teams to haul it home. But, while talking, someone drove up with a load of wood, and then there was great rejoicing. The old woman exclaimed, "Thank heaven! I'm so glad—now we will be able to keep warm."

Sylvia had quite regained her health, was very cheerful, and much inclined to talk. She inquired after the health of many of her old acquaintances, and in all respects shew that she was alive to the affairs of the day. She talked of the coming holidays, and told us what good times they used to have during Christmas and New Year, how many parties she used to attend, how they used to dance, etc., etc.

I remarked, "Did I understand you to say that you used to dance on Christmas?"

She replied, "To be sure, we did. Why, the old slaves no

more knew the meaning of Christmas than the hogs in the pen. They only knew that it was a holiday, and that they were turned loose for some fun, and of course they had it: to be sure they danced. In those days they could dance, too."

I said, "Then you think they can't dance nowadays?"

She replied, "No, not a bit. They think they can: they stomp and jump and hop and run, and like enough turn heels over head, and they call it dancing. But it isn't dancing— they don't know how to dance. They've got no steps—they don't know any steps."

"What steps did you like best when you used to dance?"

"Well, I liked the eleven times, the twelve times, and the thirteen times: these were the best steps for me. These were the steps my grandfather, Harry Compton, used to like, and all other good dancers."

"Was Harry Compton a good dancer?"

"Well, he was! He was considered the best dancer on the mountain, or that has ever been on this mountain, or anywhere in these parts. I have seen him when he was old, dance at Princeton, and everybody who saw him said he was the best dancer they ever saw."

"Was Harry Compton a large man?"

"No, he was short, but very stout, and very strong. He was considered the strongest man on the mountain, and they used to say he was the strongest Negro that ever lived, and he was very active. He could put any man upon the ground, white or black."

"Sylvia, do you think you could dance yet?"

"Yes, I could dance yet—only had a good fiddle—I like music. A good fiddle always starts the Negro, even if he's old."

"Well, do you think you'll dance this Christmas?"

"Guess not—guess I'd better think about something else. Folks of my age had better think about dying. But I like to see 'em dance—it looks good."

In the course of conversation, Sylvia adverted to the difficulty she had had with certain folks who tried to sell her land from her. Her eyes soon began to sparkle, her voice grew loud, and her words more bulky and a little sulphurous. She soon coined some pretty hard epithets, and used them with no little force.

"I asked her, "Is the gentleman who tried to sell your land from you living yet?"

Turning her face toward me, in a very positive manner, she replied:

"He's no gentleman—he's a damned rascal!"

I said, "Well, is he living?"

She replied, "I don't know whether the devil has sent for him yet or not. If he hain't yet, he will some one of these days. He pretends he's so damned good, but he'll never get to heaven. When he buried his father, he wanted to show his piety, and he had cut upon the ornament (monument, I suppose) that he placed upon his grave, a hand with one finger pointing towards heaven. That looks pretty well, but he ought to have had a bottle of whisky engraved just above the end of the finger: that would look better, would be more significant—specially to those of us who knew him."

"Why, was his father a bad man too?"

"No, his father was not a bad man, but he did like a dram of whisky most desperate well, and he could take such a soaker, too. Really, his father was a good man—was very good to the poor—and we all liked him. He was as much to be liked for his goodness as his son is to be despised for his badness. The trouble is, when the old man died, he took all

the goodness of the family with him: what is left behind is
nothing but damned trash. His son is worse than the devil
himself, and will cheat anybody he can."

While talking, I heard the voices of chickens. They seemed
to be directly behind the chair of one of our party. To let
my companions see how mountainers care for their poultry,
I said, "Don't I hear some chickens?"

"Yes, I guess you do," replied Lizzie. "We have to fetch
our chickens into the house at night, to keep them from
thieves. They steal everything up here when they can. So I
just put my chickens in this box and bring them in. As it is
snowy today, I have not put them out. They are nice ones—
you can see 'em." So saying, she raised the lid of a large box,
and there stood the birds as sleek as doves and as docile as
children.

"Sylvia, do you ever attend church?"

"Yes, sometimes. When I was young, I used to go to
church very often, but now I don't go very often. There is
no church near us, and I can't walk so far any more. I used
to walk a good way to meeting—to Pennington, to Princeton,
to Hopewell, and to Harlingen, and to camp meeting, but I
can't walk so far any more. We used to have meeting near
by, and then I always went. But the white trash broke our
meeting up, and now I don't hear preaching any more—but
I'd like to."[4]

"Did you say you used to go to camp meeting?"

"Yes. I always went to camp meeting—specially when I was
young. That was the best kind of meeting for me—I liked
that. I'd walk ten miles to a camp meeting—further, too.
They used to have great times at camp meetings. They'd turn
out from everywhere—both blacks and whites. I've seen two
thousand folks at one meeting. There was a camp meeting

about seventy-five years ago, about four miles below Trenton, near a place called Crosswicks, and I and some more of our color went down—we walked down.[5] That was the biggest camp meeting I ever attended, and the nicest one, too. The campground was a mile long—and they had such good order. There was nobody drunk, and there were no fights, and there was no noise of any kind, except what the meeting folks made—and they had a big time—the biggest kind of a time. They hollered and shouted till you'd think the devil was in 'em. I never heard such shouting—you could hear 'em to Trenton. There were four pulpits, a good way apart, and four preachers were preaching all the time. And they hollered, and the folks hollered—good God, how they hollered: I never saw such a time—I guess nobody did. I went to stay all the week, but in about three days I got a bellyful of it, and more too, and then I started home. And when I got home, I guess I was glad—I guess no nigger was ever so glad to get home. I got enough camp meeting in those three days to last a year. But the next year I heard of another camp meeting, and I wanted to go just as bad as ever."

"Did you say the white folks disturbed your meeting?"

"Yes, they broke it up. We used to have a good meeting over here, near the Rock Mills, but this white trash around here couldn't behave. They'd come into the meetinghouse and talk right out in meeting and call each other's names—and do anything to disturb us. And when quarterly meeting came, the white trash from all over came and filled the house and the space around the house, and behaved so badly and made so much noise out of doors, that we couldn't have our meeting any more."

"Well, Sylvia, this is a hard story. It's a disgrace to the more respectable white people of the neighborhood that they

have not protected the colored church. Certainly there is
much need of a church just here—indeed, I know of no place
where one is more needed. The people of this mountain
certainly need preaching to, and if the colored people try to
have a church here, there ought to be respectable white people
enough to enforce the law and see that their meetings are not
disturbed. This matter must be looked after. We'll see if this
church can't be reorganized."[6]

When the time arrived for us to draw our visit to a close,
we bade Sylvia adieu and proceeded toward the sleigh. The
paths were not shoveled, and in Lizzie's opinion there was
some danger that the ladies, in walking to the sleigh, would
get their shoes snowy, and as a consequence, before they
arrived home, would suffer cold feet. To obviate this difficulty, the kind woman took a board from the side of the
house, extended it from the door-sill to the sleigh, and thus
secured us against the effects of the snow.

NOTES

1. This seems unlikely, so far as the "growing-up" is concerned,
as the Dubois family were of course (Dutch) Reformed, as indeed
was virtually all of Hillsborough Township. But it is worth noting
that both Minna Dubois and Elizabeth Scudder Dubois were buried
in the Presbyterian Churchyard (Hallstead Borough) (Ramanthas
M. Stocker, *Centennial History of Susquehanna County, Pennsylvania*,
[Philadelphia, 1887] p. 537).

2. Not bad for a woman of 94, in fact.

3. "Sniptious": "smart, perky" (western New York, pre-1894),
"smart, spruce" (Virginia, 1829/30), "lively" (Arkansas, 1905),
"fine" (Nebraska, 1911), "neat" (western Indiana, 1911), *Dialect
Notes*, vol. I, p. 394, vol. V, p. 431, vol. III, pp. 95, 547, 590.

Also in *DAE* with reference to 1827 and 1893. The photograph was presumably taken by Frank Z. Frity of Lambertville (*Princeton Recollector*, vol. V, no. 4 [Winter 1980], p. 19). A woodcut made from the photograph appears as the frontispiece, from which one can determine whether Sylvia did in fact look sniptious.

4. There was an A. M. E. Church near Rock Mills, in the very southwestern corner of Hillsborough Township, in 1880 and for ten or fifteen years before (James P. Snell, *History of Hunterdon and Somerset Counties, New Jersey* [Philadelphia, 1881], p. 793). Whether this was Sylvia's "meeting" I am not sure.

5. The Crosswicks meeting: I have been unable to date this (I suspect 1819, a year of religious fervor in the area). Miss Gertrude Brick, Historian of Chesterfield Township (where Crosswicks is located) tells me there are no Methodist records there between 1790 and 1842. She suggests a possible location at Wesley Grove on the Crosswicks-Yardville road. (Phone conversation, June 24, 1981.)

6. This interchange is peculiar in view of the account of the "Mountain Mission" given in Snell, *History* (p. 792).

THE MOUNTAIN MISSION *

is an enterprise of recent origin, having for its object the evangelization of the districts of Sourland Mountain hitherto unreached by religious organizations. These neglected portions were more or less bordered by Reformed and Presbyterian Churches, which felt reproached at the long-continued destitution prevailing in such close proximity to them. They therefore formed an association for the support of a mountain mission. The following delegates convened near the close of the autumn of 1876 in the Reformed church of Neshanic for the purpose of consummating the association: Rev. George S. Mott, D.D. (appointed chairman) and Elder S. B. Stothoff, of the Presbyterian Church of Flemington; Rev. John Gardner and Elder D. Stryker, of the Reformed Church of Harlingen; Rev. Charles S. Converse and Elder John W.

---

* By Rev. M. N. Oliver, of Clover Hill.

Bellis, of the Presbyterian Church at Larison Corners; Rev. John Hart and Elder Peter P. Dilts, of the Reformed Church of Neshanic; Rev. W. B. Vorhees and Elder P. I. Stryker, from the Reformed Church of Blawenburg; Rev. M. N. Oliver and Elder Levi Reed, from the Reformed Church of Clover Hill; Rev. J. S. Beekman (who acted as clerk) and Elder Abram J. Prall, from the Presbyterian Church at Reaville; Elder Burniston, from the Reformed Church of South Branch; Rev. John Smock, from the Reformed Church of Readington; Rev. Herman C. Berg, from the Reformed Church of Rocky Hill; Rev. J. H. Hewit, from the Presbyterian Church at Ringos.

The association, thus formed, proceeded at once to the execution of its mission. A chapel was erected at a suitable place on the mountain, and a missionary employed to conduct religious services, organize Sabbath-schools, visit families, pray with the sick, bury the dead, and labor for souls. The following is excerpted from the report of the missionary for the year 1879, made to the association at their annual meeting:

> Regular religious services have been held in chapel twice a Sabbath during the year; attendance good; ten have been received into the membership of the church on confession; baptized sixteen, of whom five were adults; have officiated at three funerals and six marriages. The membership of the church is 34. About 40 children are enrolled in the Sabbath-school, the regular attendance of which is about 30. Two of the Sabbath-school scholars have united with the church; the remaining eight, who became church-members, were heads of families. In family visitation, am well received. There are between 30 and 40 families that make the chapel their religious home. There are about 200 families on both sides of the mountain."

The following churches have contributed for the benefit of the mission the past year: the Reformed Churches of Neshanic, Blawenburg, Clover Hill, Second Somerville, Millstone, East Millstone, Harlingen, South Branch, and the Presbyterian Churches of Ringos, Larison, Flemington, Mount

Airy, Lambertville, and Reaville. Personal contributions have also been made by Paul Tulane, of Princeton, Hon. F. T. Frelinghuysen, of Newark, Mr. Caleb S. Green, of Trenton, Mr. Harvey Fisk, of New York, and Mr. Henry H. Palmer, of New Brunswick.

The missionary in the employ of the association is Rev. F. A. Farrow. The officers are Rev. John Gardner, President; Rev. M. N. Oliver, Secretary; John B. Hopewill, Treasurer. The executive committee consists of the following ministers: Voorhees, Converse, Hart, Oliver, and Dr. Mott, with an elder from each of their churches.

APPENDIX II:
Other Documents Relating to Sylvia Dubois or Her Master

MANUMISSION OF HENRY COMPTON, SLAVE TO MILES SMITH

(Documents show Compton became Smith's slave in 1801 or 1803, and that he was born no later than 1800 and no earlier than 1781: he is presumably the son of Dorcas Compton, slave to Miles Smith and mother of Sylvia Dubois.)

Know all men by these presents that I, Henry Compton, do hereby release unto Miles Smith Esquire, all causes of action & all claims and demands against him whatever. Given under my hand and seal this (blank) day of August in the year of our Lord eighteen hundred and twenty five.

Signed Sealed and delivered in presence of (blank)

I certify that Henry Compton, formerly my slave, lived with me eighteen or twenty years, and during that time I found him honest, sober, and of general good conduct

—signed Miles Smith

From Rutgers University Library, general manuscript collection, New Brunswick, New Jersey.

New Brunswick
June 13 1825

Middlesex County To wit We do hereby certify that on this Twelfth day of November in the year of our Lord, one thousand eight hundred and twenty one, Miles Smith of the Township of Piscataway in the County of Middlesex aforesaid Brought before us, two of the overseers of the poor of the Township aforesaid, and two of the Justices of the peace of the Said County, his Slave named Henry Compton who, on view and examination, appears to us to be Sound in mind, and not under any bodily incapacity of obtaining a Support, and also is not under the age of twenty one years, nor above the age of forty years—

In Witness whereof, we have hereunto Set our hands, the day and year above written

Ephraim Runyon	Overseers of the poor of
John Dayton	the Said Township of
	Piscataway
James Dunham	Justices of the peace in
Samuel Stelle (?)	& for the Said County
	of Middlesex

(on reverse)

Certificate
Henry Compton

Miles Smith Esqr

Received in Middlesex Clerks office December 15. 1821 & recorded in Book of Manumissions folio 350 by Wm P. Deare (?) clk (?)

LETTERS OF ABRAHAM DUBOIS IN PHILADELPHIA TO HIS BROTHER MINNA DUBOIS AT GREAT BEND (1805–7)

(The Letter Book from which these letters are taken begins in 1805, so it cannot be used for evidence on the date of Minna's arrival at Great Bend. The only other papers of Abraham Dubois I have been able to discover are those in the Historical Society of Pennsylvania, marked 1792– 1809, and dealing with the West Indies and particularly with his ship, the Yorick, *captured in 1794. These are of value only in arguing against the view of William Heidgerd that Minna Dubois's capture dates from the 1790s [De- scendants of Chretien Du Bois of Wicres,* II, p. 144]: *if Minna had been at sea in the 1790s, it would almost certainly have been in his brother's ships, and if he had been captured, these papers would almost certainly contain some reference to it.)*

Minna Dubois, Luzerne   Ph'a July 17th 1805

Dear Brother

I wrote you some time ago requesting you to inform me the am't of my tax on the 20 first tracts, as well as the 27 Bo't at Sh'ffs Sale Claimed by Mr Meredith, as I found the Comm's were advertising for the tax to be paid in 3 Mo. or that they (illeg) would be sold for the tax, & I am this day informed by Mr Hodgson that the Sales for tax is to take place next month, & having not yet heard from you upon the Subject,

From Abraham Dubois Letter Book, Eleutherian Mills Library, Greenfield, Delaware.

I Renew my request that you will attend to the needful for me, at any rate write me by the Mail & inform me if any of my lands are advertized to be sold for the tax. the Claim of Mr M is not yet settled for reasons I can hardly tell. I am tired of land jobing business. I find it not only troublesome, but expensive & unprofitable—I was in hopes of paying you a Visit this season, but fear I shall not be able as I intend making a trip to the Eastward next month & shall be away at least 30 days, therefore wish to hear from you immediately.—I have the pleasure to add that we are all well & that we have an addition to the family of a Son since the last (?) of May. Please to make our best love to Sister Betsey, who we hope is well & that she is still Satisfied with that part of the country in expectation of hearing from you I Remain your Af'c Br   A Dubois

P. S. Please to say when the Sale of land for tax will take place & if the tracts are Described in Advert'z as heretofore. I am told there is a new Law respecting the sale of land for tax.   A

Minna Dubois   Philad'a 2nd Dec'r 1805

Dear Brother

On my return from Boston the 1st Oct'r I found your letter of the 30th Aug't last & I am much disappointed to find that the turnpike will not go on any part of my land, from wch I had great expectations, but now I can exp't nothing but the continuance of enormous taxes without any benefits from it. S Butler (?) was here last month & presented my transcript of tax for the 20 tracts $214 50 the tax on 27 tracts Claimed by Meredith are not assertain'd S B told me that Mr M declin'd paying the tax on them & I promised to pay it in 30

days, but have since seen the Att'y of Mr M & he tells me
that they do not refuse to pay the tax but that they wish to
have the tax suspended a few weeks untill they may make a
settlement with me I expect they'll invest on the land they
paying me the cost—I fear that Tyler will make no Sales of
land for me, & this resurvey may only be a Catchpenny Job
as it will cost 50 \$—I have long wanted to come & see your
Country, but as I am disappointed on the turnpike, 't is
probable now that I never shall, & I am now willing to take
payment for the land in turnpike stock for the land at least
in part, tho I have a very poor Opinion of the Stock. I have
only to add that we are all well as usuall and our little boy
grows finely & is now Just 6 Months old my Wife & family
Unites   in   love   with   you   &   yours   with   your
& c   AD

P. S. please to let me hear from you soon & Say if you can
make any sales of land in that way

Minna Dubois   Philad'a March 20th 1806

Dr Brother
I am just favor'd with your letter of the 11th of Feb last
from which you must not have rec'd mine dated the 2nd of
Dec'r in reply to yours of the 4th of August. mine was
forwarded to the care of Thos Wright Post Master at Wilkes
Barre. I observe wh't you say respecting my taking turnpike
shares for the land in your quarter. my last would have
informed you that I was willing to take the shares for my
land provided I was to make no other advance. I am willing
to sell evry other tract in that way divided into 4, or the one
half of each tract provided they are not to take the (? illeg
"shores"). I hope ere long to have the matter settled with

Meridith, & if I get that we can go a great lenght (sic) in the way of turnpike shares & I hope the land is tolerable good price; I am much disappointed by the turnpike not going thro my land w'h wou'd have been much in my favor— this will go by a Mr Picknole who goes on business in your County. should you see him I hope you'll render him any Civilities in your power—& if you have an oppertunity (sic) please to let us know when we may expect you here—I must also mention to you that I shall expect the old affair adjusted & finally settled when you come to town next. I have alotted that balance to pay nearly the same sum due the Estate of Brother Tyson—the Adm'r was duning me when I was in Jersey Aug't last, when I told the adm'r it was in your hands for that purpose, & wou'd soon be paid—Mr Drinker (?) has told me that he had subscribed sundry shares for land but did not say at what price for the land I have only to add that we are all well as usual. please to make our best love to Sister Betsey & believe that I am your truly Affectionate Br   A Dubois your last came via Shenango

Minna Dubois   Philad'a April 11th 1806

Dr Br
I wrote you the 20th Ult by a Mr Picknole who has not yet gone this will go by Mr Terry who has bro't me a survey of the outlines of my 20 tracts of land in your County wth some remarks &c. I have already replied to your letter of Feb last via Chenango, Wherein I agreed to take turnpike share(s) for at least ½ of each tract of those lands equally divided provided I am to make no advance in cash & the land at a fair price. I also requested to know when we are to expect you here & that I should then expect a final settlem't of the

old score(?) as the Adm'r of Tysons Estate was urging the business to a close—I need hardly mention to you that we have had uncommon weather for 6 Weeks past & the cold this day is intense—please to say when you begin to work at the turnpike & how your funds hold out &c. If I can settle the affair of the Other land with Meredith I shall be willing to vest the greater part in the turnpike stock. —We are thro Mercy, all well, & with our best love to Sister B & Self Remain Affectionately your B

AD

Minna Dubois   Ph'a 22nd May 1807

Dear Brother

Mr P Catlin on me the moment he was about to leave the City merely to say that he had seen you on his way here & that you were all well. I am much disappointed in not seeing you here in all last month, as from your letter by Dr Frazer (?) you were certainly to be here in April, & I had calculated upon it—since Mr Cruthers Return from over the mountains, I have by perseverance assertain'd that he has never yet Returned the 3 Surveys made out by Hart, & he has the Returns still by him, & is willing now either to have the Returns made or to give up the papers as we please, & I have only been waiting for your arrival here to have the matter fixt. I have taken time to examine & compare the Surveys with the Gen D'ft, & find that about 220 A's of the 414 A's survey is upon the very Summit of the Mountain extending about One & ¼ of a Mile from the River upon your line from the River, & the Other 100 Acre tract joins the upper end of the 414 Acre survey, from the River, joining Mr Drinker's line up the Creek taking in the Very tip of the Moundain about a mile further, so that the whole adjoining (~~tract~~) 320 A's there are not worth as many Cents, & as it is now laid down & Returned—as to the 100 A's below where your Mill is built, the Upper end must interfere, Mr Caruthers says, with some old Surveys, & that no encroachments has been made upon it. I find that our Warrants are dated in June 1792 which are Earlier than most of the Warrants Covering those mountains & I should suppose they may not yet be laid where they were originally intended if it is your intention to have them resurvey'd, you must Send for the Papers by some good Op'ty, or come yourself which would be more agreeable—please to let me hear from you without delay should you not come soon—We are in health thro Mercy & my Wife & family Joins in Love & Congratulations to you & yours with your truly Affectionate Br   A Dubois

Minna Dubois   Ph'a Oct'r 7th 1807

Dr Brother
Your letter from Princeton of June last, covering 50 $ for Mr Heberton, I answered by the return'g Mail, to the same place as you request'd. I have since rec'd the 3 Warrants from Mr Cruthers, & wou'd have forwarded them to you by the present Op'ty Mr Skyner (?) only that your letter mentioned yr intention of being here soon, & I wish to confer with you respecting a resurvey. I have already mentioned to you the situation of the 2 Upper tracts, & it will perhaps be best to let the other survey stand, & be return'd by Cruthers, who is Just going for the Winter season to the Western Country—if you are not coming here soon I wish you to Write me on the subject & say when you will be here—as

these surveys have never been returned there can be no limitation respecting a resurvey—how goes on the turnpike & have Corbit & you got any setlers on my land? My son Abr'm has just arr'd (?) from N Carolina where he has done nothing, or but little to advantage—my family are all well & Join in love to you & yours wth your

Affectionate Br AD

(Abraham Dubois Senr died later in October 1807)

A REMINISCENCE BY JOSEPH DUBOIS
(1812–85)

Of His Grandfather:

"My great-grandfather, Abraham Du Bois, received his portion on the death of his father, and moved to New Jersey. He had three sons: Abraham, Nicholas, and Minna. My grandfather, Minna Du Bois, was the youngest of that family. He was a wild youth, ran away, shipped and went to France. This was just before the Revolution. In the war that was then going on between France and England, my grandfather Du Bois joined the French navy. The vessel to which he belonged was captured by the English, and he and the other prisoners were taken to England and kept as prisoners in the mountains of Wales, until the war was over. He then came home. His brother Abraham, a wealthy jeweller in Philadelphia, and a large land-owner, made him an agent and sent him to Great Bend, to take care of his landed estate in this section. Several tracts here bore the warrantee name of his son, Nicholas Du Bois.

From Emily Blackman, *History of Susquehanna County* (Philadelphia, 1873), pp. 66, 72.

"Minna Du Bois was twice married; Abraham was the son of his first wife; and Jane (Mrs. Lusk), an only daughter of his last wife. The house in which the latter was born now forms a part of the Lusk House, at the south end of the bridge, where Minna Du Bois kept a public house for years, and here Benajah Strong had one before him; and Abraham Du Bois, his son, after him (1812). Mr. Du Bois died March 14, 1824, aged seventy years. His wife afterwards resided with her daughter in Montrose, where she died December 30, 1848, aged eighty years.

Of the Ferries:

"James Parmeter's ferry having become very profitable, another pioneer built a house on the opposite side of the river; and he too built a ferry boat, and opened an opposition ferry. As the road through here was fast becoming a great thoroughfare, both of these ferrymen made money. In the winter season, they found it difficult to cross with boats, owing to the floating ice in the middle of the river. As the country along the Susquehanna was mostly a wilderness, our river did not freeze entirely over as readily as now. Strong ice would form along each shore for four or five rods in width, the middle of the stream remaining for a long time open. These ferrymen would then proceed to build an ice bridge after this manner: After measuring the distance from the solid ice on each side of the river, they would commence immediately above, and laying out the width and length they would saw out of the solid shore ice a bridge, and, holding fast one end, would swing the other end across the open chasm till it rested against the solid ice on the other side; then by dipping water from the river in freezing weather they soon formed a strong and safe bridge for teams to pass, the travellers freely paying toll for crossing this ice bridge. This ferry was kept up until the fall of 1814, when the first Great Bend Bridge was completed."

A REMINISCENCE BY WILLIAM STUART
(b. 1789)

(This selection from Stuart's reminiscences is included because it covers the northeastern [Yankee-Yorker] part of Pennsylvania, including the Beach Woods [sic] and the raftsmen on the Susquehanna, at the same time [1806–7] that Sylvia was with Minna Dubois at Great Bend. Stuart was not, so far as I know, at Great Bend at this or any time—but he is an alternative source for what was going on, and not one commonly available or likely to be thought of in this connection. He does bear out Sylvia's comments on the fauna of the Beech Woods.)

My stay at Easton was four or five days, and I mounted my sick and jaded horse for the Susquehanna region. I progressed slowly, my horse being feeble, but in four days the Tunkhannock Mountains showed their cragged eminences, and through them passed the rapid waters of the Susquehanna River. I arrived at the house of my uncle, and found his family in good health and spirits, and there also the beautiful girl, whose charms kept me steady for some months previous.

From William Stuart, *Sketches of the Life of William Stuart, the First and Most Celebrated Counterfeiter of Connecticut* (Bridgeport, 1854; reprinted New Milford, 1932), pp. 19–23.

This region of country was wild and picturesque, and the people generally were Dutch and Yankees, of the most filthy, wild, and vulgar kind that could be conceived. I had just left Connecticut, and its enlightened communities, and had dropped down as it were among a race as debased and corrupt as those who have already entered the stygian pool.

But though this state of society was first so repulsive, I soon got used to it and became somewhat gratified with their rude, drinking, boisterous characters. I resolved to stay a year, and try my fortune among them. I was engaged in diverse pursuits. Sometimes I hunted bears, sometimes panthers, wolves, deer, etc., for the woods and mountains were overcharged with game. Sometimes we had frolics of the most noisy sort. We drank whiskey, not in half gills, as it is taken now, but in gallons and barrels. Every family had their whisky cask, and it was drunk by old and young, males and females, as plentifully as if it were cow's milk.

It can easily be conceived what followed such a course of life. Every evening a gang assembled at the numerous taverns to drink, tell stories, and fight. When they had become half drunk, they were noisy and quarrelsome, gouging out the eyes was one of their barbarous practices, and nearly one third of the German population had but one eye. I saw one day, a horse with one eye, carrying upon his back the husband, wife and child, each with only one eye.

This gouging they called sport, but I thought it dear. Upon every Sunday, crowds collected at the taverns, and the day was spent in drinking, swearing and fighting. The people were usually poor, as they spent their time and money at these domestic hells. The world was here abounding in lumber. We chopped down the trees, sawed them into boards and planks, made rafts, and floated them down the river to market. We stopped nights, and invariably had sprees, quarrels, fights, and in a general break-down drag-out style. In the morning we went upon our rafts and rowed down stream until night. Then another general storm broke out, and the scenes of the preceding evening were reenacted. Thus we went on till we held up at tidewater, delivered our rafts to the merchants and left them.

These rafts were numerous, and each was accompanied by three men. Fifty or sixty rafts oftentimes went on in company.

We returned up the banks of the river on foot, with kegs and guns. Whether raftsmen have reformed I have never learned; but if they continue up to this day so reckless, profane and brutal, the state of society where they congregate must be infernal.

Upon our returning tours, every night was wild with carousals, gambling, fighting and their kindred vices. For a young man like me, associating daily and nightly with these clans of wild human beasts, and entering as I did, with full soul and heart deeply into vices and petty crimes, it soured my sensibilities, steeled every kind emotion, and drove me onward to delight and glory in being an outcast from decent men. My nature was easily led at an infinite remoteness from the practice of every virtue, and like the others, I madly rushed headlong down the steep of irredeemable ruin. Before we got back our money was wasted and gone, our bodies defaced by the encounters in which we had been engaged, our clothing as tattered as an Italian Lazzaroni's, and our moral tendencies extinguished in utter darkness.

I was from the land of steady habits, having been reared in the vicinity of churches and schools, and here I was then, indulging in revelries of pandemonium. When ruminating upon this subject and those scenes, in the after calm and sober periods of my life, the remembrance of the perilous times when I was first among the foremost in daring vice, has caused me to shudder; and the advice that I would give my fellow man is, to go as far from the example I have been, as "from the centre to thrice the utmost pole."

In our returning trips, besides the rowdyism, drunkenness, profanity, gambling and debaucheries, we were by day continually annoying some man or brutally committing michievous pranks and petty thefts upon the rude population. We called at a widow woman's house and asked for milk, and while she was gone after it, we lifted the lid to her half barrel churn, I threw in the cat, and Wm. Keeler crowded the brute with the dasher to the bottom of the cream, and the lid was restored. The good woman gave us as much milk as we liked; we thanked and left her to make some butter for her family. If any reader curses me for this ingratitude, all I can say is, that I deserve his execrations, and to be executed "without the benefit of clergy."

At another time, being alone and out of money, I found a cow in the woods with a bell strapped to her neck. I approached her soothingly, then sprang and grasped the bell strap, and the cow ran like a deer through the brush, jumping and kicking at me. The bell strap broke, and I gained the noisy prize.

Evening drew on, the clouds covered up the sky, and night was near at hand, and menaced me with utter darkness in the woods. At a little opening I espied a tavern stand upon a grass plat near a bend of the river, and entered it. I told the landlord that I had no money, but that I had found a bell in the woods, and he agreed to give me supper, lodging and breakfast, and a dollar and a half for the bell.

I give these two facts as specimens of my enterprise upon

my journeys, and the heartless condition of my mind. Daily occurrences of like turpitude, were committed by me and my associates. It was then apparently a God-forsaken and God-forgotten country. Not a church or a school house in the distance of 250 miles. How could men reform? And by this continued intercourse with each other, the whole community became "earthly, sensual, devilish."

After my return from a rafting expedition, our rows, dances, frolics, gamblings, fightings, and carousals, were renewed, and although previously at these orgies there seemed no execrable condition on earth to rival them, yet in this school of infamy, our gangs saw that we had increased our wicked and diabolical propensities. The females delighted in these accessions of grossness and vulgarity, and were apt scholars to learn the rudest phrases that could shock modesty and decency. But the men were more wicked than the women. In a genuine good natured frolic and dance, the girls always manifest more elated spirits than the men. Their cheerfulness and hearty love of mirth and festivity much exceed in fulness and gleeful satisfaction. They were not cast in the roughest molds, and though rude and untaught, they graced the festive scenes with charms that such periods in their absence could never command. Such was the case in our hop at Zu. Sherwood's, near to Mrs. Hadley's, the landlady of Beach woods. This spree made me some trouble, but furnished sport for a month. Our dance was at Sherwood's, but our entertainment was furnished by Mrs. Hadley, in the immediate vicinity.

About eight o'clock in the evening, we were summoned to the supper. The weather was cold, and the Susquehanna solid as granite. Among the delicacies of the supper table, Mrs. Hadley set out in the centre an earthern pot filled with candied honey, and it was so solid it was with much difficulty that we could get the honey from the pot. While the landlady's back was turned, I rose from my seat, took up the pot of honey, carried it out of the door and put it in an oven a rod from the house.

We paid up our bills, and the old woman did not miss her honey. As we returned to the ball room, I took along the pot, broke off the earthern encasement, and set up the mess of honey on the table. Every girl and boy took what they liked, and ate it. The men filled their great mugs with whisky, sweetened with honey, and we treated ourselves and the girls as long as they could drink. The ball closed about the same time that the honey was consumed. In truth, we had a *sweet* time.

No man ever saw a company in better spirits, and well they might be. Whisky and honey loosened my tongue, and the fun and the frolic was of the nicest kind. Daylight found us at home. In the morning poor Mrs. Hadley missed her honey, and was wide awake to catch the rogue. Of course I was suspected, and old Squire Worden issued a writ against me and gave it to a squash headed constable by the name of Jonathan McMullen, to arrest me.

april 13 ## A FAMOUS NEGRESS. _1888_

The severe weather in America has killed Sylvia Dubois, the famous negress of Sour Land Mountain, New Jersey. She is said to have been 122 years old "beyond doubt." She was for years the slave of a man named Dubois. Then she was sold to a man who kept an hotel, where she became famed for her feats of strength and for the pri e-fights in which she engaged. She boasted that she was never beaten, and had knocked out scores of the strongest men. One day she got angry at her mistress and nearly killed her. She picked up her child and fled across the Susquehana and tramped all the way to Sour Land Mountain, where she lived the rest of her life. Her fondness for fighting, for liquor, and her profanity soon made her notorious. All her children died but the youngest ; who remained with her mother, and is eighty years old. It is said that she inherits all her mother's pugilistic prowess, and has maimed many men.

SILVIA DUBOIS,

BORN MARCH 5th, 1768.

SILVIA DUBOIS,

(NOW 116 YERS OLD.)

A BIOGRAFY

—OF—

The Slav who Whipt her Mistres

—AND—

GAND HER FREDOM.

BY C. W. LARISON, M. D.,

PRINCIPAL OF THE ACADEMY OF SIENC AND ART AT RINGOS, N. J.:
FORMERLY PROF. NATURAL SIENC IN THE UNIVERSITY AT LEWIS-
BURG, PA.; AUTHOR OF ELEMENTS OF ORTHOEPY;
THE TENTING SCHOL, &c., &c.

RINGOS, N. J.:
C. W. LARISON, PUBLISHER.
1883.

PREFAC.

Aş mŭeh ïntĕrĕst ạlwaş ătăehĕş tọ wŭn whö lïvş tọ à vĕrў grat aġ, ănd aş à negrĕs so old ăş Sïlvïả Dụboiş ïş sĕldŭm non, I hăv thŏt thăt ăn outlin biŏgrafў ŏv hĕr mit be desird bў the redïṇg pŭblïc. The mor so, beeaş whil gĕtïṇg the biŏgrafў ŏv the heroïn, à vảst ảmount ŏv the cŭstŭmş ănd mănĕrş ŏv the pepl wïth hwọm she lïvd ïş ạlsọ ăequird, ănd ä knŏlĕdg ŏv the waş ŏv folks ŏv à hŭndrĕd yerş àgo gand.

In ritïṇg thïs, skĕteh, I hăv bïn ăş bref ăş çïreŭmstănçĕş wŭd àlou. Aş mŭeh ŏv the măttĕr ĕntĕrïṇg ïntọ thĕ eŏmpoşïshŭn ŏv thïs bọk waş gŏtĕn frŏm hĕr, ïn à eŏloquïăl mănnĕr, ănd ăş thïs waş pụt ŭpŏn papĕr, ïn shorthănd, jŭst ăş she spok ït, ănd ăş by gïvïṇg hĕr on wŭrdş ïn the ordĕr ănd styl ïn whïeh she spok thĕm, portraş mor ŏv the cărăetĕr, ïntĕllïġĕnç, ănd forç ŏv the heroïn thăn eăn pŏsiblў be gïvĕn ïn anў ŭthĕr wa, I hăv rïtĕn the

most ĕsĕnshàl pärts ŏv ĭt, ĕxăctlў ăs̲ she re-
latĕd the făets tọ me.

The nărătĭv àbounds̲ ĭn profănĭtў, ăn ĕlemĕnt
thăt ĭs̲ fŏrĕn tọ me, ănd wŭn thăt I most eor-
dyălў despis̲, ănd sĭnçerlў dĕprecat. Bŭt,
Sĭlvĭà ĭs̲ à profan negrĕs; hĕr lăngwaġ ạlwas̲
àbounds̲ ĭn profănĭtў; ănd, tĕrs ănd forçibl ăs̲
ĭt ĭs̲, căstigat ĭt ŏv ĭts profan wŭrds̲, ănd ĭt ĭs̲
flăt ănd menĭnglĕs, ănd ŭtĕrlў fals̲ tọ conva the
ideà ĭntĕnĕd, or tọ revel hĕr cărăctĕr. In the
nărătĭv, mȳ am ĭs̲ mor tọ sho the cărăctĕr, forç
ănd spĭrĭt ŏv ĭndepĕndĕnç ŏv thĕ heroin, thăn
tọ mak out à lŏng lin ŏv yers̲; or tọ tĕl wĭth
họm she dwĕlt. Tọ ăeŏmplĭsh thĭs, I mŭst
us̲ thos wŭrds̲ ănd frases̲ peculĭăr tọ hĕrsĕlf,
hwĭeh àlon är ădequat tọ thĕ tàsk befor me.
Thĭs thĕn ĭs̲ mȳ àpŏloġў for the profănĭtў thăt
so ạbŭndàntlў ĕxĭst ĭn thĭs storў.

In the orthŏgrafў ŏv thĭs bọk, I hăv, ĭn the
man, amd tọ fŏlo the ru̲ls̲ ŏv the Spĕlĭng Reform. Thăt ĭn sŭm ĭnstànçes̲ I hav fald, thĕr
ĭs̲ no doubt. Bŭt, ĭn mĕnў ĭnstànçes̲ ĭn hwĭeh
I hav nŏt fŏlod the ădvis ŏv the Fĭlŏlŏgĭc
Soçietў, I hăv dŭn so becạs I thŏt the ădvis ŏv
thăt bŏdў, respĕetĭng thes pàrtĭculàr ĭnstànçes̲
nŏt wĕl foundĕd (ăs̲ ĭn usĭng ŏ for o ĭn the

würd or), or ĕls nŏt prăctĭc ăt thĕ prĕsĕnt tim. In the futur, pĕrhăps, sŭm ŏf thĕ changĕs tọ hwĭch I alụd wĭl be prătic. And hwĕn the redĭng pepl är prepard for thĕm, nŭn wĭl be mor rĕdy̆ tọ adŏpt thĕm thăn I. Indĕd, I lŏng tọ se thĕ tim hwĕn wŭn cărăctĕr wĭl rĕprezĕnt bŭt wŭn fon; ănd wŭn fon ĭs rĕprezĕntĕd by̆ wŭn cărăctĕr.

Bŭt, hwil I ăm nŏt wilĭng tọ adŏpt, ĭn ĕvĕry̆ ĭnstănç, jŭst nou, ĕvĕry̆ maṣur rĕcŏmĕndĕd by the Cŏmĭte ŏn thĕ Reform ŏv Englĭsh Spĕlĭng, thĕr är mĕny̆ maṣurs, nŏt rĕcŏmĕndĕd by the cŏmĭte, thăt ạr mŭch nedĕd, ănd thăt I shăl ăt wŭnç adŏpt.

Tọ fŏlo thĕ spĕlĭng nou ĭn vog, ĭṣ ŭtĕrly̆ ăbsŭrd. Sŭch a menĭnglĕṣ, jŭmblĭng ŏv cărăctĕrṣ ăṣ ŏcŭr ĭn the prĭntĭng or ritĭng ŏv würds ăṣ found ĭn most bọks ănd neuspapĕrṣ ĭṣ ŭnpárdŭnábl, ănd ĭnsŭltĭng tọ the tast ănd jŭdg̣mĕnt ŏv ạll redĕrṣ ŏv çŭltur. A feu yerṣ ȧgo, ritĕrṣ cụd nŏt safly̆ dọ ŭthĕrwiṣ thăn tọ fŏlo thĭs çĕnsurábl spĕlĭng; bŭt, sĭnç thĭs wid-sprĕd cŏnçĕrted ăcshŭn ŏv the Spĕlĭng Reformĕrṣ—mĕn ŏf thĕ hiĕst ănd bradĕst çŭltur, ănd so famŭsly̆ non ăṣ crĭtĭcs ănd techĕrṣ ĭn our Colĕg̣ĕs ănd Unĭvĕrsitĭṣ, thĕr ĭs, ăt thĕ bĕst, bŭt por ĕxcus for cŏntĭnuĭng to spĕl wŭrds wĭth áfonĭc cărăctĕrs.

As ĭt ma hăpĕn thăt sŭm ho är nŏt ăcqwantĕd wĭth thĕ Reformd spĕlĭng ŏv the Englĭsh lăngwag ma red thĭs bok, to hĕlp thĕm to lĕrn thĕ neu orthŏgrafў, ănd to façĭlitat thar prŏgrĕs ĭn redĭng thes pagĕs, I her ĭntrŏduç the ruls sŭbmĭtĕd ĭn the "Report ŏv the Amĕricàn Cŏmĭte ŏn thĕ Reform ŏv Englĭsh Spĕlĭng." In statĭng thes ruls, so fär ăs ĭt suts mў pŭrpŭs, I us thĕ lăngwag ŏv Dr. F. A. March, athŭr ŏv thĕ rĕpŏrt çitĕd.

RULS OV THE COMITE ON THE REFORM OF
ENGLISH SPELING.

1. e.—Drŏp silĕnt e hwĕn fŏnĕtĭcàlў uslĕs, ăs ĭn live, lĭv; vineyard, vĭnyàrd; believe, belev; bronze, brŏnz; single, sĭngl; engine, ĕngĭn; granite, grănĭt; eaten, etn; rained, rand, etc.

2. ea.—Drŏp a frŏm ea hăvĭng thĕ sound ŏv ĕ, ăs ĭn feather, fĕthĕr; leather, lĕthĕr; jealous, jĕlŭs, etc.

3. eau.—For beauty, us thĕ old beutў,—buty.

4. eo.—Drŏp o frŏm eo hăvĭng thĕ sound ŏv ĕ, ăs ĭn jeopardy, jĕpárdў; leopard, lĕpàrd. For yeoman, rit yomàn.

5. i.—Drŏp i ŏv parliament, pärlȧmĕnt.

6. o.—Fŏr o hăvĭn͟g the sound ŏv ŭ ĭn bŭt, rit ŭ, ăs̱ ĭn above, ȧbŭv; dozen, dŭzn; some, sŭm; tongue, tŭn͟g, etc. For women, restor wĭmĕn.

7. ou.—Drŏp o frŏm ou hăvĭn͟g thĕ sound ŏv ŭ, ăs̱ ĭn journal, jŭrnȧl; nourish, nŭrĭsh; trouble, trŭbl; rough, rŭf; tough, tŭf, etc.

8. u.—Drŏp silĕnt u ȧftĕr g befor ă, ănd ĭn nătĭv En͟glĭsh wŭrds, ăs̱ ĭn guarantee, gărȧnte; guard, gärd; guess, gĕs; guild, gĭld; guilt, gĭlt.

9. ue.—Drŏp ue ĭn apologue, ăpolŏg; catalogue, cătȧlŏg; demagogue, dĕmȧgŏg, etc.

10. y.—Spĕl rhyme, rime,—rim.

11. Dŭbl cŏnsonȧnts ma be ˈsĭmplĭfid: Fĭnȧl b, d, g, n, r, t, f, l, x, ăs̱ ĭn ebb, ĕb; add, ăd; egg, ĕg; inn, ĭn; purr, pŭr; butt, bŭt; bailiff, balĭf; dull, dŭl; buzz, bŭz; (not all). Medial befor ănŭthĕr cŏnsonȧnt, ăs̱ ĭn battle, bătl; ripple, rĭpl; written, rĭtn. Inĭshȧl ŭnăccĕntĕd prefĭxĕs̱, ănd ŭthĕr ŭnăcçĕntĕd sўlȧbls̱, ăs̱ ĭn abbreviate, ȧbrevĭat; accuse, ȧcūs; affair, ȧfar; traveller, trăvĕlĕr.

12. b.—Drŏp ȧfonĭc b ĭn bomb, bŏm; crumb, crŭm; debt, dĕt; doubt, dout; dumb, dŭm;

lamb, lam ; limb, lĭm ; numb, nŭm ; plumb, plŭm; subtle, sŭtl; succumb, sŭcŭm; thumb, thŭm.

13. c.—Chang̣ c bǎk tọ s ĭn cinder, sĭndĕr ; expence, ĕxpĕns ; fierce, fers ; hence, hĕns ; once, wŭns ; pence, pĕns ; scarce, scars ; since, sĭns ; source, sors ; thence, thĕns ; tierce, ters ; whence, hwĕns.

14. ch.—Drŏp thĕ h ŏv ch ĭn chamomile, cǎmomil ; cholera, cŏlerà ; choler, cŏlĕr ; melancholy, mĕlàncŏlў ; school, scọl ; stomach, stŭmàc.

15. d.—Chang̣ d ǎnd ed finàl tọ t hwĕn sọ pronounc̣t, ǎs̱ ĭn crossed, crŏst ; looked, lọkt, ete.

16. g.—Drŏp g ĭn feign, fan ; foreign, fŏrĕn ; sovereign, sŏvĕrĕn.

17. gh.—Drŏp h ĭn aghast, àgǎst : burgh, bŭrg : ghost, gost.

Drŏp gh ĭn haughty, hàtў : though, tho : through, thrụ.

Chang̣ gh ĭntọ f hwar ĭt hǎs̱ thǎt sound, ǎs̱ ĭn cough, cŏf : enough, enŭf : laughter, làftĕr : tough, tŭf.

18. l.—Drŏp l ĭn could, cụd.

19. p.—Drŏp p ĭn receipt, reçet,

20. s.—Drŏp s ĭn aisle, il : demesne, demen :
island, ilánd.

Chang̣ s intọ z in dĭstĭnctĭv wŭrdṣ, ăṣ ĭn
abuse, ábuz (verb) : house, hoᵫz (verb) : rise,
riz (verb) : etc.

21. sc.—Drŏp c ĭn scent, sĕnt : scythe, sȳth.

22. tch.—Drŏp t ăṣ ĭn catch, căeh; pitch,
pĭeh; witch, wĭeh, etc.

23. w.—Drŏp w ĭn whole, hol.

24. ph.—Rit f for ph, ăṣ in philosophy, fĭl-
ŏsofȳ; sphere, sfer, etc.

Thĕ ábŭv rụlṣ gratlȳ ăd ŭs ĭn ĭmprọvĭng
Englĭsh spĕlĭng; yĕt thĕr är mĕnȳ dĭfĭcŭltĭs
thăt tha dọ nŏt hĕlp ŭs sŏlv. Tọ sŭrmount
thes, I ăd á feᵫ thăt sem tọ me quit ăṣ nĕçĕs-
arȳ ăṣ thoṣ mad by thĕ ábŭv namd filŏlog̣ĭsts :

1. Silĕnt vouĕls.—Drŏp ạll silĕnt or áfonĭc
vouĕlṣ, ăṣ ĭn goose, gọs; loose, lọs; food, fọd;
book, bọk; great, grat; gain, gan.

2. i.—Rit ĭ for e or ee hwĕn so soundĕd, ăṣ
ĭn been, bĭn.

3. a.—Rit ĕ for a hwĕn a hăs the sound ŏv ĕ
ăṣ in any, ĕnȳ; maṇȳ, mĕnȳ.

4. e.—Rit a for e whĕn e hăs thĕ sound ŏv a,
ăṣ ĭn eight, at; they, tha.

5. w.—U<u>s</u> w onl<u>y</u> ăs á cŏnsonánt. Rit u̱ for w ĭn dĭfᴛʜŏng̲s ĭn hwie̱h w hăs ᴛʜĕ souud ŏv u̱, ăs in new, neu̱; stew, steu̱.

6. o.—U<u>s</u> o ă<u>s</u> á vouĕl onl<u>y</u>. Hwĕn o hă<u>s</u> ᴛʜĕ sound ŏv w, rit w, ă<u>s</u> ĭn one, wŭn; once, wŭn<u>s</u>.

7. u.—Hwĕn u ĭ<u>s</u> equĭválĕnt to̱ w, rit w, ă<u>s</u> ĭn language, lăng̲wag̲; lĭngŭal, lĭng̲wàl.

8. i.—Rit y for i hwĕn i hă<u>s</u> ᴛʜĕ sound ŏv y, ă<u>s</u> ĭn pinion, pĭnyŭn; minion, mĭnyŭn.

9. c, t, s.—Rit s̱h for c, t, and s, hwĕn c, t and s hă<u>s</u> ᴛʜĕ sound ŏv s̱h, ă<u>s</u> ĭn ocean, os̱hŭn; social, sos̱hàl; nation, nas̱hŭn; notion, nos̱hŭn; mission, mĭs̱hŭn; pa̱ssio̱n, p̤ăs̱hŭn.

10. f.—Rit v for f hwĕṉ f hăs ᴛʜĕ sound ŏv v, ă<u>s</u> ĭn of, ŏv.

The ábŭv ru̱l<u>s</u>, go̱d ă<u>s</u> ᴛʜa är, ĭf us̱d, wĭl mak ăn Eng̲lĭsh orᴛʜŏgraf<u>y</u> vĕr<u>y</u> lĭtl bĕtĕr ᴛʜăn ᴛʜĕ wŭn hĭᴛʜĕrto̱ ĭn us. Indĕd, to̱ do̱ mŭe̱h, ĭn ᴛʜĕ ĭmprovmĕnt ŏv Eng̲lĭsh orᴛʜŏ-graf<u>y</u>, we mŭst hăv á bĕtĕr ălfabĕt. Thĕ wŭn ĭn g̲ĕnĕràl us ĭ<u>s</u> nŏt sŭfĭshĕnt. In our ălfabĕt ᴛʜĕr s̱hu̱d be ăt lest wŭn cărăctĕr for ĕvĕr<u>y</u> sĭmpl fon; ănd ee̱h cărăctĕr s̱hu̱d a̱lwa<u>s</u> be ca̱ld by ᴛʜe sound, or fon, ĭt ĭ<u>s</u> ĭntĕndĕd to rĕprĕs-ĕnt. Bŭt, ĭn our lăng̲wag̲ ᴛʜĕr är ᴛʜĭrt<u>y</u>-sĕvĕn wĕl defind fon<u>s</u>; hwil ĭn our ălfabĕt thĕr är onl<u>y</u> twĕnt<u>y</u> six cărăctĕr<u>s</u>. And, wh<u>a</u>t maks thĕ mătĕr wŭrs, for ŏv the<u>s</u> cărăctĕr<u>s</u>, a, i, u and x, rĕpre<u>s</u>ĕnts cŏmpound fon<u>s</u>---a begĭnĭ<u>n</u>g with á sound hĕrd onl<u>y</u> ĭn thĕ ĭnĭshál ănd ĕsĕnshál ŏv a, ănd thĕn ĕndĭ<u>n</u>g ĭn á <u>s</u>ound hĕrd ĭn the ĕsĕnshál ănd vănĭsh ŏv e. i ĭs equál to äe; u ĭ<u>s</u> equál to yu, x is equal to ks or gs. Hĕnç, ĭn reălit<u>y</u>, we hăv twĕnt<u>y</u>-t<u>u</u> cărrăctĕr<u>s</u> t<u>o</u> rĕpre<u>s</u>ĕnt thĭrt<u>y</u>-thre sĭmpl fon<u>s</u>, ănd for cărăctĕr<u>s</u> thăt rĕpre<u>s</u>ĕnt cŏmpound fon<u>s</u>.

T<u>o</u> ĭmpr<u>o</u>v thĕ ălfábĕt, thĕn we mŭst ĕnlár<u>g</u> ĭt. Thĭs we d<u>o</u> by u<u>s</u>ĭ<u>n</u>g eeh ŏv thĕ vouĕl cărăctĕr<u>s</u> ĭn thĕ old ălfábĕt, without diácrĭtĭç märks t<u>o</u> rĕpre<u>s</u>ĕnt thĕ souund, or fon, hĕrd ĭn ŭttĕrĭ<u>n</u>g ĭt; thăt ĭs, wc u<u>s</u>e ĭts nam sound. Hĕnç whĕn ĕn<u>y</u> vouĕl hă<u>s</u> no diácrĭtĭc märk, ĭt hă<u>s</u> ĭts nam sound, ă<u>s</u> a ĭn ape,=ap; e ĭn eve,= ev; u ĭn tune,=tun; o ĭn old, i ĭn unite,=unit; Bŭt, t<u>o</u> rĕpre<u>s</u>ĕnt ŭthĕr vouĕl fon<u>s</u>, the<u>s</u> vouĕl cărăctĕr<u>s</u> mŏdifid by diácrĭtĭc märks är u<u>s</u>d. Thŭs, á rĕpre<u>s</u>ĕnts thĕ vouĕl fon ĭn thĕ wŭrd ásk, <u>a</u> ĭ<u>n</u> <u>a</u>ll, a ĭn wh<u>a</u>t, ă ĭn ăt; ĕ ĭn mĕt; ĭ ĭn ĭt; ŏ ĭn nŏt, <u>o</u> ĭn bo<u>o</u>t,=b<u>o</u>t; <u>o</u> ĭn b<u>o</u>ok,=b<u>o</u>k; ŭ ĭn bŭt, <u>u</u> ĭn r<u>u</u>de,=r<u>u</u>d; <u>u</u> ĭn f<u>u</u>ll,=f<u>u</u>l; <u>y</u> ĭn ç<u>y</u>st; ȳ ĭn m<u>y</u>.

Sŭm ŏv the cŏnsonȧnt cărăctĕrs rĕpreṣĕnt mor thăn wŭn fon. Sŭch är c, g, n, s, th, x, z; ăṣ for ĭnstȧnç, c ĭn corn and c ĭn ced; g ĭn gun,—gŭn, and g ĭn gem—ġĕm; n ĭn no, ănd n ĭn link,—lĭṇk, or siṇg; s ĭn sin,—sĭn, ănd s ĭn his,—hĭṣ; th ĭn them,—thĕm ănd th ĭn thing—, thĭṇg; x ĭn fix,—fĭx, ănd x ĭn exist,—exĭst; z ĭn zone,—zon, ănd z ĭn azure,—ăzhur.

The fĭrst sound ȧbŭv ĭnstȧnçt ĭs thĕ wŭn hwĭch ĭs thĕ mor freqꞏuĕntlẏ hĕrd. Hĕnç, we ma çal ĭt thĕ fĭrst sound. Tọ rĕpreṣĕnt thĭs (the fĭrst sound) we wĭl uṣ the sĕvĕrȧl cŏnsonȧnt cărăctĕrs, her çĭtĕd wĭthout diȧcrĭtĭc märks; ănd tọ ĭṇdicat the sĕcŏnd sound ŏv ech ŏv the sam cărăctĕrs, we wĭl uṣ çĕrtĭn märks. Thŭs, tọ rĕpreṣĕnt the sĕcŏnd sound ŏv c, we wĭl uṣ c märdt thŭs ç; ănd tọ rĕpreṣĕnt the sĕcŭnd sound ŏf g, we wĭl uṣ g märkt thŭs ġ; the secŭnd sound ŏv n we wĭl ĭndicat thŭs ṇ; ănd ŏv th thus th, (the fĭrst sound beĭṇg rĕpreṣĕntĕd by th); ănd ov x thŭs x; ănd ov z thŭs zh. Hĕnç, our ălfabĕt wĭl ăper ăṣ the ărangmĕnt ŏv cărăcters belo,

Alfabet Usd in the Orthografy ov this Bok.

VOUEL CARACTERS.

a	ale, fate,=al, fat.
ă	ădd, făt,=ăd, făt.
ä	ärm, fäthĕr.
à	àsk, glàss.
ạ	ạll, tạlk.
ạ	whạt, wạnder.

e	eve, mete=ev, met.
ĕ	ĕnd, mĕt.

i	içe, fine=iç, fin.
ĭ	ĭn, fĭn.

o	old, note=not.
ŏ=ạ	ŏdd=ŏd, nŏt, whạt.
ọ	prọve=prọv, dọ, tọ.
ọ	wọlf, wọl, bọok=bọk.

u	uṣe, tube=uṣ, tub.
ŭ	ŭs, tŭb.
ụ=ọ	rụde=rụd, dọ.
ụ=ọ	bụll=bụl, pụt, wọlf,

ȳ=i	flȳ, içe=iç.
y̆=ĭ	cy̆st, pĭn.

CONSONANT CARACTERS, AND THE SOUNDS OR FONS THA REPRESENT.

---

b	bärn, rob.
c	ca̤ll, colt.
ç	çede, traçe.
c̶h	c̶hild, muc̶h.
d	dale, săd.
f	fame, leaf.
g	go, găg.
ġ	ġĕm, ġĭn.
h	ha̤ll, hăt.
j=ġ	jär, joke, ġĕm.
k=c	keep, kĭn̲g, ca̤ll.
l	lĕft, bĕll.
m	make, aġe.
n	nĕt, tĕn.
n̲	lĭn̲k, ŭn̲cle, same
p	pay, ape.
q̶u	q̶ueen, cŏnq̶uĕst.
r	rĭp, fär.
s	same, yĕs, çede.
s̲	hăs̲, ȧmus̲e,
s̶h	s̶hĕlf, flĕs̶h.
t	tone, nŏt.
t̶h̶	t̶h̶ĭn̲g, brĕat̶h̶.
t̶h	t̶hine, wĭt̶h.
v	vane, wave.
w	wĕt, wa̤s̲.

hw	hweat, hweel.
x	expĕct, fŏx=fŏks.
x̱	exĭst=ĕgsĭst.
y	yạwn, yĕt.
z	zone, maze.
z-h	azure=azhure.

In prĭntĭng the bọk, I hăv uṣd the dïácrĭtĭc tȳp prepard tọ prĭnt mȳ bọk ĕntitld Elements ŏv Orthoepy. Thĭs maks the spĕlĭng ŏv the wŭrds—ăs the spĕlĭng ŏv ĕvĕrȳ wŭrd shụd be —fonĭc. (For á discŭshŭn ŏv fonĭcs ănd fonĭc spĕlĭng, se mȳ "Elements ŏv Orthoepy," or mȳ Fonĭc Spĕlĕr and Sȳlábatĕr.)

Bȳ usĭng the dïácrĭtĭc tȳp ănd foloĭng the fonĭc orthŏgráfȳ, the nŭmbĕr ŏv pagĕṣ, ĭn the bọk ĭṣ about wŭn fĭfth lĕs thăn wụd be, hăd I folod the áfonĭc spĕlĭng. Bȳ usĭng the dïácrĭtĭc tȳp, no doubt ĭṣ lĕft respĕctĭng the pronŭnçĭashŭn ov ĕnȳ wŭrd; by thĭs mĕthŏd, eeh fon ĭn á wŭrd ĭs rĕprĕṣĕntĕd bȳ á sutábl cărăctĕr; ănd wĭth feu ĕxçĕpshŭnṣ thĕr ĭṣ no cărăctĕr ĭn á wŭrd thăt dŭs nŏt rĕprĕṣĕnt á fon.

C. W. LARISON.

ACADEMY OV SIENC AND ART,

RINGOS, N. J., Agust 1st, 1883.

THE BIOGRAFY

OF

SILVIA DUBOIS.

The twĕntў sĕvĕnth ŏv Jănuarў 1883 da̤nd frŏstў ănd drerў.   The mĕrcŭrў pointĕd to̤ 20° a̤bŭv zero.   The skȳ wa̤s̠ ovĕrca̤st ănd so̤n the wĕthĕr ăperd thrĕtĕnĭng.   Hĭls̠ ănd dals̠, mountĭns̠ ănd vălўs̠, ŭpla̤nds̠ ănd lĕs̠, wĕr cŭvĕrd wĭth sno; ănd, sav the numĕrŭs̠ bold arĕa̤s ŏv wo̤ds̠ ănd the sprĕdĭng bo̤us ŏv leflĕs orcha̤rds̠, the prŏspĕct wa̤s̠ quit ärctĭc.

The chĭllў ar ca̤s̠d the cătl to̤ reman ĭn thar stals̠, or to̤ snŭgl to̤gĕthĕr ŭpŏn the le-sid ŏv bĭldĭngs.   The poltrў refus̠d to dȩçĕnd frŏm thar ro̤st.   The spăro hŭvĕrĭng ĭts lĭtl frŏst-bĭtĕn fet, ŭtĕrd ĭts shärp chĭrp ĭn a̤ plantĭv wa.   Whil the sno bĭrd, ĭn quĕst ŏv wed-sed, bĭsilў hŏpt ovĕr the frozĕn crŭst, or dĭlĭgĕntlў flĭtĕd a̤mŭng the dĕd brănchĕs̠ ŏv

ămbrŏsĭá, scarçlў takĭng the tim tọ ŭtĕr hĭs
shrĭl nots---ehe-de-de-de---so egĕr wạs he tọ
find fọd for hĭs mornĭng mel, ănd thĕn tọ
hastĕn tọ hĭs shĕltĕrd hạnt.

Bŭt, thĕ slaĭng wạs gọd ănd the carṣ ŏv
bĭsў lif forçt mĕnў á cŏtĕr frŏm hĭs hom tọ
brav the frĭgĭd ar ŏv the ehĭlў mornĭng.
Horsĕṣ stĕpt quĭk, lit ănd fre, ănd the jĭngl ŏv
sla bĕlṣ ĕcod frŏm the f or cŏmĕrṣ ŏv the hori-
zŭn. Bŭt, the fŭrў mŭfs cŭvĕrĭng the hĕdṣ
ănd taçĕṣ ŏv the wĕl robd păsĕngĕrṣ told wĕl
thặt no wŭn lĕft hĭs hom thặt mornĭng tọ
sla-rid for plạṣur.

It wạs Sătŭrda; ănd, ặṣ the dutĭṣ ŏv the
scọl-rọm dĭd nŏt demănd our labor for the da,
we tŭrnd our ătĕnshŭn tọ the ặbjĕct, ănd the
agĕd. Acordĭnglў, ábout 7 o'clŏk A. M.,
we ădjŭstĕd our răpĭngṣ, mountĕd the sla
ănd dirĕctĕd our wa tọ Cedár Sŭmmĭt, the
most ĕlevatĕd, porshŭn ŏv the Sourlánd Mountĭn. Răpĭdlў we spĕd álŏng. And, ặṣ we
reeht the brou ŏv the mountĭn, f or á momĕnt
we pạṣd tọ sŭrva the lăndscap. Towạrd the
wĕst, north ănd est, the viu wạs ŭnŏbstrŭetĕd,
ănd the prŏspĕet wàs grănd.

Elĕvatĕd 400 fĕt ábŭv thĕ Rĕdshal Văllў, wĕ

scǎnnd t̶h̶ĕ basĭn ŏv t̶h̶e Rǎritȧn frŏm t̶h̶e sorç
ŏv t̶h̶e strem tǫ ĭts ĕxĭt ĭnto t̶h̶e se. The bold
mountĭns t̶h̶ǎt skĭrt ĭt ŏn t̶h̶e nor̶t̶h, ros̲ g̶ĕntlў
ŭp ǎnd semd tǫ slop so g̶rǎduȧlў towȧrd t̶h̶e
nor̶t̶h t̶h̶ǎt t̶h̶a semd nols ǎnd hĭlls̲. The
plan, t̶h̶o rolĭn̲g ǎnd rĭg̶d, s̲emd ĕntirlў lĕvĕl.
Evĕrўhwǎr wǫs sno. Inded, t̶h̶e drerў samnĕs
ŏv t̶h̶e snoў fleç wǫs onlў relevd by spärç areas̲
ŏv wǫd lȧnds̲, ǎnd t̶h̶e lŏn̲g line ŏv perĭn̲g
fĕnçĕs̲. Evĕn t̶h̶e dĭstȧnt vĭlag̶ĕs̲ cǫd härdlў
be descrid, so c̶o̶mpletlў wĕr t̶h̶a ĕnvĕlopt ĭn
t̶h̶e fleç ŏv sno. Bŭt, nerĕr by, frŏm t̶h̶e c̶h̶ĭm-
nў ŏv mĕnў ȧ färm-ho̶u̶s ǎsçĕndĕd t̶h̶e sǫtў
smok, ĭn cŭrlĭn̲g fĕstǫns̲.

Onwȧrd we hǎstĕnd, ovĕr ȧ rod t̶h̶ǎt meǎn-
dĕrd no̶u̶ ȧmĭd ǎn ŭmbrag̶ŭs fŏrĕst, no̶u̶
ȧmĭd rŏkў areas̲ ovĕr-gron wĭth çedȧrs̲, no̶u̶
ȧmĭd t̶h̶e smǎl rŏkў fĕlds̲ ŏv t̶h̶e mountĭn
färmĕr. Evĕrўhwĕr t̶h̶e fĕt̶h̶ĕrў bo̶u̶s̲ ŏv t̶h̶e
çedȧrs̲ t̶h̶ǎt skĭrtĕd t̶h̶ĕ wa wĕr pĕndȧnt wĭth
sno---ȧ bĕutĭfụl spĕctȧcl. The bränc̶h̶ĕs̲ ŏv
t̶h̶e grat oks mantand t̶h̶ar lit sŏmbr gra,
ǎdĭn̲g drerĭnĕs tǫ t̶h̶e wĭntĕr sĕn. The ovȧl
bǎks ŏv t̶h̶e hug̶ rŏks lĭftĕd ȧ mo̶u̶nd ŏv sno,
lik t̶h̶e ho̶u̶s̲ĕs̲ ŏv t̶h̶e Esquĭmos. The mo̶u̶n-
tĭnĕrs̲ hŭts, fär remǫvd frŏm t̶h̶e rod, ȧwa bǎk

ner sŭm sprĭṉg, or ŭpŏn the brĭnk ŏv sŭm
plăshĭṉg rĭl, ĕxhĭbĭtĕd no sinṉ ŏv lif, sav the
soṭỹ cŏlŭm ŏv cŭrlĭṉg smok that lazilỹ ăsc̣ĕnd-
ĕd ámĭd the fŏrĕst bous.

From the man rod tọ eeh mountĭnĕrṉ hŭt,
or tọ spärc̣ grọps ŏv squălĭd sĕttlmĕnts, fọt-
päthṉ, or nắro bỹ-waṉ, ĕxtĕnd băk, sŭmtimṉ,
for milṉ, meăndĕrĭṉg ámĭd huġ rŏks, thĭkĕts
ŏv c̣edárṉ, ŭmbraġŭs fŏrĕsts, thru märshĕs ănd
swạmps, ănd, ovĕr stremṉ that är nŏt ĕvĕrỹ-
hwĕr fordĕd. Thĕṉ by-waṉ är bĕst non tọ
thĕ mountĭnĕrs. Thar stŏk ŏy ġeogräfĭc nŏl-
ĕdġ cŏnsĭsts manlỹ ĭn ăn ăcquantánc̣ ŏv theṉ
windĭṉg waṉ. And, whil eeh mountĭnĕr, ĭn
the därkĕst nit fŏloṉ eeh, ănd ĕnỹ wŭn ŏv theṉ
bỹ-waṉ, wĭth ăṉ mŭeh c̣ĕrtĭntỹ ănd ăṉ mŭeh
dĕxtĕrĭtỹ ăṉ á căt trăvĕrsĕs á bem ĭn the nit,
or hĕr meăndĕrĭṉg páth thru á glọmỹ ha-mou,
á pĕrsŭn nŏt skĭld ĭn the waṉ ŏv the mountĭnĕrṉ, wụd, ăt mĭd-da, be nŏt mor sŭcc̣ĕsful
ĭn hĭṉ jŭrnỹĭṉg her than ĭn the lăbỹrĭnth ŏv
Eġỹpt, or ŏv Cŏrĭnth. Acordĭnglỹ, hwĕn we
hăd ărivd ăt the cornĕr ăt hwĭeh the rod ĕx-
tĕndṉ est-wárd tọ Rŏk Mĭlṉ, tọ led our wa tọ
thĕ hŭt ŏf Sỹlvĭá Dụbois, we ĕmployd wŭn

ho profĕst to be ăcquantĕd wĭth thes meăndĕrĭng päths.

To me, the sit ăt whĭch we lĕft the man rod to go ĭn to Sȳlvĭa's mănshŭn lŏkt no mor lik a rod thăn dĭd ĕnȳ ŭthĕr hålf rŏd ŏv ground ŭpŏn the sam sid ŏv the rod, for the låst hålf mil. But, fath ĭn our gid, ĭnduçt ŭs to fŏlo hĭm ĭmplĭçĭtlȳ whĕrĕvĕr hĕ lĕd. The wa was vĕrȳ crŏkĕd. Pĕrhăps, nŏt a sĭngl rŏd ŏv the påth ĕxtĕndĕd ĭn the same dĭrĕcshŭn. Nor, cud we se fär åhĕd ŏv ŭs, sŭmtims nŏt ä rŏd. Bŭt, ŏn we movd, ăround huǵ rŏks, betwen lärǵ tres, ovĕr lärǵ stons, thru năro ănd dănǵĕrŭs pås was, nou åmĭd a thĭkĕt ŏv çedårs, or a groth ŏv brămbls, or a cŏps ŏv bushĕs, or a spårs fŏrĕst ŏv ŭmbraǵŭs oks ănd hĭkorĭs. Sŭmtims the rod was rŭtȳ, sŭmtims sidlĭng, sŭmtĭms ŭp a shärp nol, sŭmtims doun a step bănk; nĕvĕr lĕvĕl; sŭmtĭms stonȳ, ănd alwas dănǵĕrŭs. Bŭt, by ănd by a vĭstå ăppĕrd. We wĕr ŏn a slit ĕmĭnĕnç. Opĕnĭng ŭp befor ŭs wås ăn areå ŏv lănd clerd ŏv tres, bushĕs ănd brămbls, fĕnçt ănd färmd. It ĭs thĕ prŏpĕrtȳ ŏv Elĭzåbĕth, the yŭngĕst dåtĕr ŏv Sȳlvĭä Dubois. Upŏn ĭt, hĕr mŏdĕst mănshŭn risĕs, a hŭt tĕn fet squar, bĭlt ŏv lŏgs,

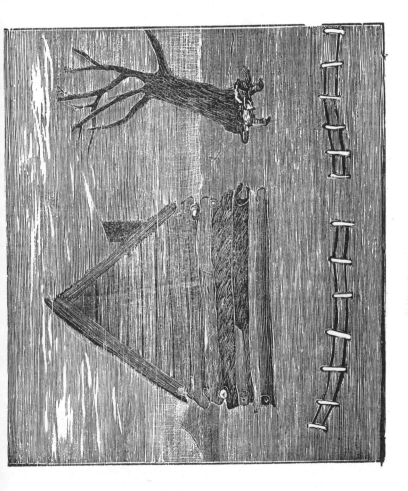

roft with bords, unadornd with poreh, piazza, colonad or veranda. Primativ simplicity enters into every fas ov its arcitetcur. It contans not an element that is not absolutly neded. Ner by stands the scragling branehes ov a ded apl tre, and beneth it is the shelter for the fathful dog. Around the area is a fenc bilt in the most economic wa;—in sum places it is mad ov crutehes with wun pol, in sum places with crutehes and tu pols, in sum places ther är tu staks and a rider, in uther places it is mad ov rals so arang'd that wun end rests upon the ground whil the uther is elevated by mens ov staks fixt acros anuther inclining ral.

Pering abuv the sno, her and thar, wer staks ov maz, cabag, ben-vins, pe-brush and uther evidences that the enclosd area, during the spring sumer and atumnal munths, had bin tild, and had yelded a sparc suply to the tenánts ov the soil.

Wen from the eminenc we had survad the hut and its environs, we decended to the fenc that enclosd the lot, fastend, and blanketd our horses and advanct toward the habitashun. The dor is dubl---consisting ov an upper and

å nĕthĕr pärt. The ŭpĕr pärt stọd åjär, ănd
ĭn the çĕntĕr ŏv the opĕnĭng ăpĕrd the fụl,
round faç ŏv å lärg, bŭxŭm negrĕs,—the onĕr
ănd proprietor ŏv thĕ mănshŭn whĭeh we vĭsĭtĕd,
ănd the yŭngĕst dạghtĕr ŏv Sĭlvĭå Dụbois, the
ladў ŏv họm we hăd hĕrd so mŭeh tạlk. Our
vĭsĭt wạs å sŭrprṣ. Yĕt, wĭth märkt eŏmpla-
sånç ănd thăt hŏspitălĭtў thăt căractĕrizes the
ferlĕs mountĭner, we wĕr ĭnvĭtĕd ĭn, ănd băd
tọ be setĕd bȳ the stov.

The rọm wạs nŏt wĕl litĕd. And ăṣ I wạṣ
sĭtĭng down, I notĭçt, sĭtĭng ŭpŏn å ehar, å
dŭskў form closlў snŭgld ŭp ĭn the năro
spaç, betwĕn the stov ănd the wạl. Aṣ mȳ yṣ
(eyes) becam ăeŏmodatĕd tọ the degre ŏv
litnĕs ŏv the rọm, I sạ thăt thĭs dŭskў form
wạṣ the ĕldĕrlў ladў thăt we deṣird tọ se,—that
she hăd fĭxt hĕrsĕlf her ĭn the wạrmĕst pärt ŏv
the rom, ănd thăt she wạṣ åslep.

I scănd hĕr closlў. Tho sĭtĭng, her slep wăṣ
ăṣ trănquĭl ăṣ thăt ŏv å bab. Hĕr hĕd, tid ŭp
wĭth å hăndkĕrehĭf, åftĕr the usụål mănĕr ŏv
cŭlŭrd ladĭṣ, wạṣ boud forwård, so thăt the
ehĭn rĕstĕd ŭpŏn hĕr flĕshў ehĕst. Hĕr hănds
wĕr foldĕd ŭpŏn hĕr lăp. Hĕr fĕt wĕr ĕxtĕndĕd

beneŧh ŧhe stov. Hĕr countenånç wạs̱ sever, bŭt seren.

Hĕr ăpărĕl wạs̱ nŏt Parĭs̱ĭàn : yĕt, ĭt wås̱ rĕs̱ŭnåblў hol, ănd nŏt dĭrtў. Thĕr semd tọ be enŭf ŏv ĭt, ănd ădjŭstĕd ĕntirlў ĭn ăcordånç wĭŧh ŧhe ġenyŭs ŏv ŧhe Afrĭeàn raç. Inded, ŧhe spĕctåcl wås̱ sŭeh ŧhăt ĭt elĭçĭtĕd ŧhe ĕx- prĕs̱hŭn (ŧhŏt, nŏt mad): "Wĕl! yu är ăt hom ĭn ŧhe ĕnjoymĕnt ŏv lif, jŭst ăs̱ yu wụd hăv ĭt."

Cạs̱hŭslў, bŭt crĭtĭcålў, I sŭrvad ŧhe rọm ănd ŧhe fŭrnitur. The lŏg̱s̱ cŏmpos̱ĭṉg ŧhe wạl wĕr nŏt ĕntirlў strat, ănd ŧhe ĭntĕrspaçĕs̱ betwen ŧhĕm, ĭn sŭm plạçĕs̱, wĕr larġ. At wŭn tim, ŧhĕs̱ ĭntĕrspaçĕs̱ hăd bĭn fĭld wĭŧh mŭd,— ănd ŧhĕn, no doubt, ŧhe hous wạs̱ cŏmpăra- tĭvlў wạrm. Bŭt, nou, ĭn mĕnў plạçĕs̱, bȳ frŏst ănd ran, ănd bȳ bŭg̱ ănd mouç, ŧhe mŭd hăs̱ crŭmbld ănd fạlĕn out; ănd, ŧhe opĕnĭṉgs̱ ădmĭt àlik ŧhe lit ănd ŧhe wĭnd. Wĭŧhĭn reeh ŏv mȳ ehar, I cŭd pàs mȳ hănd betwen ŧhe lŏg̱s̱, ŭntĭl ĭt wạs̱ ĕntirlў out ŏv dors̱ ; ănd, ĭn sŭm plạçĕs̱, I cụd se lit ŧhrụ à crĕvĭç tụ fet lŏṉg; ĭn ŭŧhĕrs̱, I cụd pàs mȳ fĭṉgĕrs̱ àlŏṉg ăn opĕn spaç betwen ŧhe lŏg̱s̱ frŏm tĕn tọ fĭten ĭnehĕs̱. Thrụ ŧhĕs̱ opĕn spaçĕs̱, ŧhe wĭnd wạs̱ pàsĭṉg ăt à răpĭd rat.

The ĭnĕr sŭrfáç ŏv the wạl wạṣ nŏt evĕn. Eeh lŏg shod ĭts bärkў cŏntur, and eeh ĭntĕrspaç ĭts claў lĕdġ, or ĭts opĕn spaç. Cálçimĭn ănd whit-wạsh dĭd nŏt ăper; ănd wạl-papĕr wĭth gĭldĕd bordĕr wạṣ wạntĭng. The çelĭng ĭs wạntĭng. In ĭts stĕd ĭs the bar rọf, or the splĭntĕrў sŭrfáç ŏv sŭm ralṣ thăt ĕxtĕnd frŏm wạl tọ wạl, for the sŭpport ŏv sŭeh thĭngṣ ăṣ är ĭn the wa, ĭf lўĭng ŭpŏn the flor.

In erĕctĭng the ĕdifĭc, the lŏgṣ ĭn the sŭthĕrn fáçad hăd bĕn lad ŭp tọ the hit ŏv 4½ fet, wĭth ăn opĕn spaç ner the çenter, tọ sĕrv ăṣ à dor. The nĕxt laĕr ŏv lŏgṣ ĕxtĕnd ĕntirlў ăround, formĭng the plats for the rọf ănd the lĭntĕl ŏv the dor. Frŏm theṣ lŏg-plats ăsçĕnd, ăt à shărp ĭnçlinashŭn, tọ the rĭdġ-pol, the ráftĕrṣ, hwĭeh ĭn sŭm plaçes är cŭvĕrd wĭth shĭnglṣ ; ĭn ŭthĕrṣ, wĭth bordṣ or bärk.

Upŏn ethĕr sid ŏv the dor, frŏm the lŏg-plat thăt căps the frŏnt wạl, tọ ĭts countĕrpárt ŭpŏn the băk wạl, ĕxtĕnd ok ralṣ, wĭth the flăt splĭntĕrў sid downwárdṣ. Thĭs formṣ, ŭpŏn ethĕr sid ŏv the dor, a smạl lŏft, ŭpŏn hwĭeh är pild bŭndlṣ ŏv clothṣ, bĕd-clothṣ ănd bĕdĭng, ănd I no nŏt hwạt ĕls. Tọ gĕt ŭpŏn theṣ lŏfts, thĕr är nethĕr stĕps nor ladĕr ; ănd yet tha är hăndў. Stăndīng ŭpŏn the flŏr, a tạl pěrsŭn căn reeh ạlmost tọ ĕnў pärt ŏv thĕm, ănd take doun, or pụt àwa, ĕnўthīng dĕsird. I notīçt thăt the ehars thăt wĕr nŏt ĭn us hăd bĭn plaçt ŭpŏn wŭn ŏv thes lŏfts, out ŏv the wa.

So lo ĭs the lĭntĕl, thăt ĭn the ăct ŏv ĕntĕrīng the dor, a pěrsŭn ĭs obligd tọ stọp; ănd, hwĕn risīng ŭp, àftĕr ĕntĕrīng, wĕr he nŏt carfụl tọ be ĭn the opĕn spaç betwen the lŏfts, he wụd băng hĭs hĕd àganst the ral flor. Altho thĭs wạs mў fīrst vĭsĭt, I wạs fortunat enŭf, ŭpŏn ĕntĕrīng, tọ be ĭn the rit posīshŭn. Bŭt, I wạs nŏt a lĭtl sŭrprisd ăs I lọkt àbout ănd found thăt hwil mў fĕt ănd lĕgs, ănd the loĕr pärt ŏv mў bŏdў wĕr doun stars, mў sholdĕrs, ärms ănd hĕd wĕr ŭp stars. Houĕvĕr, thĕ sŭrpris dĭd nŏt ŭnfĭt me for sŭrvaīng the lŏfts, thar ărangmĕnts ănd thar cŏntĕnts. Pĕrhăps, I wụd hăy sŭrvad thes àpärtmĕnts ănd thar cŏntĕnts lŏngĕr, ănd mor crĭtĭcàlў; bŭt, whĕn wĕl ĕngagd ĭn veuīng thes thĭngs, the thŏt ŏeŭrd: Whăt ma tha be dọīng belo; ma mў nĕthĕr pärts nŏt be ĭn sŭm dangĕr; or ăt the lest, ma tha nŏt demănd mў ătĕnshŭn. Acŏrdĭnglў I stọpt doun, ăçĕptĕd a prŏfĕrd ehar, ănd setĕd mўsĕlf ĭn a

spaç thăt semd to be the most out ŏv the wa,
ănd begăn, as ăforsĕd, a crĭtĭcál sŭrva ŏv the
ĕnvirŭns ŏv mȳ posĭshŭn.

The flor semd to be mad ŏy bords ănd splĭt
wod, lad ŭpŏn the ground, ănd pĕrhăps poundĕd
ŭpŏn, ŭntĭl nerlȳ lĕvĕl. I sa no pŭdls ŏv
stăndĭng watĕr, ănd yĕt thĕ flor was nŏt ĕntirlȳ
drȳ. The ĭntĕrspaçĕs betwen the flor-bords wud
ĕsilȳ hăv ăloud me to ăsçĕrtan the quălĭtȳ ŏv
the soil ŭpŏn whĭeh thĕ hous ĭs bĭlt. Altho
thes ĭntĕrspaçĕs wĕr tŏlĕráblȳ wĕl fĭld wĭth
cla, yĕt the flor sŭmhwat remindĕd me ŏv the
ăperánç ŏv a cordŭroy rod.

The lŏgs out ŏv hwĭeh thĭs hous ĭs bĭlt,
sĕrvd a tĕrm ŏv yers ĭn the wal ŏv ăn ŏldĕr hous.
The prĭmatĭv hous hwĭeh was ăn ĕrlĭĕr mănshŭn ŏn thĭs lŏt, was bĭlt a lŏng hwil ágo. In
the cors ŏv tim the ĕnds ŏv the lŏgs ŏv thăt
hous rŏtĕd ŏf, ănd the ĕdifĭç beeam ŭnsaf.
therŭpŏn, wŭn áftĕrnon about 18 yers ágo, Elĭzábĕth cŏnvokt hĕr nabŭrs, ĭn the capăçĭtȳ ŏv a
frŏlĭc, as sŭeh găthĕrĭngs är her cald, to recŏn-
strŭct hĕr mănshŭn. Acordĭng to hĕr plăn, tha
tok doun the old bĭldĭng, nŏteht the lŏgs băk
a sutábl dĭstánç frŏm the ĕnd, ănd pild thĕm
ŭp ĭn sŭeh a wa thăt, out ŏv the usábl matĕrĭál

ŏv the old hous tha cŏnstrŭctĕd the prĕṣĕnt ĕdifĭc. We är told thăt the old hous wäṣ sŭmhwạt lärgĕr ŏn the ground, sŭmhwȧt hiĕr, ănd in ĕvĕrẙ wa mor stẙlĭsh thăn the prĕṣĕnt manshŭn.

The houshold fŭrnitur—so fär ăṣ I cụld se—cŏnsĭstĕd ŏv ăn old-tim cọk stọv, ȧ dĭnĕr pŏt, ȧ wạtĕr pal, sĭx chars, ȧ smal cŭbärd ănd sŭm bĕd-clothṣ thăt ăperd tọ hăv bĭn lŏṇg ĭn us, ănd nŏt wĕl protĕctĕd frŏm dĭrt.

The cọk stọv ĭṣ wŭn ŏv thăt pătĕrn hwĭch wäṣ ĭn us frŏm 30 tọ 40 yerṣ ȧgo. It wạṣ mad for bŭrnĭṇg wọd. It ĭṣ nou mŭch the wŭrs for war. Thĕr ĭṣ yĕt remănĭṇg ŏv hwạt it wŭns wạṣ, ȧ pärt ŏv ceh fir-dŏr, ănd ȧ cŏnsĭdĕrȧbl ŏv the top plats. Bŭt, the fir iṣ wĕl ard; ĭt hăṣ ăn ȧbŭndȧnç ŏv drȧft frŏm ĕvĕrẙ sid It stăndṣ clos ŭp ĭn the southwest cornĕr, ĭn ȧ diăgonȧl mănĕr, ĭn sŭch ȧ wa thăt the pip-ĕnd ĭṣ toärd the cornĕr, ănd the fir-ĕnd toärd the çĕntĕr ŏv the hous. The smok finds exĭt thrụ tụ joints ŏv pip, thăt ĕxtĕnd frŏm the stọv ạlmost tọ the rọf. Frŏm the rọf ŭpwȧrd ĕxtĕndṣ ȧ kĭnd ŏv chĭmnẙ, mad ŏv ȧ peç ŏv shet-irŏn, bĕnt ạlmost ĭntọ ȧ çẙlĭndĕr, wĭth făntăstĭc scŏlŏps ȧround the tŏp—wĕthĕr the wŭrk ŏv

ăn ärtiẓàn, or the rĕsŭlt ŏv the dĭsĭntĕgratĭng
ĭnflụĕnç ŏv rŭst, I dọ nŏt no. Altho the
spaç betwen the pip ănd the chĭmnў ĭẓ lärg̣,
sŭmhow the spärks ănd the smok—thăt ĭẓ sŭm
ŏv thĕm—folo thĭs ĭntĕrŭptĕd flu ŭp ănd out
ŏv the hous.

Altho I sạ, out ŏv dorẓ, no pil ŏv wọd frŏm
hwĭch tha cụd drạ—ănd I thĭnk I sạ nŏt à sĭng̣l
stĭck, the stov wạẓ wĕl fĕd, the spärks rŭshĭng
ŭp the ĭntĕrŭptĕd smok-wa furĭŭslў. And, ạltho
mў băk wạẓ à lĭtl cŏld, mў shĭnẓ ănd neẓ wĕr
about ăẓ hŏt ăẓ I hăv ĕvĕr hăd thĕm, ănd mў
ўs (eyes) wĕr ăẓ wĕl fĭld wĭth smọk ăẓ tha
hăv ĕvĕr bĭn, nŏt ĕxçĕptĭng the tims durĭng
hwĭch I hăv bĭn' ătĕndĭng à fir ĭn à smok-
hous.

The dĭner-pŏt wạẓ ămpl, ănd ăpĕrd tọ hăv sen
sĕrvĭç. Of cours, ĭt wạẓ ŭpŏn the stov—the
wạtĕr ĭn ĭt, boilĭng furĭŭslў; bŭt frŏm ĭt, I fald
tọ detĕct ĕnў odŭr ŏv sẹthĭng pŏtag—bef or
mŭtŭn, pork or chĭkĕn.

The chạrẓ wĕr bŏtŭmd wĭth rŭsh, ănd tha
wĕr ĭn gọd repar.

Alŏng thĕ wạl, ŭpŏn the wĕst sid ŏv the rọm,
stọd à bŏx or cŭbärd, about 3 fet lŏng, 18
ĭnchẹs wid ănd $2\frac{1}{2}$ fet hi, pantĕd ănd ärmd wĭth

dors. Upŏn ĭt wąs å tĭn kĕrosen lămp thăt bŭrnd wĭthout å chĭmnў; ănd, jŭdġĭng frŏm the crŭst ŏv sǫt ănd lămp-blăk ŭpŏn the ral͜çclĭng dĭrĕctlў åbŏv the plaç ĭt ŏcupyd, ĭt smokt wĕl—ĕvĕn ĭf ĭt fald tǫ lĭt the rǫm.

Thes wĕr the onlў ärtĭcls ŏv fŭrnitur thăt I są. Thăt thĕr wĕr ŭthĕrs, ĕxçĕptĭng sŭch ąs ma hăv bĭn ĭn the cŭbärd, ĭs härdlў pŏsibl.

Durĭng the tim I wąs mākĭng the sŭrva, thĕr wąs nŏt sĭlenç. All the hwĭl we cŏnvĕrst. Our tąlk ràn sŏshåblў, ănd our host wąs ąs cŏmplåçĕnt ąs å Frĕnch bĕl.

At lĕngth, we ănounçt thăt we hăd cŭm tǫ ĭntĕrvew thĕ aġĕd ladў, Mrs. Sĭlvĭå Dŭbois. Herŭpŏn, hĕr dątĕr årousd hĕr mŭthĕr, told hĕr thăt pärtĭs hăd cąld tǫ se hĕr, ănd ĭntrodŭçt ŭs tǫ our heroin. Our gretĭngs wĕr nŏt vĕrў formål, nor mŭch prolŏngd. Bŭt hwĭl ĕxchångĭng så͜luts, our hŏst, for å mŏmĕnt, fred frŏm ĕntĕrtan͜ĭng ŭs, adjŭstĕd thĭngs åbout the rǫm, mad ĭn͜ĕfåbl ăpŏloġĭs respĕctĭng the åperånç ŏv the åpärtmĕnt, ănd ĕxtĕndĕd tǫ ŭs sŭch politnĕs ănd sŭch ătĕnshŭn, ąs mad ŭs fel thăt we wĕr wĕlcŭm gĕsts.

I hăd sen Sĭlvĭå ŏn å formĕr ocåshŭn, ănd

neu sŭmthĭng ŏv hĕr ĭdĭosy̆ncrasĕs. Indĕd, I hăd, durĭng à former ĭntĕrvu, hĕrd hĕr relat măny̆ ŏv the most ĭmportànt ĭnstànçĕs ŏv hĕr lif. So, hwat fŏloş, ĭn thĭs cŏloquy̆, tų sŭm ĕxtĕnt, I hăd hĕrd hĕr relat befor, ănd waş, ăt thĭs tim, drạn out, by̆ à serĭş ŏv prepárd qwĕsy̆ŭns, ĭn the ordĕr ĭn hwĭeh ĭt ĭş her statĕd, so thăt tọ the redĕr ĭt wụd be sŭmhwat coherĕnt.

Sĭlvĭà ĭş lärġ ŏv statur. In hĕr pämy̆ daş, she hăş bĕn nŏt lĕs thăn 5 fet 10 ĭnehĕs hi. She ĭnformş me thăt she usuàly̆ wad mor thăn 200 ĭbs. She ĭs wĕl proporshŭnd, ŏv à nĕrvo-ly̆mfătĭc tĕmpĕràmĕnt, ănd ĭş stĭl capabl ŏv grat ĕndurànç. Yers àgo, she waş non tọ be the strŏngĕst pĕrsŭn ĭn the sĕtlmĕnt, ănd the wŭn họ hăd the gratĕst ĕndurànç. She waş ĭndŭstrĭŭs, ănd waş usuàly̆ ĭn grat reqwĕst durĭng the hous-clenĭng ănd sop makĭng seşŭn ŏv the yer. Evĕry̆ bŏdy̆ wäntĕd Sĭlvĭà tọ hĕlp clen hous, ănd tọ hĕlp mak sop. She waş so strŏng she cụd lĭft ĕny̆thĭng thăt nedĕd tọ be mọvd, ănd cụd cäry̆ ĕny̆thĭng thăt hăd tọ be totĕd; ănd she waş so wĭlĭng tọ ŭş hĕr strĕngth thăt hĕr pŏpulărĭty̆ waş ĭnĕfàbl. So Sĭlvĭà wĕnt ĕvĕry̆hwĕr, ănd ĕvĕry̆ bŏdy̆ neu hĕr—ĕspĕshàly̆ the children, ho, ăs a rul, wĕr wŭndĕrfulў áfrad ŏv hĕr.

Acordĭng to hĕr on ăcount, to children she was nŏt vĕrў woĭng. On the cŏntrarў, she usd to tak delit ĭn tĕlĭng thĕm gŏblĭn storĭs, ănd ĭn makĭng thĕm áfrad ŏv hĕr. She usd to tĕl thĕm thăt she wŭd kidnăp thĕm, ănd thăt she wŭd swálo thĕm aliv; ănd, ĭt ĭs sĕd, to children, she lŏkt ăs ĭf she mit do sŭch thĭngs.

Usuálў, children kĕpt out ŏv hĕr wa. Usuálў, hwĕn tha sa hĕr cŭmĭng, tha sat rĕfug ĭn the cŭmpanў ŏv oldĕr folks,—ĭn sŭm secludĭd plac,— or ĭn a fot-rac. As a jok, she tĕls a storў respĕctĭng ăn ŏcŭrĕnc ĭn the boy-hod ŏv a cĕrtĭn ĭndivĭduál nou wĕl ădvánct ĭn yers. He, a lĭtl mor bold thăn the ăvĕrag boy ŏv 10 yers, ŏn wŭn ŏcashŭn, vĕnturd to be a lĭtl sasў to hĕr, ănd for the tim, kĕpt out ŏv hĕr wa. Bŭt a fĕw das áftĕr, hwil he was bĭsў plaĭng ĭn a gärden, ăround hwĭch wás a hi pĭckĕt fenc, Silvĭă ĕntĕrd the gat ábout the tim the lăd sa hĕr. To trў hĭs mĕtál, she ĕxclamd: Nou I'll hăv yu, sĭr! Up he bounct! Evĕrў lĭmb wás ĭn moshŭn! The hi pal-fenc was a triflĭng barĭer—wŭn áful yĕl he găv, ănd thĕn thru the răsbĕrў brĭers ănd ovĕr the fenc he wĕnt lik á cát ; ănd, houlĭng lŭstilў ăs he răn, dĭsăpĕrd from veu, bў crepĭng ŭndĕr ăn old bărak.

Hĕr lŭv ŏv fredŭm ĭs boundlĕs. To be fre ĭs the al-ĭmportánt thĭng wĭth Sĭlvĭá. Bŏnd-aġ, or evĕn restrant, ĭs to ner ákĭn to dĕth for Sĭlvĭá. Fredŭm ĭs the gol ; fredŭm ŏv speeh, fredŭm ŏv labŭr, fredŭm ŏv thĕ păshŭns, fre-dŭm ŏv the ăpetit—ŭnrestrand ĭn al thĭngs. To ĕnjoy thĭs, she wud go to ĕnў ĕxtrems—evĕn to the ĕxtrems ŏv lĭvĭng ŭpŏn the hărĭtў ŏv hĕr aqwantánçĕs, ĭn the hŭt ĭn hwĭĥ we found hĕr,—áwa frŏm çĭvĭlizashŭn ănd cŭltur, wĭth bŭt lĭtl to et, wĭth lĕs to war, ănd the porĕst kind ŏv shĕltĕr. Thŭs she gans the ŏb-jĕct ŏv hĕr desĭr. And, she ĭs ĭnded fre—ĕvĕrў păshŭn ĭs fre, ĕvĕrў desĭr ĭs grătifĭd. Lĕs re-stránt I nĕvĕr sa ĭn ĕnў pĕrsŭn—nor ĭnded cud thĕr be.

The old ladў dĭd nŏt áwak frŏm hĕr slŭmbĕr qwĭklў. Nor dĭd she qwĭklў cŏmprehĕnd thăt she hăd vĭsĭtors. Bŭt, ăs aġĕd foks usuálў do, she áwok slolў,—á pärt ŏv hĕr ăt á tim, ăs ĭt wĕr. At fĭrst, she movd hĕr hănds ănd ärms ; thĕn hĕr fet ănd lĕgs ; thĕn rŭbd hĕr faç ; thĕn she movd hĕr bŏdў ŭpŏn the har ; ănd ĭn the cors ŏv sŭm mĭnĭts, she begăn tọ reáliz thăt she hăd gĕsts, ănd thăt she mŭst ĕntĕrtan thĕm. Tharŭpŏn, ȧdjŭstĭng hĕr cloths, ănd qwĭklў tŭrnĭng hĕr hĕd toȧrd me, she ejăculatĕd: "Họ är thes?" Tọ thĭs ĭntĕrogashŭn hĕr dạtĕr replid: "Hwy, mŏmў! Dr. Lärison, hĭs dạtĕr, ănd Mĭs Pral. Tha wạnt tọ se yu —tha wạnt tọ tạk wĭth yu."

Qwĭklў ănd stĕrnlў she replid: "Wạnt tọ se me! I don't no hwȳ tha shụd wạnt tọ se me; sŭch ăn old thĭng ạs I ăm,—prĕtў ner dĕd nou, ănd Gŏd nọs I ạt tọ hăv bĭn dĕd lŏng ȧgo."

Herŭpŏn, I begán tọ ĭnqwir ȧbout hĕr hĕlth. She ĭnformd me thăt she wạs wĕl—ănd thăt she wạs ạlwạs wĕl; ĕxçĕpt sŭmtims she sŭfĕrd "colds." She sĕd thăt she hăd nĕvĕr hăd ȧ spĕl ŏv sever sĭknĕs, ănd dĭd nŏt ĭntĕnd tọ hăv; thăt "tant no ụs tọ be sĭk; foks don't fcl wĕl wĕn tham sĭk; tha fel bĕst wĕn tham wĕl."

"Jŭst so, Sĭlvĭȧ," I replid; "bŭt, ĭt scms thăt foks căn't ạlwạs be wĕl—sĭknĕs wĭl cŭm sŭmtims."

Tọ thĭs cŏmmĕnt the old ladў hastĭlў replid: Thă wŭdĕnt be sĭk hȧf so mŭch ĭf tha'd behav 'ĕm sĕlvs, ănd sta ăt hom, ănd et plan vĭtȧls. Tha wạnt tọ rŭn ạll ovĕr, ănd be ĭntọ ạll kind

ŏv nĭgår shins, ănd stŭf 'ĕmsĕlvs wĭth ạll kinds
ŏv things ; ănd thar gŭts wont stănd ĭt. Thĕn
tha gĕt sĭk ; ănd lik enŭf sĕnd for å dŏctŏr—
ănd whĕn he cŭms, ĭf thar nŏt prĕtў carfụl,
tha'l hăv å hĕl ŏv å tim ; for he's shur tọ
go rit for the guts, fŭst păs ; nĕvĕr neu wŭn ŏv
'ĕm tọ mĭs. A bĭg dos ŏv calomĕl ănd jäläp
tọ begĭn bĭsinĕs, ănd thĕn thĕ wạr ĭs begŭn.
Thĕs dọctŏrs, tha'v gŏt no mĕrcў ŏn yu, 'spĕsh-
ålў ĭf yur blăk. Ah ! I'v sen 'ĕm, mĕnў å tim,
bŭt, thay nĕvĕr cŭm áftĕr me, I nĕvĕr gav 'ĕm
å chănç,—nŏt the fŭst tim.

When I hăd gron qwiĕt frŏm å fĭt ŏv láftĕr,
provokt bў the old wọmản's stўl, ăs mŭch ăs
frŏm the mătĕr spokĕn, I told hĕr thăt I hăd
cŭm tọ tạk wĭth hĕr,—tọ lĕrn hwạt I cŭd respĕctĭng hĕr grat ạg, hĕr cors ŏv lif, the hĭstorў
ŏv hĕr fămĭlў, the cŭstŭms ŏv the pepl họ
lĭvd å çĕnturў or mor ảgo, hĕr prĕsĕnt wĕlfar
ănd hĕr futur prŏspĕcts.

Wĭth thĭs statmĕnt Sĭlvĭå semd plesd, ănd
ănounçt thăt she wạs rĕdў ănd wĭlĭng tọ ĭnform me respĕctĭng mătĕrs ăs fär ăs she wạs
abl. At wŭns, she ăsumd ăn ătitud, ănd ăn ar
thăt shod she wạs " ạll ătĕnshŭn " ănd rĕdў tọ
tạk. I hăd providĕd mўsĕlf wĭth papĕr ănd

pĕnçĭl tọ tak doun ĭn short-hănd, hĕr lăṇgwaġ̇
ăṣ ĭt fĕl frŏm hĕr mouth. Respĕctĭṇg thĭs, I
ĭnformd hĕr, ănd reqwĕstĕd the prĭvĭlĕġ̇ thăt I
miġht prĭnt ănd pŭblĭsh ănẏthĭṇg thăt she told
me. Tọ thĭs reqwĕst she replĭd : "Most ŏv
foks thĭnk thăt nĭġ̇ĕrs hăn't no ăcount ; bŭt,
ĭf yu thĭnk hwạt I tĕl yu ĭṣ wŭrth pŭblĭshĭṇg,
I wĭl be glăd ĭf yu dọ ĭt. T'wont dọ me no
gọd : bŭt ma be 'twĭl sŭmbŏdẏ ĕls. I'v lĭvd
ȧ gọd hwil, ănd hăv sen ȧ gọd del, ănd ĭf I
shụd tĕl yu ạl I'v sen, ĭt wụd mak the har
stănd ŭp ạl ovĕr yur hĕd."

Bȳ thĭs tim, ĭt hăd fụlẏ ăperd thăt Sĭlvĭă,
ĭn hĕr on wa, wạṣ nŏt ȧ lĭtl relĭġ̇ŭs, ănd wạṣ
wĕl uṣd tọ spekĭṇg the nam ŏv the Suprem
Beĭṇg ; ănd hwạt ĭṣ mor remärkȧbl ĭn ȧ wọmăn,
she semd tọ be so famĭlyȧr wĭth ạll thoṣ wŭrdṣ
ĕxprĕsĭv ŏv the ătrĭbuts ŏv Gŏd. Inded, I hăv
sĕldŭmlẏ non ȧ clĕrġ̇ẏmȧn, ĕvĕn hwĕn ăn ĕxçĕlĕnt Hebrụ ănd Grek scŏlȧr, tọ be mor famĭlyȧr wĭth theṣ tĕrmṣ thăn Sĭlvĭă, nor mor ĭn the
hăbĭt ŏv usĭṇg thĕm. And yĕt, betwen Sĭlvĭă
ănd ȧ clĕrġ̇ẏmȧn, thĕr semd tọ be ȧ märkt dĭfĕrĕnç ĭn the wa ĭn hwĭch ech uṣd thĕm. For,
hwil the clĕrġ̇ẏmȧn uṣĕṣ theṣ tĕrmṣ manlẏ ĭn
spekĭṇg ŏv the gọdnĕs ănd ŏmnĭpotĕnç ŏv Gŏd,

ănd ĭn ĭnvokĭng Hĭs̱ blĕsĭng, Sĭlvĭå semd tọ
us̱ ᵼhĕm ĭn ăn ĭntĕrjĕcsʜŭnȧl, ŏr ăn ădjĕctĭvȧl
wa tọ ĕmbĕlĭsʜ hĕr lăng̱wag̱, ănd tọ gĭv forç tọ
hĕr ĕxprĕsʜŭns̱.   And, ŏv ạl ᵼhăt I hăv ĕvĕr
lĭsĕnd tọ, I hăv nŏt hĕrd ĕnȳ wŭn hăndl ᵼhes̱
tĕrms̱ mor retŏrĭcȧlȳ, or yĕt mor ĭn ăcordȧnç
wĭᵼh ᵼhe prĭnçĭpls̱ ŏv ĕlocusʜŭn. And, ăs̱ ĭt wĭl
detrăct vĕrȳ gratlȳ frŏm ᵼhe mĕrĭts ŏv hĕr dĭs-
cors, ĭn cas I omĭt ᵼhĭs pärt ŏv hĕr lăng̱wȧg̱, I
bĕg̱ mȳ redĕrs̱ ᵼhe prĭvĭlĕg̱ ŏv levĭng ᵼhe wŭrds̱
ĭn hĕr frȧzĕs̱, jŭst ăs̱ sʜe ŭtĕrd ᵼhĕm, ăs̱ mŭᵼh
ăs̱ ĭs̱ barȧbl.

Hwil Sĭlvĭå's̱ famĭlĭȧrĭtȳ wĭᵼh ᵼhe titls̱ wĭᵼh
hwĭᵼh Jehovå ĭs̱ wŭnt tọ be ădrĕst, ĭs̱ ĕxçed-
ĭng̱lȳ grat, hĕr nolĕdg̱ ŏv ᵼhăt ŭᵼhĕr beĭng̱ cạld
ᵼhe Dĕvĭl, ĭs̱, bȳ no mens̱ lĭmĭtĕd.   If hĭs̱
cărăctĕr hăs̱ ĕvĕr bĭn bĕtĕr portrad bȳ ĕnȳ
ŭᵼhĕr pĕrsŭn, or ĭf he hăs̱ ĕver bĭn ădrĕst bȳ,
or non bȳ, ĕnȳ ŭᵼhĕr tĕrms̱ ᵼhăn ᵼhos̱ sʜe us̱d,
ĭt hăs̱ nŏt cŭm tọ mȳ nŏlĕdg̱.   Inded, ᵼt semd
ᵼhăt ĕvĕrȳ tĭtl, ăpĕlasʜŭn, ănd ĕpĭᵼhĕt, ᵼhăt
hăd ĕvĕr bĭn us̱d ĭn rĕfĕrĕnç tọ hĭs̱ Satănĭc
Măjĕstȳ, sʜe hăndld wĭᵼh peculĭȧr fredŭm ănd
es̱.   Inded, ᵼhe prolĭfĭcnĕs̱ ŏv hĕr mind, ĭn ᵼhĭs
dirĕcsʜŭn, ĭs̱ trănsĕndȧnt.   For hwĕr rots wĭᵼh
ᵼhe most ĕxqwĭs̱ĭt prefĭxĕs̱ ănd sŭfĭx̱ĕs̱, fal tọ

sĕrv hĕr pŭrpos, she ĕxtĕmporaneŭslў ănd wĭthout hĕsitashŭn, coins ăn ovĕrflo ŏv sĕlf-ĕx-
planĭng cŏmpounds, thăt sem to fulў met the
demănd ĕvĕn ŏv hĕr on ĕxtrem casĕs.

Nor ĭs she bărĕn ŏv ideás respĕctĭng thos
ĭmăgĭnarў beĭngs, cald bȳ the lĕrnĕd, Farĭs,
Nȳmfs, Sprits, Elfs, Demons, ănd the lik. To
hĕr, ĕvĕrў grŏt ănd cornĕr, ĕvĕrў wod ănd
swamp, hĭl ănd mĕdo, ĭs ĭnhăbĭtĕd bȳ thĕs ĭm-
agĭnĕrў beĭngs, ho är çeslĕslў plȳĭng thar ärts
ĭn ĭntĕrferĭng wĭth humàn àfars—workĭng to
this pĕrsŭn wĕlth ănd hapĭnĕs,—to thăt wŭn,
povĕrtў ănd wo.

THE COLLOQUY.

I begăn mȳ întĕrogashŭng bȳ saĭng, I ĕxpĕct yu hăv ạlwaȿ bĭn prĕtȳ wĕl ăcquantĕd
wĭth the pepl lĭvĭng ŭpŏn thĭs mountĭn. Tọ
thĭs remărk she quĭklȳ replid:

Yes! And I tĕl yu thăt tha är the wŭrst
sĕt ŏv folks thăt hăȿ ĕvĕr lĭvd; thĕȳ lȳ ănd
stel, ănd ehet, ănd rŏb, and mŭrdĕr, tọ. Hwȳ!
yu wụd'nt belev hou băd tha är; tha'd ehet
the vĕrȳ dĕvĭl, ĭf he waȿ on ĕrth; ănd tha'd lȳ
hĭm out ŏv hĭȿ posĕshŭnȿ, tọ. Hwȳ, a̤ pĕrsŭn
ĭȿ ĭn dangĕr ŏv hĭȿ lif ŭp her, ănd he căn't kep
nŏthĭn'. Tha'd stel the brĕd out ŏv a̤ blind
nĭgĕr'ȿ mouth, ănd then mŭrdĕr hĭm ĭf he
told ŏv ĭt. Thăt's the wa ĭt goȿ ŭp her—tha'r
wŭs thăn the dĕvĭl hĭmsĕlf.

Bŭt, I replid, thĕr mŭst be sŭm gọd wŭnȿ
a̤mŭng thĕm. Tọ thĭs she ejăculatĕd: No, ther
ant; nŏt wŭn; thar äl bad, ănd sŭm är wŭȿ.
Yu nĕvĕr sen sŭeh folks; thar the dămdĕst
thăt ĕvĕr lĭvd.

Wĕl, thĕn, hou do tha lĭv? sĕd I.

Liv! Hwȳ, tha don't lĭv—tha onlȳ sta—ănd hărdlȳ thăt; à god mĕnȳ ŏv thĕm don't sta lŏng ĭn the sam plaç, nethĕr; tha'r à sĕt ŏf dămd tŭrtls; tha cărȳ al tha'v gŏt ŏn thar băks —ănd thăt ant mŭch, nethĕr,—ănd thĕn thar rĕdȳ to gĕt up ănd gĕt out, ĕnȳ tim; ănd yu căch 'ĕm ĭf ȳu want to.

Wĕl, ĭf tha är so băd, do ĕnȳ ŏv thĕm lĭv togĕthĕr, or dŭs ech wŭn lĭv àlon? I ĭnqwird.

To thĭs she replid: Lĭv togĕthĕr! Gĕs tha do; to mĕnȳ ŏv 'em. Hwy! ĭn sŭm ŏv thĕm shăntĭs thĕr är à dŭzĕn or mor,—hwits ănd blăks, ănd al cŭlŭrs—ănd nŏthn' to et, ănd nŏthn' to war, ănd no wod to bŭrn,—ănd hwat căn tha do—thà hăv to stel.

And thĕn thĕr ĭs no dĭstĭncshŭn ŏv cŭlŭr ŭp her? sĕd I.

No, nŏt à bĭt. The nĭgĕrs ănd whits al lĭv togĕthĕr. The hwits är jŭst ăs god ăs the nĭgĕrs, ănd both är ăs băd ăs the dĕvĭl căn mak 'ĕm.

Wel, thĕn, do the negros mărȳ the whits?

Hwĕn tha want to; bŭt, tha don't do mŭch mărȳĭng ŭp her—tha don't hăv to—ănd thĕn ĭts no us,—ĭts to mŭch trŭbl.

Wĕl, thĕn, hou àbout the chĭldrĕn, är thĕr ĕnў?

Yĕs; à plĕntў ŏv 'ĕm; ănd al cŭlŭrs—blăk, ănd whit, ănd ўelo—ănd ĕnў ŭthĕr cŭlŭr thăt yu hăv ĕvĕr sen, bŭt blu; thĕr ant no blu wŭns yĕt.

Wĕl, ĭf thĕr parĕnts är nŏt mărĭd, hou do tha brĭng ŭp the chĭldrĕn?

Brĭng 'ĕm ŭp! Tha don't brĭng 'ĕm ŭp. Hwy, ăs son ăs tha är born, ĕvĕrў dĕvĭl ŏv 'ĕm ĭs for hĭmsĕlf, ănd the dĕvĭl's for 'ĕm al. Thăt's hou thăt gos. And I tĕl yu, tha hăv à blamd hărd tim ŏv ĭt, to.

And thĕn, hou do tha nam the chĭldrĕn?

Nam 'ĕm! Hwy, tha nam 'ĕm àftĕr thar dădĭ's, to be sur—ĭf tha no ho tha är. Bŭt, thăt don't mak ĕnў ŏds; cas, befor tha är gron ŭp, hàf ŏv 'em don't no thar on yŭng wŭns from ĕnўbŏdў ĕls's, ănd the ŭthĕr hàf ŏv 'ĕm wudn't on 'ĕm ĭf tha dĭd; ănd the yŭng wŭns ant no bĕtĕr—tha ŏfĕn swar tha hăd no dădĭs'. Yu se, jŭst ăs son ăs tha gĕt bĭg enŭf, tha trăvĕl out to gĕt sŭmthĭng to et, ănd ĭf the fed is prĕtў god, ma be tha'l sta—nĕvĕr gĕt băk; ănd ĭf thà cŭm băk, tha find so mĕnў mor ĭn the nĕst, tha căn't sta ĭf tha want to. Hwў! nŭn

ŏv 'ĕm thăt's gọd for ĕnȳthĭng ĕvĕr stas her.
Tha go àwa hwĕn tha är smạl, ănd ġĕt wŭrk
ănd sta. Yu'l find foks born ŏn thĭs mountĭn,
lĭv'n ĭn Prĭnçtŭn, Neu Brŭnswĭk, ĭn Trĕntŭn,
ĭn Neu York, ănd the dĕvĭl nọs hwĕr ạl; ănd
ĭf tha är driv'n tem for sŭm bĭg-bŭgs, or är wa-
tĕrs ĭn sŭm grat hotĕl, tha'l nĕvĕr on tha wĕr
born on thĭs mountĭn, nŏt à bĭt ŏv ĭt. Tha no
bĕtĕr. Bŭt, ĭf wŭn tŭrns out tọ be à pọr dĕvĭl,
ănd ġĕts ĭntọ sŭm băd scrap—thăt fĕlo ĭs sur
tọ cŭm băk tọ the mountĭn. Thăt's the wa tha
kep the rănks fụl—fụl ŏv the scoundrĕls thăt
căn't sta ĕnȳ hwĕr els; thăt's the wă ĭt gos
wĭth the foks her.

Hàv yu ạlwas lĭvd ŏn thĭs mountĭn, Sĭlvĭà?

No; I wạs born ŏn thĭs mountĭn ĭn ăn old
tăvĕrn thăt usd tọ stănd ner the Rŏk Mĭls; ĭt
stọd ŭpŏn the lănd nou ond bȳ Rĭchàrd Scŏt.
The old hotĕl wạs ond ănd kĕpt bȳ Rĭchàrd
Cŭmptŭn; ĭt wạs torn doun à lŏng hwil àgo,
ănd nou yu căn't tĕl the spŏt ŏn hwĭch ĭt stọd.
Mȳ parĕnts wĕr slavs; ănd hwĕn mȳ màstĕr
movd doun tọ Neshănĭc, I wĕnt ạlŏng wĭth
thĕm; ănd, hwĕn mȳ màstĕr went tọ Grat Bĕnd,
ŏn the Sŭsqwehănà, I wĕnt wĭth hĭm thar.
Aftĕrwàrds I ĭvd lĭn Neu Brŭnswĭk, ănd ĭn

Prĭnçtŭn, ănd ĭn ŭthĕr placĕṣ. I cam băk tọ
the mountĭn becaṣ I ĭnhĕrĭtĕd à hous ănd lŏt ŏv
lănd, ăt mȳ fäthĕr'ṣ dĕth. Thăt's hwạt brŏt me
băk tọ the mountĭn.

Ho wạṣ yur fäthĕr?

Mȳ fäthĕr wạṣ Cŭfȳ Bard, à slav tọ Jŏn
Bard. He (Cŭfȳ) wạṣ à fĭfĕr ĭn the bătl ŏv
Prĭnçtŭn. He uṣd tọ be à fĭfĕr for the mĭnĭt
mĕn, ĭn the daṣ ŏv the Rĕvoluṣhŭn.

Ho wäṣ yur mŭthĕr?

Mȳ mŭthĕr wäṣ Dorcŭs Cŭmptŭn, à slav tọ
Rĭehard Cŭmptŭn, the proprietor ŏv the hotĕl,
ăt Rŏk Mĭlṣ. Hwĕn I wạṣ tọ yerṣ old, mȳ
mŭthĕr bŏt hĕr tim ŏv Rĭehàrd Cŭmptŭn,—
Mĭnĭcàl Dụbois goĭng hĕr securĭtȳ for the pamĕnt ŏv the mŭnȳ. Aṣ mȳ mŭthĕr fald tọ mak
pamĕnt ăt the tim ăpointĕd, she becam the prŏpĕrtȳ ŏv Mĭnĭcàl Dụbois. Wĭth thĭs falur tọ
mak pamĕnt, Dụbois wạṣ gratlȳ dĭsăpointĕd,
ănd mŭeh dĭspleṣd, ăṣ he dĭd nŏt wĭsh tọ fạl ạr
tọ mȳ mŭthĕr ănd hĕr ehĭldrĕn, ăṣ slavṣ tọ hĭm.
So he trátĕd mŭthĕr bădlȳ—ŏfĕn tĭmṣ cruĕlȳ.
On wŭn ŏcaṣyŭn, hwĕn hĕr bab wạṣ bŭt thre
dàṣ old, he whĭpt hĕr wĭth ăn ŏx-găd, becaṣ
she dĭdn't hold à hŏg hwil he yokt ĭt; ĭt wạṣ
ĭn Märeh; the ground wạṣ wĕt ănd slĭpĕrȳ,

ănd the hŏg prọvd tọ strŏng for hĕr, ŭndĕr the çĭrcŭmstăn̤çĕs̲. Frŏm the ĕxpọşyur ănd the whĭpĭng, ſhe becàm severlў sĭk wĭth puĕrperàl fevĕr; bŭt, àftĕr à lŏng hwil ſhe recŏvĕrd.

Undĕr the slav lạs̲ ŏv Neu Jĕrsў, hwĕn the slav thŏt the mästĕr tọ sever, ănd the slav ănd the mästĕr dĭd nŏt gĕt àlong harmonĭŭslў, the slav hăd à rit tọ hŭnt à neu mästĕr. Acord-ĭnglў, mў mŭthĕr Dọrcŭs, wĕnt ĭn qwĕst ŏv à neu mästĕr; ănd, ăṣ Mr. Wm. Bard uṣd tọ sĕnd thĭngs̲ for hĕr ănd hĕr ehĭldrĕn tọ et, hwĕn Du-bois nĕglĕctĕd, or refuṣd tọ fŭrnĭſh enŭf tọ săt-ĭsfy thar cravĭng stŭmăcs, ſhe àskt hĭm (Bard), tọ bў hĕr. Thĭs he dĭd. And ſhe likt hĭm wĕl; bŭt ſhe wạs̲ ămbĭſhŭs tọ be fre. Acord-ĭnglў, ſhe bŏt hĕr tim ŏv Bard, bŭt fald tọ mak pamĕnt, ănd retŭrnd tọ hĭm hĭs̲ slav.

She wạs̲ thĕn sold to Milṣ Smith, ho wạs̲ à kind mästĕr, ănd à gọd măn. Bŭt, ſhe wạs̲ ămbĭſhŭs tọ be fre—ṣo ŏv, Smĭth ſhe bŏt hĕr tim, ănd wĕnt àwa tọ wŭrk, ănd tọ lĭv wĭth strängĕrs̲. But, ăṣ ſhe fald tọ mak pamĕnt ăt the ăpointĕd tim, ſhe wạs̲ takĕn băk à slav, ănd spĕnt the remandĕr ŏv hĕr daṣ wĭth him, ănd wạs̲ bĕrĭd àbout 45 yerṣ àgo ŭpŏn hĭs̲ homstĕd.

Ov corṣ, I remand à slav tọ Mĭnĭcàl Dụbois.

He dĭd nŏt tret me crŭelў. I trid tǫ pleṣ hĭm, ănd he trid tǫ pleṣ me; ănd we gŏt álong tog̈ĕthĕr prĕtў wĕl—ĕxçĕptĭng sumtimṣ I wṵd be á lĭtl refrăctorў, ănd thĕn he wṵd gĭv me á sever flŏg̈ĭng. Hwĕn I wąṣ ábout fiv yerṣ old, he mǫvd ŭpŏn á färm ner the vĭlag̈ ŏv Flagtoṵn. Hwil ther, I hăd gǫd timṣ—á plĕntў tǫ et, á plĕntў ŏv clothṣ, ănd á plĕntў ŏv fun— onlў mў mĭstrĕs wąṣ tĕriblў păshunąt, ănd tĕriblў croṣ tǫ me. I dĭd nŏt lik hĕr, ănd she dĭd nŏt lik me; so she uṣd tǫ bĕat me bădlў. On wun ŏcashun, I dĭd sumthing thăt dĭd not sut hĕr. Aṣ uṣuál, she scoldĕd me. Then I wąṣ sáçў. Herupŏn, she whĭpt me untĭl she mărkt me so bădlў thăt I wĭl nĕvĕr loṣ the scärṣ. Yu căn se the scärṣ her upŏn mў hed, tǫ-da; ănd I wĭl nĕvĕr loṣ thĕm, ĭf I lĭv ănuthĕr hundrĕd yerṣ.

Hwĕn I wąṣ ábout tĕn yerṣ old, the bătl ov Mŭnmuth ŏcurd. I remĕmbĕr vĕrў wĕl hwĕn mў mästĕr cum hom frŏm thăt bătl. Chĕrĭs wĕr rip, ănd we wĕr g̈ăthĕrĭng härvĕst. He wąṣ ăn ŏffiçĕr; but I dǫ nōt no hĭṣ rănk. He told grat storĭṣ ábout the bătl, ănd ŏv the bravĕrў ŏv the Neu Jĕrsў mĭlĭshá; ănd ábout the cŏnduct ŏv G̈ĕnĕrál Wáshĭngtun. He sĕd

tha whĭpt the Brĭtĭsh bădlў—but ĭt wạs á dĕspĕrat fit. He told us thăt the bătl ŏcurd ŏn
the hŏtĕst da he ĕvĕr sạ; he sĕd he cam ner
pĕrĭshĭng frŏm thĕ ĕxçĕs ŏv het ănd from thĭrst;
ănd thăt á grat mĕnў dĭd di for the wạnt ŏv
wạtĕr.

I ạlso remĕmbĕr hwĕn mў fäthĕr ănd uthĕrs
returnĕd frŏm the bătls ŏv Trĕntun ănd Prĭnçtun,—but I wạs yungĕr thĕn, ănd onlў remĕmbĕr thăt ĭt wạs wĭntĕr, ănd thăt tha cŏmpland
thăt tha hăd suffĕrd so mueh frŏm cold ănd
ĕxposur.

Befor the bătl ŏv Prĭnçtun, mў mästĕr hăd
bĭn á prĭsunĕr ŏv wạr. He hăd bĭn căpturd
hwil fitĭng ŏn the wạtĕr, sumwhĕr ner Neu
York. I uṣd tọ her hĭm tĕl hou he ănd sĕvĕrál
uthĕrs wĕr croudĕd ĭntọ á vĕrў smạl rọm ĭn
the hold ŏv á vĕsĕl—the trăp-dor securlў fäst-
ĕnd doun, ănd the suplў ŏv frĕsh ar so com-
pletlў shut ŏf, thăt almost ạl họ wĕr thus ĭm-
prĭsund, did ĭn á fĕw hours. In thĭs plaç tha
wĕr kĕpt tụ das. Dụbois, bў brethĭng wĭth
hĭs mouth ĭn clos cŏntăct wĭth á nal-hol, hĕld
out untĭl he wàs removd. Tụ or thre uthĕrs
wĕr fortunat enuf tọ finð sum uthĕr defĕcts ĭn

the wod-wurk, thru hwĭch à scăntў suplў ŏv ar cam.

Hwĕn I wås ĭn mȳ 14th yer, mȳ mästĕr movd frŏm Flăgtoun to hĭs färm ålŏṉg the Susqwhănà Rĭvĕr. Thĭs färm ĭs the lănd ŏn hwĭch the vĭlaġ cald Grat Bĕnd hăs bĭn bĭlt. Hwĕn we movd upŏn the färm, thĕr wås but wun uthĕr hous ĭn the sĕtlmĕnt for the dĭstånç ŏv sĕvĕrál mils. Thes tu housĕs wĕr bĭlt ŏv lŏgs. The wun upŏn mȳ mästĕrs färm hăd bĭn kĕpt ăs à tăvĕrn; ănd hwĕn he movd ĭnto ĭt, he kĕpt ĭt ăs à tăvĕrn. The plaç wås non ăs Grat Bĕnd. It wås ăn ĭmportánt stŏpĭṉg plaç for trăvĕlĕrs on thar wa to the Lak Cuntrĭs, ănd to uthĕr plaçs wĕstwård. Also, ĭt wås à plaç much vĭsĭtĕd bȳ botmĕn goĭṉg doun ănd up the rĭvĕr. Her, to, cam grat numbĕrs ŏv huntĕrs ănd drovĕrs. In făct, ĕvĕn ĭn thes das, Grat Bĕnd wås ăn ĭmportánt plaç.

In movĭṉg to Grat Bĕnd, we wĕnt ĭn tu wăguns. We tok wĭth us tu cous; thĕs I drov al the wa thar. Aftĕr we crŏst the Dĕlàwar ăt Estun, the rod ĕxtĕndĕd thru à grat fŏrĕst, wĭth onlў her ănd thar à clerd păteh, ănd à smal lŏg hut. Ĕvĕn the tăvĕrns wĕr onlў lŏg huts—sumtims wĭth but wun rom

doun stars ănd wŭn ŭp stars. Thĕn thĕr wŭd
be tu or thre bĕds ĭn the rọm ŭp stars, ănd
wŭn ĭn the rọm doun stars.

The grat fŏrĕst wạs cạld the Bech Wọds.
It wạs so bĭg thặt we wạs sĭx das ĭn goĭng
thru ĭt. Sŭmtims we wŭd go ȧ hȧlf da without pȧsĭng ȧ hous, or metĭng ȧ pĕrsŭn. The
wọds wạs ful ŏv bars, pănthĕrs, wild-căts ănd
the lik. About thes I hăd hĕrd ȧ grat mĕnў
wild storĭs. So I mad shur tọ kep mў cous
prĕtў clos tọ the wăgŭns.

Usuȧlў, we stŏpt ovĕr nit ăt ȧ hotĕl. Bŭt,
ăs the housĕs wĕr smạl, ŏfĕn ĭt wŭd hăpĕn thặt
ŭthĕrs hăd stŏpt befor we ărivd, ănd the lŏdg-
ĭng rọms wŭd ạl be ŏcupid. Thĕn we wŭd slep
ĭn our wăgŭns, or ĭn the out-bĭldĭngs. In thos
das, trăvĕlĕrs hăd tọ gĕt ȧlŏng the bĕst wa tha
cụd.

As mў mästĕr sạ thặt the sit ŭpŏn whĭch he
lĭvd wạs favŭrȧbl tọ bĭsinĕs, durĭng the thĭrd
sŭmĕr ȧftĕr our ărivȧl, he erĕctĕd ȧ lärg neu
fram hous—the fĭrst hous, nŏt bĭlt ŏv lŏgs, ĭn
Grat Bĕnd. Thĕn, he begăn tọ dọ ȧ lärg bĭsinĕs, ănd becam ȧ vĕrў prŏminĕnt măn thar, ăs
he wạs hwil he lĭvd ĭn Neu Jĕrsў.

Alrĕdў sĕvĕrȧl pĕpl hăd mọvd tọ the nabŭrhǫd, hăd erĕctĕd lŏg houṣĕ̱ṣ, clerd the lăndṣ, ănd begŭn tǫ cŭltivat feldṣ, ănd raṣ stŏk. Vĕry̆ sǫn, ĭn the vĭlag, stor-houṣĕ̱ṣ ănd mĭlṣ wĕr bĭlt. Inded, Grat Bĕnd begăn tǫ be the çĕntĕr ŏv á lärġ ănd thrivĭng sĕtlmĕnt.

At thĭs tim hŭntĕrs uṣd tǫ cŭm tǫ thĭs point tǫ trad; tǫ sĕl der-met, bar-met, wĭld tŭrky̆ṣ ănd the lĭk, ănd tǫ ĕxehǎng the skĭnṣ ŏv wild ănimàlṣ for sŭeh cŏmŏditĭṣ ăṣ tha wĭsht. At our tăvĕrn, tha uṣd tǫ stǎ; ănd tha wĕr á jŏly̆ sĕt ŏy fĕloṣ; I likt tǫ se thĕm cŭm—thĕr wàṣ fŭn thĕn.

Thĕr waṣ á fĕry̆ àcrŏs the Sŭsqwehǎnǎ ǎt Grat Bĕnd. The bot ŭpŏn our sid wàṣ ond bȳ mȳ mästĕr; the wŭn ŭpŏn the ŭthĕr sid wàṣ ond bȳ Cǎptĭn Hateh. I sǫn lĕrnd tǫ mǎnaġ the bot ăṣ wĕl ăṣ ĕny̆ wŭn cųd, ănd ŏfĕn uṣd tǫ fĕry̆ temṣ àcrŏs àlon. The foks hǫ wĕr ăc-qwantĕd wĭth me, ŭṣd tǫ prĕfĕr me tǫ tak thĕm ăcrŏs, ĕvĕn hwĕn the fĕry̆mĕn wĕr àbout. Bŭt, Cǎptĭn Hǎteh dĭd nŏt lik me. I uṣd tǫ stel hĭ̱ṣ cŭstŭmĕrṣ. Hwĕn I lăndĕd mȳ bot ŭpŏn hĭ̱ṣ sid, ĭf ĕny̆ bŏdy̆ wàṣ thar thǎt wạntĕd tǫ cŭm ovĕr tǫ the Bĕnd, bĕfor he neu ĭt, I wųd hŭry̆ thĕm ĭntǫ mȳ bot ănd pųsh ŏf frŏm the shor, ănd lev hĭm swarĭng. Yų se the

mŭnў I gŏt for fĕtehĭng băk à lod wạṣ min;
ănd, I stol mĕnў à lod frŏm old Hăteh; I ạlwaṣ
dĭd, ĕvĕrў tim I cụd.

Alŏng wĭth the fĕrў bot, ạlwaṣ wĕr wŭn or
tụ skĭfs. Theṣ we tọk àlŏng tọ hăv ĭn rĕdĭnĕs
ĭn cas ŏv ạcĭdĕnt. Hwĕn the lod wạṣ hĕvў, or
hwĕn ĭt wạṣ wĭndў, tụ or mor fĕrўmĕn wĕr re-
qwird. At sŭeh timṣ, I wụd hĕlp thĕm àcrŏs,
bŭt I ạlwaṣ cŭm băk àlon ĭn à skĭf. In thĭs
wa I gŏt so thăt I cụd hăndl the skĭf fĭrst rat,
ănd wạṣ vĕrў fŏnd ŏv usĭng ĭt. Ofĕn timṣ I
usd tọ tak sĭngl păsĕngĕrṣ ovĕr the fĕrў ĭn à
skĭf; sŭmtimṣ tụ or mor ăt wŭnç. Thĭs I likt,
ănd tha usd tọ pa me wĕl tọ dọ ĭt. I hăd à gọd
nam for mănăgĭng the skĭf—tha ụsd tọ sa thăt,
ĭn usĭng the skĭf I cụd bet ĕnў măn ŏn the
Susqwehănà,—ănd I ạlwaṣ dĭd bet ạl thăt raçt
wĭth me.

Ofĕntimṣ hwĕn the fĕrўmĕn wĕr ăt dĭnĕr,
sŭm wŭn wụd cŭm tọ the fĕrў tọ crŏs. Tha
wụd hŏlo tọ lĕt ŭs no thăt sŭm wŭn wạntĕd
tọ crŏs. Thĕn thĕr wụd be à raç. I'd skĭp
out, ănd doun tọ the whạrf so sọn thăt I'd hăv
'ĕm lodĕd ănd pụsht ŏf befor ĕnў wŭn ĕls cụd
gĕt thar—ănd thĕn I'd gĕt the fe. I tĕl yu, ĭf
tha dĭd nŏt ehŭk nif ănd fork, ănd rŭn ăt wŭnç,

'twas no us—tha cud'nt run with me,—the fe
was gŏn. I'v gŏt mĕnў å shĭlĭṇg that wa, ănd
mĕnў å gọd drĭnk, tọ.

I åskt: Was yur mästĕr wĭlĭṇg thăt yu shụd
ehet the fĕrўmán out ŏv hĭs fes ĭn thăt wa?

She replid: He dĭd nŏt car; he thŏt I was
smärt for doĭṇg ĭt. And sŭmtims, ĭf I hăd nŏt
bĭn ĭn the hăbĭt ŏv hŭrўĭṇg thĭṇgs ŭp ĭn thĭs
wa, pepl wụd hăv watĕd ăt the fĕrў bў the
hour,—bŭt yu se tha dĭd'nt hăv tọ wat hwĕn I
was åbout, ănd thĭs ĭs hwӯ tha likt mĕ, ănd
hwӯ mў mästĕr likt me, tọ.

Wĕl, Sĭlvĭå; hwåt kind ŏv tims dĭd yu hăv
hwil ăt Grat Bĕnd?

What kĭnd ŏv tims? Hwӯ, fïrst rat tims!
Thĕr wĕr plĕntў ŏv frolĭcs, ănd I usd tọ go
ănd dånç al nit,—foks cụd dånç thĕn. Hwӯ!
thĕr wĕr sŭm ŏv the bĕst dånçĕrs ŭp thar thăt
I ĕvĕr sa; foks neu hou tọ dånç ĭn thos das.

Thĕn yu thĭnk thăt the yŭṇg foks ŏv thĭs
naborhọd don't no hou tọ dånç?

I no tha don't; I'v sen 'ĕm trӯ, ănd tha
căn't dånç å bĭt. Tha'v gŏt no stĕp.

Hăv yu sen ĕnўbŏdў trӯ tọ dånç vĕrў låtlў?

Yĕs; låst wĭntĕr tha mad å pärtў ovĕr

her, ăt wŭn ŏv the nabŭrs, ănd tha ĭnvĭtĕd me over; ănd I wĕnt. Tha hăd à fĭdl, ănd tha trid to dànç—bŭt tha cụd'nt—nŏt à dămd à wŭn ŏv 'ĕm.

Wĕl! hwạt wạs the mătĕr?

Hwạt wạs the mătĕr! Hwȳ! tha hăd no stĕp,—yu căn't dànç ŭnlĕs yu hăv the stĕp; ănd tha wĕr ăs ạkwàrd ăs the dĕvĭl; ănd thĕn thà wĕr so dămd clŭmsȳ. Hwȳ, ĭf tha went to crŏs thar lĕgs, tha'd fạl doun.

Thĕn yu thĭnk thăt to dànç wĕl, ĭt ĭs nĕçesarȳ to crŏs the lĕgs?

Sŭmtims ĭt ĭs,—nobŏdȳ căn dànç mŭch wĭthout crŏsĭng the lĕgs; bŭt tha cụdn't do ĭt —tha'd gĕt tăngld ĭn the rĭgĭn ănd căpsiz. Hwȳ! tha căntĕrd ovĕr the flor lik so mĕnȳ he gots.

Wĕl, dĭd yu sho thĕm hou to dànç?

Wĕl, yĕs; I tọk à stĕp or tụ; bŭt I cụdn't do ĭt ăs I usd to hwĕn I wạs yŭng. Tha thŏt I dĭd wĕl; bŭt tha don't no—tha'v nĕvĕr sen gọd dànçĭng. Hwȳ! hwĕn I wạs yŭng, I'd crŏs mȳ fet nĭntȳ-nin tims ĭn a mĭnĭt, ănd nĕvĕr mĭs the tim, strĭk hel or to wĭth eqwàl es, ănd go thrụ the fĭgurs ăs nĭmbl ăs à wĭtch. Bŭt nou tha'r so clŭmsȳ thăt hwĕn

wŭn taks à fǫt ŏf frŏm the flor, sŭmbŏdў hăs̱
tǫ hold hĭm ŭp hwil he shaks ĭt. And then hwĕn
tha rel tha pṳsh ănd croud lik à yok ŏv yṳ̄ng
sters̱, ănd tha băng eeh ŭther ŭntĭl tha är ĭn
danger ŏv thar livs̱.

Yes, Sĭlvĭà, the ärt ŏv dánçĭng hăs̱ fạlĕn
ĭntǫ declin, ănd I ăm sŏrў tor ĭt. The yṳ̄ng
foks ŏv thĭs gĕnĕrashŭn är nŏt onlў clŭms̱ў
ănd ạkwàrd, bŭt tha är băd fĭgurs̱ ; ther ĭs̱
nŭthĭng ĭn thar sports tǫ devĕlŏp à gǫd form,
ănd ăs̱ à cŏnseqwĕnç, thĭs gĕnĕrashŭn ĭs̱ cărăc-
tĕrizd bў băd devĕlŏpmĕnt—wek bŏdĭs̱ wĭth
ŭglў façes, ănd pǫr minds̱.

Herŭpŏn Sĭlvĭà bgăn tǫ sa :

Bŭt, tha thĭnk thar grat thĭngs̱ ănd vĕrў
hăndsŭm. Bŭt tha ant ; thar pǫr, scrŏnў mor-
tàls̱—mak no ăperànç, ănd căn't dǫ nŏthĭng.
Hwў ! the mĕn ŏv the aġ ov mў mästĕr, lǫkt
brav. Tha wĕr tạl ănd cŏmăndĭng, ănd stout
ŏv lĭmb, ănd ġraçfụl ănd hăndў ; tha hăd gǫd
façĕs, grat hi forhĕds̱—ănd lärġ brit ȳs (eyes)
ănd brŏd mouths̱ wĭth gǫd teth. Tha stǫd ŭp
strat, ănd wạlkt wĭth frĕdŭm ănd es̱. I tĕl yu,
ĭn thos̱ ŏld tims̱, ther wĕr gǫd lǫkĭng mĕn,—
brav lǫkĭng mĕn, tha wĕr ạl s̱o ; Gĕnĕràl Washĭngtŭn wạs̱, ănd Làfaĕt wạs̱, ănd mў mästĕr wạs̱

ănd ạl the grat mĕn thặt I ĕvĕr sạ wĕr, ănd tha wĕr ạl gọd dȧnçẹrs; ănd dȧnçt hwĕnĕvĕr tha hăd ȧ chȧnç. Tha uṣd tọ sȧ thặt Gĕnĕrȧl Washĭngtŭn wạṣ the most beutĭful dạnçĕr ĭn Amĕricȧ—thặt he cụd ĕvĕn bet the Marcŭs de Lȧfaĕt.

The big yankĭs frŏm York Stat ănd Neu Englȧnd, uṣd tọ cŭm tọ our hous, ănd tha wĕr vĕrў fin lọkĭng mĕn—ạl ŏv 'ĕm wĕr. And tha wĕr vĕrў tạl, ănd vĕrў strat, ănd vĕrў dĭgnĭfid; ănd thȧr wivṣ wĕr wĕl formd ănd beutĭful, ănd vĕrў dĭgnĭfid wimĕn. And tha wĕr ạl vĕrў polit—hăd the best ŏv mȧnĕrs—wĕr the mŏst acŏmplĭsht foks I ĕvĕr sạ. And tha wĕr ạl gọd dȧnçĕrs—the best ŏv dȧnçẹrs—ănd tha nĕvĕr gŏt tĭrd ŏv dȧnçĭng. Evĕn the old mĕn ănd old wimĕn dȧnçt—ănd tha wĕr jŭst ăṣ gọd figurs ăṣ yu ĕvĕr sạ, ănd vĕrў graçful.

I se, Sĭlvĭȧ, thặt yu hăd gọd timṣ hwĕn ȧt the Grat Bŏnd.

Ges we hăd! Hwĕn mў mästĕr mọvd ĭntọ hĭṣ neu hous, we hăd ȧ bĭg tim. Al the grănd foks wĕr thar, ănd I tĕl yu, thĭngs wĕr livlў. We hăd ȧ plĕntў ŏv brăndў, ănd tha uṣd ĭt, tọ —ȧ bĭg tim I tĕl yu; ăў! ăў! the bĭgĕst kind ŏv ȧ tim.

Dĭd yu us ĕnў brănдў?

Wĕl, I dĭd; bŭt nŏt tĭl towǎrds nit; I hǎd tọ mŭch tọ dọ; I hǎd tọ se tọ the rĕst; I neu hwĕr ĕvĕrўthĭng wạs, ănd I hǎd tọ hĕlp thĕm gĕt thĕm. Bŭt, I lọkt out for mўsĕlf. Thĕr wạs wŭn kĕg ŏv brănдў thǎt I neu wạs mad vĕrў gọd, for I. hĕlpt mak ĭt; wĕ usd tọ mak our on brănдў, ănd I ạlwas hĕlpt mў mästĕr mak ĭt, ănd neu jŭst ạs wĕl hou tọ dọ ĭt ạs ĕnўbŏdў.

I lĕft thĭs kĕg tĭl ĭt wạs the lǎst thĭng tọ be mọvd; thĕn, hwĕn I ănd ȧ çĕrtĭn fĕlo begǎn tọ mọv ĭt, we cŏnclụdĕd thǎt we wụd se ĭf ĭt hǎd kĕpt wĕl; we hǎd no cŭp, so we drạwd ĭt out ĭn ăn ĕrthĕn pŏt; ănd thĕn he drănk; ănd thĕn I drănk—tĭl we drănk ạl we cụd; bŭt stĭl thĕr wạs sŭm lĕft ĭn the pŏt, ănd we cụdn't gĕt ĭt băk ĭn the kĕg, for we hǎd no fŭnĕl; we dĭdn't wạnt tọ thro ĭt ȧwa, thǎt lọkt tọ wastfụl; so, we cŏnclụdĕd we'd drĭnk ĭt ŭp; so, he drănk ănd I drănk, tĭl ĭt wạs gŏn. Thĭs mad ŭs prĕtў fụl; bŭt we stärtĕd wĭth the kĕg; bў ănd bў ĭt begŭn tọ be tọ hevў—ănd thĕn ĭt gŏt doun, ănd thĕn we gŏt doun; ănd thĕn I neu thĕr'd be ȧ tim, becạs I neu ĭf mў mästĕr sạ me, I'd gĕt ȧ hĕl ŏv ȧ lĭk'n. And sŭm ŏv the

rĕst neu thăt tọ. And tha dĭdn't wạnt tọ se
me lĭkt, sọ tha gŏt me ŭp, ănd hĕlpt me ŏf towärd the hous tọ pụt me tọ bed.

I usd tọ be sŭbjĕct tọ the crămps, ănd sŭmtims I usd tọ hăv ĭt vĕrў băd,—so thăt mỹ
mĭstrĕs usd tọ gĭv me mĕdĭçĭn for ĭt ; ănd, wŭns
à lĭtl hwĭl befor, I wạs so bàd wĭth ĭt thăt
she thŏt I wạs going tọ di wĭth ĭt. Wĕl, I
thŏt nou I hăd bĕtĕr hăv the crămp, ănd thĕn
mabe I wụdn't gĕt lĭkt. So I begăn tọ hăv
pan—ănd sọn ĭt gŏt prĕtў băd—wors thăn I'd
ĕvĕr hăd ĭt befor; ănỹhou, I mad mor fŭs thăn
I ĕvĕr hăd befor, ănd yĕld ă gọd del louder.

Prĕtў sọn tha cạld mĭsỹ, ănd she wạs ạwfụlỹ
fritĕnd ; she thŏt I wụd di, shur ; she sĕd she'd
nĕvĕr sen me so wek wĭth ĭt befor.

So she hăd me cărĭd ănd plaçt ŭpŏn the
trŭndl–bĕd, ĭn hĕr on rọm, ănd ătĕndĕd tọ me
nịçlў. She gav me sŭm mĕdĭçĭn hwĭeh she
thŏt hĕlpt me ặmazĭnglў ; bŭt befor the mĕdĭçĭn cụd dọ ĕnỹ gọd the rŭm stŏpt ạl mỹ yĕlĭng,
ănd grŭntĭng tọ ; ĭn făçt, I wạs so drŭnk thăt
I cụdn't se, her, nor fel. For ạhwil, I thŏt I
wạs dĕd ; bŭt bỹ ănd bỹ the brăndỹ begăn tọ
war ŏf, ănd I begăn tọ se. I cạshŭslỹ sqŭrmd
ároụnd tọ se wĕthĕr ĕnỹbŏdỹ wạs ábout, ănd

thar săt mĭsў, fănĭng me. I cạshŭlў opĕnd mў
ȳs (eyes) jŭst the lest bĭt, tọ se hou she lọkt;
she lọkt vĕrў pĭtўfụl—I wạs tọ drŭnk tọ läf;
bŭt "Mȳ God," thŏt I, "ĭf yu onlў neu hwȧt
I ăm dọĭng, yu'd thro thăt făn ȧwa ănd gĭv
me hĕl."

At nit, mȳ mästĕr cam tọ bĕd vĕrў lat.
Hwĕn he cam ĭn tọ ŭndrĕs, I wạs makĭng bĕ-
lev thăt I wạs ȧslep. I dĭdn't dar tọ gĕt wĕl
tọ sọn. At wŭns, mĭstrĕs begăn tọ tĕl
hĭm hou sĭk I wạs; ănd hou ner I cam tọ dy-
ĭng,—bŭt I dĭdn't fọl hĭm. He lọkt ăt me ȧ
lĭtl, ănd thĕn wĕnt tọ bĕd. He sed : "Pạ!
she's onlў drŭnk—she's bĭn drĭnkĭng wĭth the
men. Go tọ slep—she'l be ạl rit ĭn the mornĭng." And so I wạs, tọ; bŭt, thăt cụrd me
ŏv drĭnkĭng.

Thĕn yu nĕvĕr drănk ȧftĕr thăt?

I nĕvĕr gŏt drŭnk ȧftĕr thăt. Sŭmtims
hwĕn ŭthĕrs hăv bĭn drĭnkĭng, I hăv takn ȧ
drăm, tọ; bŭt, I dĭdn't gĕt drŭnk—I nĕvĕr dọ.
I no mȳ mạsur, ănd I tak no mor.

Dĭd yur mĭstrĕs ĕvĕr fĭnd out thăt yu wĕr
deçevĭng hĕr hwĕn yu wĕr drŭnk?

I gçs nŏt; ĭf she hăd, she'd ȧ kĭld me—ĭf
she cụd; bŭt, I hăv lȧft ạbout ĭt ȧ grat mĕnў

tims. I spoild hĕr fŭn for thăt nit—she hăd to lev hĕr cŭmpánў ănd tak car ŏv me,—ĭt wạs prĕtў härd for hĕr; for she hăd á grat del ŏv bĭg cŭmpánў thar thăt nit, ănd she wạs hĕl for cŭmpạnў.

Wĕl; yur mĭstrĕs wạs álwạs kĭnd to yu, wạsn't she?

Kĭnd to me; hwȳ, she wạs the vĕrў dĕvĭl hĭmsĕlf. Hwȳ, she'd lĕvĕl me wĭth ĕnўthĭng she cụd gĕt hold ŏv—clŭb, stĭk ŏv wọd, tŏngs, fir-shŭvĕl, nif, ăx, hătehĕt; ĕnўthĭng thăt wạs hăndўĕst; ănd thĕn she wạs so dămd qwĭk ábout ĭt, to. I tĕl yu, ĭf I ĭntĕndĕd to sạç hĕr, I mad shur to be ŏf áwạs.

Wĕl; dĭd she ĕvĕr hĭt yu?

Yes, ŏfĕn; wŭns she nŏçt me tĭl I wạs so stĭf thăt she thŏt I wạs ded; wŭns áftĕr thăt, becạs I wạs á lĭtl sạçў, she lĕvĕld me wĭth the fir-shŭvĕl ănd brok mȳ pat. She thŏt I wạs ded thĕn, bŭt I wạsn't.

Brok yur pat?

Yĕs; brok mȳ skŭl; yu cán pụt yur fĭngĕrs her, ĭn the plaç hwar thĕ brak wạs, ĭn the sid ŏv mȳ hĕd, yĕt. She smăsht ĭt rit ĭn—she dĭdn't do thĭngs to the hálvs.

Herŭpŏn I ĕxămĭnd Sĭlvĭȧ's hĕd, ănd found thặt, ăt sŭm tim, lŏng ȧgo, the skŭl hăd bĭn brokĕn ănd deprĕst for ȧ spaç nŏt lĕs thăn thre ĭnehĕṣ ; thặt the deprĕst frăgmĕnt hăd nŏt bĭn ĕlevatĕd, ăṣ sŭrgĕnṣ nou dǫ, ănd thặt ĭn cŏnse- qwĕnç, thĕr ĭṣ, tǫ thĭs da, ȧ deprĕshŭn ĭn hwĭeh I căn bĕrÿ ȧ lärg pärt; ŏv the ĭndĕx fĭnger.

Upŏn hĕr hĕd, I found numĕrŭs ŭthĕr scärṣ most ŏv hwĭeh Sĭlvĭȧ sĕṣ, är the reṣult ŏv woundṣ ĭnflĭctĕd bȳ hĕr mĭstrĕs Bŭt she sĕṣ sŭm ŏv them är nŏt.   Theṣ är, ăcordĭng tǫ hĕr tĕl, the reṣults ŏv woundṣ ĭncŭrd durĭng ŭthĕr warṣ,—waġd ặftĕr she gand hĕr fredŭm.   For, ĭn the strŭgl for lif, Sĭlvĭȧ ĭncŭrd mĕnÿ ȧ cŏm- băt ; ănd, ặltho she älwaṣ căm ŏf frŏm the feld vĭctorĭŭs, sŭmtĭmṣ she dĭd nŏt cŭm ŏf ŭn- scăthd.

In hĕr fits, ĭt ĭṣ sĕd, she ĕngaġd ȧlik măn or womȧn, blăk or hwit—best or bĭrd—ĕnÿthĭng bŭt Gŏd or dĕvĭl.

Acordĭng tǫ hĕr tĕl, she card bŭt lĭtl for fĭst or fǫt ; bŭt sŭmtimṣ hwĕn tha cam doun ŭpŏn hĕr wĭth wǫd ănd stel, she dĭd wĭnç ȧ lĭtl. Bŭt wo! tǫ the cŏmbătȧnt thặt dard tǫ reṣort tǫ thoṣ ŭnfar ĭmplemĕnts ŏv war.   At bĕst, ĕvĕn wĭth theṣ, tha cǫd onlÿ wound hĕr,—jŭst enuf

to ĕxăspĕrat hĕr to do jŭstĭc to the ŏcashun.
For, hwĕn rĭgd for a fĭst fit, nĕvĕr enŭf stod
befor hĕr, nor găthĕrd áround hĕr, to dĭscŭmfĭt
hĕr, or to kep hĕr ŭpŏn the sod.

Respectĭng her pro-wĕs, Sĭlvĭă's tĕstimonў ĭs
nŏt al that I hăv găthĕrd. Dĭfĕrĕnt mĕn, whŏs
vĕnĕrábl lŏks sho that tha är old enŭf to remĕmbĕr sens that tha wĭtnĕst sĭxtў ănd sĕv-
ĕntў yers ágo, tĕl me that tha hăv sen Sĭlvĭă ĭn
bătl mĕnў á tim, ănd that hĕr cŭrag, ănd hĕr
ábĭlĭtў was alwas ădeqwat to ĕnў ĕmĕrġĕncў.

Houĕvĕr, tradĭshŭn stats, that Sĭlvĭă was
nĕthĕr qwärĕlsŭm nor ăgrĕsĭv. On the cŏntrarў, she was deçidĕdlў á peç-makĕr; ănd sŭm
ŏv hĕr most notwŭrthў fets wĕr ăcomphlĭst
hwĕn sŭprĕsĭng á rou, or, pärtĭng cŏmbătánts;
ĭnded, hĕr prĕsĕnç ŏfĕn prĕvĕntĕd á fit. Be-
càs, ĭf the fit begăn cŏntrarў to hĕr wĭl, ŏfĕn-
tims she, to mak thĕm mor obedĭĕnt ĭn the
futur, ănd to tĕrifў ŭthĕrs ŏv á qwarelsŭm or
á pugĭlistĭc natur, wud sevĕrlў whĭp both the
cŏmbătánts.

Nor was she lĕs liklў to ĭntĕrfer ĭn casĕs
hwĕr thĕr was á fre fit. In casĕs ĭn hwĭch frŏm
fiv to tĕn wĕr ĭn á fit, Sĭlvĭă hăs ŏfĕn bĭn non
to wad ĭn, to sez wĕrĕvĕr hand-holt was esĭĕst,

ănd tọ thro wŭn negro ĭn wŭn dĭrĕcshŭn, ănd
ănŭthĕr ĭn ănŭthĕr dĭrĕcshhŭn, untĭl the làst
fēlo wạs hŭrld frŏm the àrenà ŏv fit ; ănd, ŏfĕn
tims she thrụ thĕm wĭth sŭeh forç, thăt the
dăsh ŭpŏn the ground ŭnfītĕd thĕm for fŭrthĕr
àcshŭn, or for retŭrnĭng tọ the batl; sŭeh fets,
oĭng tọ hĕr grat siz, ănd gratĕr strĕnth, she
ăcŏmplĭsht wĭth ez; ănd, ĭt ĭs sed, thăt sŭeh
wĕr hĕr delĭbĕrashŭns, thăt she wụd retŭrn
frŏm sŭeh sens ĭn the ŭtmost cŏmposur.

Wĕl, Sĭlvĭà, hwăt dĭd yur mästĕr sa àbout
sŭeh ăs wạs dŭn bȳ yur mĭstrĕs ?

Sa ! hwȳ he neu hou păshŭnat she wạs. He
sạ hĕr kĭk me ĭn the stŭmăç wŭn da sọ bădlȳ,
thăt he ĭntĕrferd. I wạs nŏt gron ŭp, thĕn ; I
wàs tọ yung tọ stănd sŭeh. He dĭdn't tĕl hĕr
sọ hwĕn I wạs bȳ ; bŭt, I hăv hĕrd hĭm tĕl hĕr
hwĕn tha thŏt I wạs nŏt lĭstĕnĭng, thăt she wạs
tọ sever—thăt sŭeh wŭrk wụd nŏt do—she'd
kĭl me nĕxt.

Wĕl, dĭd hĭs remŏnstrátĭng wĭth hĕr mak hĕr
ĕnȳ bĕtĕr ?

Nŏt à bĭt; mad hĕr wŭrs—jŭst pụt the dĕvĭl
ĭn hĕr. And thĕn, jŭs ăs sọn ăs he wạs out ŏv

the wa, ĭf I wạṣ à lĭtl sạçy̆, or à lĭtl nĕglĕctfụl,
I'd cătch hĕl àgĕn.

Bŭt I fĭxt hĕr—I pad hĕr ŭp for ạl hĕr
spŭnk; I mad ŭp mȳ mind thăt hwĕn I grụ
ŭp I wụd dọ ĭt; ănd hwĕn I hăd à gọd chănç,
hwĕn sŭm ŏv hĕr grănd cŭmpàny̆ wạṣ àround,
I fĭxt hĕr.

Wĕl, hwăt dĭd yu dọ?

I nŏkt hĕr doun, ănd blămd ner kĭld hĕr.

Wĕl; hwar ănd hou dĭd thăt hăpĕn?

It hăpĕnd ĭn the bär-rọm; thar wạṣ sŭm
grănd foks stŏpĭng thar, ănd she wạntĕd thĭngs
tọ lọk prĕty̆ stȳlĭsh; ănd sọ she sĕt me tọ scrŭb-
ĭng ŭp the bär-rọm.   I fĕlt à lĭtl grŭm, ănd
dĭdn't dọ ĭt tọ sut hĕr; she scoldĕd me àbout
ĭt, ănd I sạçt hĕr; she strŭk me wĭth hĕr hănd.
Thĭnk's I, ĭt's à gọd tĭm nou tọ drĕs yu out,
ănd dămd ĭf I wŏn't dọ ĭt; I sĕt doun mȳ tọlṣ,
ănd sqwård for à fit.   The fĭrst hwăk, I strŭk
hĕr à hĕl ŏv à blo wĭth my fĭst.   I dĭdn't nŏk
hĕr ĕntĭrly̆ thrụ the pănĕlṣ ŏv the dọr; bŭt hĕr
lăndĭng àgănst the dor mad à tĕrĭbl smăsh, ănd
I hŭrt hĕr so bădly̆ thăt ạl wĕr fritĕnd out ov
thar wĭts, ănd I dĭdn't no mȳsĕlf bŭt thăt I'd
kĭld the old dĕvĭl.

Wĕr thĕr ćny̆ wŭn ĭn the bär-rọm, thĕn?

It wạs fụl ŏv foks ; sŭm ŏv thĕm wĕr Jĕrsў foks, họ wĕr goĭng frŏm the Lak Cŭntrĭs̱ hom, tọ vĭsĭt thar frĕnds̱ ; sŭm wĕr drovĕrs̱, ŏn thar wa tọ the wĕst, ănd sŭm wĕr hŭntĕrs̱ ănd botmĕn staĭng à hwil tọ rĕst.

Hwạt dĭd tha dọ hwĕn tha sạs̱ yu nŏk yur mĭstrĕs doᴜn?

Do ! hwȳ, tha wĕr goĭng tọ tak hĕr pärt, ŏv cors̱ ; bŭt I jŭst săt doᴜn the slŏp bŭkĕt ănd stratĕnd ŭp, ănd smăkt mȳ fĭsts ăt 'ĕm, ănd tŏld 'ĕm tọ wad ĭn, ĭf tha dard, ănd I'd thràsh ĕvĕrў dĕvĭl ŏv 'ĕm ; ănd thĕr wạs̱n't à dămd à wŭn thăt dard tọ cŭm.

Wĕl, hwăt nĕxt ?

Thĕn I gŏt oᴜt, ănd prĕtў qwĭk, tọ. I neᴜ ĭt wụdn't dọ tọ sta thar ; so I wĕnt doᴜn tọ Chenăng Point ; ănd thar wĕnt tọ wŭrk.

Hwar wạs̱ yur mästĕr, dŭrĭng thĭs fracŭs ?

He ! he wạs̱ gŏn tọ tĕnd cort at Wilksbar. He wạs̱ à grănd-jŭry-mán, ănd hăd tọ be gŏn à gọd mĕnў das̱. He ŏfĕn sĕrvd ăs̱ grănd jurў-mán, ănd thĕn he wạs̱ álwas̱ gŏn à wek or tụ. Thĭngs̱ wụd hăv gŏn bĕtĕr ĭf he hăd bĭn hom.

Hwĕn he cam hom, hwạt dĭd he do ?

He sĕnt for me tọ cŭm băk.

Dĭd yu go ?

Ov cors, I dĭd, I hăd tọ gọ ; I wạṣ à slav,
ănd ĭf I dĭdn't gọ, he wụd hăv brŏt me, ănd ĭn
à hŭrȳ, tọ ; ĭn thoṣ daṣ, the mästĕrs mad the
nĭgĕrṣ mind ; ănd hwĕn he spok, I neu I mŭst
oba.

Thĕm old mästĕrs, hwĕn tha gŏt măd, hăd
no mĕrcȳ on à nĭgĕr—tha'd cŭt à nĭgĕr ạl ŭp
ĭn à hŭrȳ—cŭt 'ĕm ạl ŭp ĭntọ strĭngṣ, jŭst lev
the lif—thăt's ạl ; I'v sen 'ĕm dọ ĭt, mĕnȳ à
tim.

Wĕl, hwăt dĭd yur mästĕr sa hwĕn yu cam
băk ?

He dĭdn't scọld me mŭeh ; he told me thăt,
ăṣ mȳ mĭstrĕs ănd I gŏt àlọng so bădlȳ, ĭf I
wụd tak mȳ ehild ănd go tọ Neu Jĕrsȳ, ănd
sta thar, he wụd gĭv me fre ; I told hĭm I wụd
go.   It wạṣ lat ăt nit ; he rot me à pàs, gav ĭt
tọ me, ånd ĕrlȳ the nĕxt mornĭng I sĕt out for
Flăgtoun, N. J.

It semṣ thăt yu gŏt àlọng wĭth yur mästĕr
mŭeh bĕtĕr thăn yu dĭd wĭth yur mĭstrĕs ?

Yĕṣ ; I gŏt àlọng wĭth hĭm, fĭrst rat ; he
wạṣ à gọd măn ; ănd à grat măn, tọ; ạl the
grănd foks lĭkt Mĭnĭcàl Dụbois.   Hwĕn the
grat mĕn hăd thar metĭngs, Mĭnĭcàl Dụbois
wạṣ ạlwaṣ ĭnvitĕd tọ be wĭth 'ĕm ; ănd he ạlwaṣ

wĕnt, to̤; he waṣ ȧwa frŏm hom ȧ grat del; he hăd ȧ grat del ŏv bĭsnĕs, ănd he waṣ non a̤l ovĕr the cŭntry̆. I likt mȳ mästĕr, ănd ĕvĕry̆ bŏdy̆ likt hĭm.

He nĕvĕr whĭpt me ŭnlĕs he waṣ s̄hur thăt I desĕrvĕd ĭt; he uṣd to̤ lĕt me go to̤ frŏlĭcs ănd ba̤ls, ănd to̤ hăv go̤d timṣ ȧwa frŏm hom, with ŭthĕr blak foks, whĕnĕvĕr I wa̤ntĕd to̤; he waṣ ȧ go̤d măn ănd ȧ go̤d mästĕr; bŭt, hwĕn he told me I mŭst cŭm hom frŏm ȧ ba̤l ăt ȧ çĕrtĭn tim, hwĕn the tim cam, the jĭg waṣ out—I neu I mŭst go; ĭt wṳdn't do̤ to̤ dĭsȧpoint Mĭnĭcȧl Dṳbois.

Dĭd pärtĭṣ ŏfĕn ŏcŭr?

Yĕs; ănd I a̤lwaṣ wĕnt, to̤; Old Mĭnĭcȧl wṳd a̤lwaṣ lĕt me go, becaṳṣ I waṣ ȧ go̤d ne- grĕṣ, ănd a̤lwaṣ trid to̤ pleṣ hĭm; I hăd go̤d timṣ hwĕn he waṣ ȧround, ănd he a̤lwaṣ dŭn thĭngṣ rit; bŭt yu mŭstn't gĕt hĭm măd.

In the lŏng nits ŏv wĭntĕr, we ŏfĕn hăd frŏl- ĭcs, a̤lmŏst ĕvĕry̆ wek; we'd härdly̆ gĕt ŏvĕr wŭn frŏlĭç wĕn we'd begĭn to̤ fĭx for ȧnŭthĕr.

Thĕn thĕr waṣ the holĭdaṣ—Crĭstmȧs, ănd Neu Yĕr, ănd Estĕr, ănd the Forth ov Jŭlȳ, ănd Gĕnerȧl Tranĭng. Bŭt, the bĭgĕst ŏv 'ĕm a̤l waṣ gĕnerȧl tranĭng. Thăt waṣ the bĭgĕst

da for the nĭgĕrs—I tĕl yu thăt wạs the bĭgĕst
da. The nĭgĕrs wĕr ạl out tọ gĕnerȧl tranĭng
—lĭtl ănd bĭg—old ănd yung; ănd thĕn tha'd
hăv sŭm rŭm—ạlwạs hăd rŭm ăt gĕnerȧl tran-
ĭngs—ănd thĕn yu'd hĕr 'ĕm lȧf ȧ mil—ănd
hwĕn tha gŏt ĭntọ ȧ fit, yu'd hĕr 'em yĕl mor
thăn fiv milṣ.

Dĭd the nĭgĕrs yĕl hwĕn tha fạt?

The couärds dĭd—wŭrs than ĕnȳthĭng yu
ĕvĕr hĕrd—wŭrs thăn ĕnȳthĭng bŭt ȧ couärdlȳ
nĭgĕr.

Hwar dĭd yu hold yur frŏlĭcs?

Thĕr wạs ȧ grat mĕnȳ nĭgĕrs ȧround the
nabŭrhọd ŏv Grat Bĕnd, ănd sŭmtims wĕ'd
met ăt wŭn mästĕr's hous, ănd sŭmtims ăt ănŭthĕr'ṣ. We wạs shụr tọ hăv ȧ fĭdl, ănd ȧ
frŏlĭk, ănd ȧ fĭrst rat tim; bŭt nŭn ŏv 'ĕm hăd
ȧ bĕtĕr tim thăn mȳsĕlf—I likt frŏlĭcs. I cụd
dȧnç ạl nit, ănd fel ăṣ jŏlȳ ăṣ ȧ wĭch ạl nĕxt da.
I nĕvĕr tird ăt frŏlĭcs—nŏt I; nŏr ăt gĕnerȧl
tranĭng, nethĕr.

Dĭd yu sa yur mästĕr uṣd tọ mak his on
brăndȳ?

Yĕs; he ŏfĕn mad ĭt—ạlwạs mad hĭs peȧh
brăndȳ; ĕnȳ wŭn căn mak peȧh brăndȳ—the
bĕst thăt wạs ĕvĕr drŭnk; yu jŭst bŭrn ȧbout

for pounds ŏv drid pĕehĕs ŭntĭl yu căn rŭb
them tǫ poudĕr ĭn yur hănds ; yu mŭst bŭrn
'ĕm ĭn à pŏt that hăs à vĕrў tĭt cŭvĕr ŏn. Thĕn
rŭb 'ĕm fin ĭn yur hănds ; or, ĭf sŭm peçĕs är
tǫ härd for that, pound them fin wĭth à hămĕr.
Thĕn pŭt thĭs poudĕr ŏv bŭrnt peehĕs ĭntǫ à
bărĕl ŏv neu ăpl hwĭskў, ănd ĭn for wĕks, ĭf yu
shak the bărĕl ĕvĕry da, yu wĭl hăv à bărĕl ŏv
peeh brăndў gǫd ĕnŭf for ĕnў bŏdў.

Yu mąk ăpl brăndў ĭn ąlmost the sam wa ;
yu bŭrn àbout for pounds ŏv ăpls drid wĭth the
skĭns ŏn. Mak them ĭntǫ poudĕr, ănd pŭt 'ĕm
ĭn à bărĕl ŏv neu ăpl hwĭskў, ănd shak the
bărĕl ĕvĕrў da for for weks. In for weks, yu
hăv à bărĕl ŏv ăpl brăndў bĕtĕr than ĕnў yu
ĕvĕr są. A lĭtl ŏv that wĭl mak à fĕlo tąlk—
ănd wŏn't bŭrn hĭs gŭts out, nĕthĕr. Foks
usd tŏ drĭnk brăndў rit àlŏng—drănk ĭt ĕvĕrў
da—drănk à plĕntў ŏv ĭt, ănd dĭdn't gĕt the
măn-à-poehe, nor the delĕrĭŭm trĕmĕns, nethĕr.
Hwў, the brăndў usd tǫ be gǫd—tastĕd gǫd,
ănd wąs plĕsent tǫ drĭnk ; yu căn't gĕt nŭn
sŭeh nou—nŏt à bĭt ŏv ĭt. A drĭnk ŏv brăndў
nou, bŭrns lik fir—bŭrns ąl the wa doun—gǫs
thrų the gŭts wŭrs than à shet ŏv rĕd-hŏt sănd
păpĕr.

SILVIA A FRE NEGRES.

Hou dĭd yu go tọ Flăgtoun?

On fọt, tọ be shụr; I cam rit doun thrụ the Beeh Wọdṣ, ạl ȧlon, ĕxçĕptĭng mȳ yuṇg wŭn ĭn mȳ ärmṣ; sŭmtimṣ I dĭdn't se ȧ pĕrsŭn for ȧ hȧf ȧ da; sŭmtimṣ I dĭdn't gĕt hạlf enŭf tọ et, ănd nĕvĕr hăd ĕnȳ bĕd tọ slep ĭn; I jŭst slept ĕnȳhwar. Mȳ babȳ wạṣ ȧbout ȧ yer ănd ȧ hȧf old, ănd I hăd tọ cărȳ ĭt ạl the wa. The wọd wạṣ fụl ŏv pănthĕrṣ, barṣ, wild-căts ănd wọlvṣ; I ŏfĕn sạ 'ĕm ĭn the datim, ănd ạlwaṣ hĕrd 'ĕm houlĭṇg ĭn the nit. O! thăt old pănthĕr—hwĕn he hould, ĭt mad the har stănd ŭp al ovĕr mȳ hĕd.

At Estŭn, I wĕnt on bord ov ȧ rȧft tọ go doun the Dĕlȧwar. A măn bȳ the nạm ŏv Brĭnk, hăd hĭṣ wif ănd fămĭlȳ ŏn bord ŏv ȧ rȧft, bound for Filȧdĕlĭfȧ; I wĕnt ŏn bord tọ hĕlp the wĭf, for mȳ păsaġ; tha wĕr niç foks, ănd I hăd ȧ gọd tim; I lĕft the rȧft nŏt fär

frŏm Trĕntŭn, bŭt I dọ nŏt no ĕxăctlў hwar—
thar wạs no toun ăt the plăç ăt hwĭch I gŏt ŏf
the ráft.

Thĕn I proçedĕd dirĕctlў tọ Flăgtoun, tọ se
mў mŭther; I dĭd nŏt fĭnd hĕr thar—she hăd
moyd tọ Neu Brŭnswĭk.   On mў wa, á măn
cạld tọ me, ăskĭng me, " Họs nĭgĕr är yu?"
I replĭd, I'm no măn's nĭgĕr—I belŏng tọ Gŏd
—I belŏng tọ no măn.

He thĕn sĕd : Hwar är yu goĭng ? I replĭd :
Thăt's nŭn ŏv yur bĭsnĕs—I'm fre; I go hwar
I plẹs.

He cam towärd me; I săt doun mў yung
wŭn, shod hĭm mў fĭst, ănd lọkt ăt hĭm; ănd I
gĕs he sạ t'wạs no us; he mozed ŏf, tĕlĭng me
thăt he wụd hăv me ărĕstĕd ăs sọn ăs he cụd
fĭnd á măġĭstrat.

Yu se thăt ĭn thọs dạs, the negrọs wĕr ạl
slavs, ănd tha wĕr sĕnt nohwar, nŏr áloud tọ
tọ go ĕnўhwar wĭthout á pás; ănd hwĕn ĕnў-
wŭn mĕt á negro whọ wạs nŏt wĭth hĭs mästĕr, he hăd á rit tọ dĕmănd ŏv hĭm họs negro
he wạs; ănd ĭf the negro dĭd nŏt sho hĭs pás,
or dĭd nŏt gĭv gọd ĕvidĕnç họs he wạs, he
wạs ărĕstĕd ăt wŭns, ănd kĕpt ŭntĭl hĭs mästĕr cam for hĭm, pád hwatĕvĕr chärġĕs wĕr

mad, ănd tǫk hǐm áwa. Yu se, ǐn thǫs daṣ, ĕnÿbŏdÿ hăd athŏrǐtÿ tǫ ărĕst vagrant negroṣ. Tha gŏt pa for ărĕstǐng thĕm, ănd chärgd for thar kepǐng tǐl thar mästĕr redemd thĕm. Bŭt, he dǐdn't ărĕst me—nŏt á bǐt.

Hwĕn I gŏt tǫ Neu Brŭnṣwǐk, I found mÿ mŭthĕr; sǫn áftĕr, I wĕnt tǫ wŭrk, ănd remand ǐn Neu Brŭnṣwǐk sĕvĕrál yerṣ. Frŏm Neu Brŭnṣwǐk I wĕnt tǫ Prǐnçtŭn tǫ wŭrk for Victŏr Toulan. I remand ǐn hǐṣ fămǐlÿ ă lŏng hwil; I wŭrkt for hǐm hwĕn Paŭl Toulan waṣ á child; I wŭrkt thar hwĕn he waṣ born. Victŏr Toulan waṣ á grat măn, ănd á gǫd măn; ănd he uṣd hǐṣ sĕrvánts wĕl; ănd Paul waṣ á nǐç boy, ănd Mădám Toulan waṣ á gǫd wǫmán; ănd I likt 'ĕm ąl, ănd ąl the sĕrvánts likt 'ĕm.

Aftĕr á lŏng hwil, I vǐsǐtĕd mÿ grăndfáthĕr, Hărÿ Cŭmptŭn, hǫ lǐvd ăt the forks ŏv the rod, ner thǐs plaç; he waṣ thĕn ăn old măn; tha sa he waṣ mor thăn á hŭndrĕd yerṣ old, ánd I gĕs he waṣ; bŭt he waṣ yĕt qwit ăctǐv; he wąntĕd me tǫ sta wǐth hǐm ănd tak cąr ŏv hǐm, ănd I stad; ănd ăt hǐṣ dĕth, I ǐnherǐtĕd hǐṣ prŏpĕrtÿ. I lǐvd ŏn the old homstĕd ŭntǐl á feu yerṣ ágo, hwĕn thĕm dămd dĕmocrăts set fir to mȳ hous, ănd bŭrnd ŭp mȳ hom ănd ạl thăt I hăd. Sĭnç thăt tim, I hăv lĭvd ăt thĭs plaç, wĭth mȳ yun̠gĕst dạtĕr.

Wĕl, Sĭlvĭă, yu hăv lĭvd á lŏn̠g hwil, ănd hăv sŭfĕrd á grat mĕnȳ hărdshĭps, ănd, I expĕçt thăt y̌u är tird ŏv lĭvĭn̠g.

No, I ant; I'd lik to lĭv ănŭthĕr hŭndrĕd yers yĕt—ănd I dŏn't no bŭt I wĭl, to; mȳ teth är god, ănd ĭf I căn gĕt enŭf to et, I dŏn't no hwȳ I shụd di; thĕr's no us ĭn din̠g—yu ant god for ĕnȳthĭn̠g áftĕr yu är dĕd.

Wĕl, Sĭlvĭă, I ĕxpĕçt yu är wĕl ăqwantĕd wĭth thĭs mountĭn, ănd wĭth ạl the foks thăt lĭv on ĭt.

Yĕs, I no ĕvĕrȳ fot ŏv it—ĕvĕrȳ hol ănd cornĕr ŏv ĭt; ĕvĕrȳ plaç hwar ĕnȳbŏdȳ lĭvs̠, or ĕvĕr hăs̠ lĭvd. And I no the foks, to; ạnd sŭm ŏv 'ĕm är prĕtȳ băd wŭns̠, to; ĭn făct, tha är ạl băd, ănd sŭm ŏv thĕm är wŭrs. Hwạt the dĕvĭl wĭl ĕvĕr do wĭth thĕm hwĕn he hăs̠ to tạk 'ĕm, I dŏn't no. Shurlȳ he dŏn't wạnt 'ĕm, ănd wụdn't hăv 'ĕm ĭf he cụd help ĭt. The onlȳ resŭn thăt sŭm ŏv thĕs̠ foks ŭp her dŏn't di sonĕr thăn tha do ĭs̠, the dĕvĭl wŏn't hăv thĕm; He jŭst pụts ŏf tăken thĕm, becạs he nos̠ hwạt á tim he'l hăv hwĕn he gĕts 'ĕm. Hwȳ! sŭm

ŏv thĕm är stärvd tọ dĕth lŏng enŭf befor tha
di ; bŭt, tha căn't di—thĕr's no plaç for thĕm
tọ go tọ åftĕr tha är dĕd. Tha ȧn't fit tọ go tọ
hĕvĕn, ănd the dĕvĭl wŏn't hăv 'ĕm, ănd so tha
hăv tọ sta her. Hwȳ, thĭs mountĭn ĭs wŭrs thăn
hĕl ĭtsĕlf ; hwȳ, ĭf sŭm ŏv thes foks don't behav bĕtĕr, åftĕr tha go ĭntọ the ĭnfĕrnȧl regŭns
thăn tha do hwil her, the dĕvĭl wĭl hăv ȧ tim ŏv
ĭt.   He'l nĕvĕr mănag 'ĕm ; he'l hăv tọ cạl ȧ
cŏngrĕs ănd hăv ăn ȧmĕndmĕnt fĭxt tọ the
cŏnstitushŭn.   A brĭmston fir won't dọ ; ĭt wĭl
nĕvĕr faz 'ĕm ; ĭt don't her. I'v sen ĭt trĭd, ănd
ĭt don't dọ ăt ạl—onlȳ maks 'ĕm wŭrs.

Wĕl, Sĭlvĭȧ, yu tĕl ȧ prĕtȳ härd storȳ åbout
yur nabŭrs.

Tĕl ȧ härd storȳ ! I tĕl the trụth ; ănd I cụd
tĕl mor ŏv ĭt ; hwȳ, yu dont no 'ĕm ; thĕr ĭs
mor foks kĭld ŭp her thăn ĕnȳbŏdȳ nos ŏv ; ănd
yu no sŭmbŏdȳ ĭs kĭld ŭp her ĕvĕrȳ yer ; ănd
nobŏdȳ ĭs ĕvĕr hăngd for ĭt ; ănd ĭt gĕts wŭrs
ănd wŭrs.   If tha kĭl ĕnȳbŏdȳ ŭp her, tha jŭst
tak the mŭrdĕrĕrs ŏf tọ Flĕmĭngtŭn ănd kĕp
'ĕm ĭn jal åhwil tĭl tha hăv ȧ triȧl, ănd then tha
tŭrn 'ĕm out tọ cŭm băk her, ănd thĕn tha är
wŭrs thăn tha wĕr befor ; tha jŭst kĭl ĕnȳbŏdȳ
thĕn.

And tha stel! hwȳ, yu wŭd'nt belev hou mŭeh tha stel; tha don't stel mŭeh ŏv wŭn ănŭthĕr, becạs thăt wŭldn't do; ĭf tha wĕr cạt ăt thăt, tha'd gĕt kĭld dămd son, ănd thĕn tha 'ant gŏt mŭeh to be stold. Bŭt tha go ŏf frŏm the mountĭn, doun ĭnto the vălĭs, ănd thar tha stel ĕnȳthĭng tha căn find—shĕp ănd ehĭckĕns, ănd gran, ănd met, ănd cloths—ănd ĕnȳthĭng ĕls thăt tha căn et or war; ănd, nobŏdȳ căn find ĕnȳthĭng thăt hăs bĭn stolĕn bȳ the foks ŭp her, for, hwĕn ĕnȳthĭng ĭs to be stolĕn, tha ạl no ábout ĭt, ănd tha ạl lȳ for eeh ŭthĕr, ănd tha ạl no hwar ĭt ĭs to be hĭd, ănd tha ạl hĕlp to kep foks frọm findĭng ĭt; so ĭt dŭs no gọd to hŭnt ŭp her for stolĕn gọds. And thĕn tha no so dămd wĕl hou to hid thĭngs, to; tha don't hid hwạt tha stel, ĭn thar housĕs, ŭntĭl ạl the housĕs hăv bĭn sĕreht; hwĕn tha stel ĕnȳthĭng tha hid ĭt ĭn sŭm hol thăt nobŏdȳ bŭt mountĭnĕrs no ŏv; or ĕls ŭndĕr sŭm rŏks, or ŭndĕr sŭm wọd, hwar nobŏdȳ bŭt the mountĭnĕrs wụd thĭnk ŏv lọkĭng. Thăt ĭs the wa tha do bĭsnĕs ŭp her; ănd ĭf yu tĕl 'em ŏv ĭt, tha'l kĭl yu—dămd ĭf tha won't.

And Sĭlvĭå, yu hăv lĭvd rit her, ĭn the mĭdst

ŏv thĕm for fĭftў yerṣ wĭthout fạlĭng ĭntọ thar
waṣ?

Yĕs; ănd lŏn̯gĕr tọ. I no 'ĕm; I'v bĭn tọ
'ĕm—bŭt tha hăv nĕvĕr trŭbld me mŭeh—tha
no ĭt wụd'nt dọ; tha no I'd gĭv 'ĕm thăt.

(So saĭng, she brŏt hĕr rit fĭst ĭntọ hĕr lĕft
hănd ŭntĭl the smăk cụd be hĕrd fĭfty yärdṣ.)

Wĕl, Sĭlvĭȧ, hwạt dọ yu thĭnk ŏt tọ be dŭn
wĭth thĕṣ băd foks?

Ot tọ be dŭn wĭth 'ĕm? Hwȳ, sŭm ŏv 'ĕm
ŏt tọ be hăngd rit ŭp bȳ the nĕk; ănd sŭm ŏv
'ĕm ŏt tọ be tid ŭp ănd lĭkt nerlȳ tọ dĕth—tid
rit ŭp tọ ȧ post ănd lĭkt tĭl wĭthĭn ăn ĭneh ŏv
the lif. Thăt's hwạt ŏt tọ be dŭn wĭth 'ĕm—
thăt's the wa I'd sĕrv 'ĕm. I'd tak 'ĕm ŭp tọ
Flĕmĭngtŭn, ănd lĭk 'ĕm tĭl tha'd nĕvĕr wạnt
tọ be lĭkt ȧgĕn.

Hăv yu ĕvĕr bĭn tọ Flĕmĭngtŭn, Sĭlvĭȧ?

Bĭn hwar?

Bĭn tọ Flĕmĭngtŭn?

Bĭn tọ thăt dămd Flĕmĭngtŭn?—yĕs, I'v bĭn
thar; ănd ĭt ĭṣ the dămdĕst plaç ĭn the wŭrld.

Hwȳ, Sĭlvĭȧ, hwạt hăv yu ȧgĕnst Flĕmĭngtŭn?

I'v gŏt enŭf ȧgĕnst ĭt. Yu căn't gĕt ĕnȳthĭng thar wĭthout mŭnȳ; nobŏdȳ ĭṣ eŏnsĭd-

ĕrd ĕnȳthĭn̲g thar ŭnlĕs he hă̱s mŭnȳ; nobŏdȳ
wĭl tĕl yu ĕnȳthĭn̲g thar ŭnlĕs yu gĭv 'ĕm
mŭnȳ; ĭf yu a̲sk a la̲yĕr ĕnȳthĭn̲g, he won't
tĕl yu a bĭt ŭntĭl he gĕts yur mŭnȳ. Yu căn't
gĕt jŭstĭ̱c thar ŭnlĕs yu hăv sŭm mŭnȳ; ănd
yu căn't gĕt ĭt thĕn—beca̱s, ĭf ănŭther pĕrsŭn
hă̱s mor mŭnȳ thăn yu hăv, tha'l a̲l ŏv 'ĕm—
ĕvĕrȳ dămd la̲yĕr, the jŭd̲g, ănd the jury, go
for hĭm, ănd a po̱r bŏdȳ hă̱s no sho ăt a̲l. I no
'ĕm—I'v bĭn to̱ 'ĕm—thar a băd sĕt.

Hăv yu bĭn to̱ the la̲yĕr̲s ăt Flĕmĭn̲gtŭn,
Sĭlvĭa?

Yes, I hăv—bŭt, ĭt dĭdn't do̱ ĕnȳ go̱d; the̱s
dămd S——'s hăv bĭn trȳĭn̲g to̱ gĕt mȳ prŏpĕrtȳ awa frŏm me for mĕnȳ yer̲s, ănd I wa̲ntĕd
to̱ cŏnsŭlt a la̲yĕr to̱ gĕt hĭm to̱ pu̱t the̱s dĕvĭls
thru̱; bŭt I cu̱dn't; nŏt a dămd a la̲yĕr wu̱d tak
mȳ cas, bĕca̱s I hăd no mŭnȳ; thă sĕd tha cu̱d
nŏt ta̲lk wĭthout mŭnȳ; tha cu̱dn't do̱ ĕnȳ-
thĭn̲g for me ŭnlĕs I pad 'ĕm sŭm mŭnȳ.

Hwȳ dĭdn't yu pa thĕm sŭm mŭnȳ?

Pa 'ĕm! I cu̱dn't—I hădn't a cĕnt to̱ mȳ
nam.

Wĕl, Sĭlvĭa, hou dĭd yu fel hwĕn tha told yu
thăt tha cu̱d do̱ nŭthĭn̲g for yu wĭthout yu
gav thĕm sŭm mŭnȳ?

Fel! I fĕlt lik kĭkĭng thar dămd trips out. Tha thĭnk tha är so dămd bĭg becąs tha är drĕst ŭp à lĭtl; ănd tha är tǫ dămd proud tǫ be deçĕnt. If tha'd cŭm over ŏn the moun-tĭn we'd sho 'ĕm; we'd skĭn ĕvĕrȳ dĕvĭl ŏv 'em —I'd dǫ ĭt mȳsĕlf, ąs old ąs I ăm. I'd jŭst lik tǫ put mȳ fĭst àgĕnst thar ȳs (eyes).

(So saĭng, she brŏt the fĭst àgĕnst the hănd, ŭntĭl ĭt smăkt àloud.)

War yu ĕvĕr ăt Flĕmĭngtŭn hwĕn yu wĕr nŏt cŏnsŭltĭng ląyĕrs?

Yĕs, ŏ fĕn. I usd tǫ go hwĕnĕvĕr thĕr wąs ĕnȳ doĭngs thar; hwĕnĕvĕr thĕr wąs gĕnĕràl tranĭng, ănd hwĕnĕvĕr the bĭg mĕn hăd thar mĕtĭngs thar. Al the nĭgĕrs usd tǫ go tǫ Flĕmĭngtŭn ŏn thos bĭg dąs; ănd thĕn thad gĕt lĭkt—gŏd Gŏd, hou thad gĕt lĭkt! Hwȳ, thad ti'm rit ŭp ănd lĭck'm tǫ dĕth—cŭt 'ĕm ĭnto peçĕs—cŭt 'ĕm ąl ĭnto strĭngs.

Dĭd yu ĕvĕr se thĕm hwĭp the negrǫs?

Se 'ĕm! yĕs, I hăv; se 'ĕm lĭk à dŭzĕn ŏv 'ĕm ăt à tim. Ti 'ĕm rit ŭp tǫ à post, ănd gĭv 'ĕm hĕl, rit ŏn the bar-băk—fĕteh the blǫd ĕvĕrȳ tim; ànd tha'd hŏlĕr! Gǫd Gŏd! tha'd houl tĭl yu cụd her 'ĕm à mil; ănd thĕn, hwĕn tha hăd cŭt the băk ąl ĭn slĭts, tha'd put sąlt

ĭn the găshĕs̱ ; ănd thĕn tha'd houl, Lord Gŏd!
no pănthĕr ĭn the bĕeh wọds̱ ĕvĕr mad hȧlf so
mŭeh noi̱s̱.

Thăt's the wa tha fĭxt the nĭgĕr ĭn old tims̱,
thĕm dămd Flĕmĭngtŏnĕrs̱—tha thĭnk tha är
so dămd bĭg.

Hwạt dĭd the negros̱ dọ, thăt tha hwĭpt thĕm
so bădlẙ?

Hwẙ, ŏv cọrs tha'd gĕt sŭm hwĭskẙ, ănd thĕn
tha'd gĕt ĭntọ ȧ kĭntẙ-koy, ănd mak ă noi̱s̱ pĕrhăps; tha'd gĕt ĭntọ ȧ rou or ȧ fit, ănd thĕn sŭm-
bŏdẙ wụd gĕt hŭrt; ănd thĕn the wŭn thăt
gŏt hŭrt wụd cŏmplan tọ the ạthŏritĭs̱, ănd
thĕn the cŏnstȧbls̱ wụd be ȧftĕr the nĭgĕrs̱ ;—
and hwĕn tha cạt'm tha'd ti 'ĕm rit ŭp wĭthout
jŭdg or jụrẙ, ănd pụl ŏf the shĭrt, ănd pụt ĭt
rit ŏn the bar hid.   Mẙ Gŏd, hou tha'd lĭk 'ĕm
—cŭt the hid ạl ĭn găshĕs.

That's the wa tha us̱d tọ fĭx the old slavs̱;
gĭy 'ĕm ȧ hŏlidȧ tọ hăv ȧ lĭtl sport, ănd thĕn
ĭf tha hȧd čnẙ fŭn, lĭk 'ĕm tĭl tha'd hăv ȧ sor
băk tĭl the nĕxt hŏlida cŭm.

Wĕl, Sĭlvĭȧ, wụd tha wạnt tọ go tọ the nĕxt
hŏlidȧ?

Yes, the nĭgĕrs̱ ạlwas̱ wạntĕd tọ go, băk sor
or wĕl ; nĕvĕr neu wŭn tọ mĭs hwĕn hĭs̱ mästĕr

told hĭm he cụd go.   Thĕn he'd be shụr tọ gĕt
lĭkt wŭrs thăn he wạs befor; becạs sŭm nĭgĕrs
cụdn't hăv à hŏlidà wĭthout gĕtĭng ĭntọ à fĭt,
thĕn he'd be shụr tọ gĕt tid ŭp ănd lĭkt.

During the tim Sĭlvĭà wạs ănsĕrĭng the làst
few qwĕstyŭns, she bệçam so ĕxçĭtĕd, so ĕloqwĕnt ĭn hĕr own wa, ănd so ĭndŭlgĕnt ĭn hĕr
profan ĕpĭthĕts, thăt I ferd thăt I wụd nŏt be
àbl tọ tak doun ạl thăt she sĕd, nŏr be àbl tọ
fĭt ŭp for the prĕs hwạt I dĭd tak doun.   Inded, hwĕn she begăn tọ tĕl àbout the tretmĕnt
ŏv the negros during the das ŏv slavĕrў, she
ăt wŭns wăxt ĕloqwĕnt, ănd sọn becam so ve-
hemĕnt, thăt I dĭd nŏt no hwĕthĕr ĭt wạs wis
tọ prŏsecut mў ĭnqwirўs ĕnў fŭrthĕr ĭn thĭs dirĕcshŭn.   At ạlmost the fĭrst qwĕstyŭn, I thŏt
I smĕlt the fŭms ŏv brĭmston; ănd ạs we proçedĕd, the sulfŭrŭs odŭr bệçam so strŏng, thăt
I ferd thăt bў hĕr pouĕrful gĕstĭculàshŭn ănd
the pels ŏv hĕr tĕrĭfĭc lăngwag, she hăd rĕnt
the crŭst ŏv the crth sŭmhwĕr ner hwar she
săt, ănd the fums frŏm the ĭnfĕrnál regŭns wĕr
ăsçĕndĭng thrụ the fĭshŭr ĭntọ the àpàrtmĕnt
ĭn hwĭeh we săt.   Inded, the ătmŏsfer wạs dĕ-
çidĕdlў ehokў, ănd Ī shụd hăv àskt for à bĕtĕr

vĕntĭlashŭn, bŭt for the făct thăt, hwĭehĕvĕr wa I lọkt, the opĕn spaçẹs̱ betwen the lŏg̱s̱ álo̱ud me tọ se the swaĭn̲g fŏrĕst trẹs̱, ănd gav the perçĭn̲g wĭnd á fre cŭrĕnt tọ mȳ ehĭlȳ băk ănd tọ mȳ ehĭlĭĕr er̲s̱.

Reflĕctĭn̲g thăt thĭs, thĕn, nătu̱rálȳ wŭd be á lĭtl ĕxçĭtĭn̲g tọ ăn old slav, I cŏnclụdĕd tọ rŭn the rĭsk ŏv the swĭn̲g ŏv hĕr bĭg fĭst, ănd the ĭncresĭn̲g ehŏkȳnĕs ŏv the sŭlfŭrŭs ătmŏsfer, ănd proçẹdĕd ạ̱s̱ folo̱s̱ :

Wĕr yu ăt Flĕmĭn̲gtŭn hwĕn the lĭtl negro wạs̱ hăn̲gd for mŭrdĕrĭn̲g hĭs̱ mĭstrĕs̱?

Yĕs̱ ; ănd thăt wạs̱ the dămdĕst tim I ĕvĕr sạ. The nĭgĕr̲s̱ qwărĕld ănd fo̱ut, ănd po̱undĕd eeh ŭthĕr, ănd bĭt eeh ŭthĕr̲s̱ er̲s̱ ŏf ; ănd thĕn po̱undĕd eeh ŭthĕr̲s̱ nos̲ẹs̱ do̱un, bŭn̲gd eeh ŭthĕr̲s̱ ȳs̱ (eyes) ănd sŭm gŏt blamd ner kĭld. And thĕn thĕm dămd Flĕmĭn̲gtŏnĕr̲s̱ gŏt áftĕr 'ĕm, ănd tha tid 'ĕm ŭp, ănd lĭkt 'ĕm wĭtho̱ut mĕrcȳ—cut 'ĕm ạl ŭp—cŭt 'ĕm ạl ĭn strĭn̲gs̱ ; jŭst lĕft the lif—no mor.

Thăt wạs̱ á grat tim, I'l nĕvĕr forgĕt thăt.

Wĕl, Sĭlvĭá, dĭd the negrọs̱ nŏt desĕrv tọ be hwĭpt sŭmtĭms̱?

Yĕs̱, sŭmtĭms̱—mŏst ạlwas̱, I ĕxpĕct. Thạ

hăd tọ lĭk 'ĕm, thĕr wạs no ŭthĕr wa ; tha hăd
tọ mak 'ĕm mind ; the nĭgĕrs thăt behavd wĕl
nĕvĕr gŏt lĭkt ; bŭt sŭm wụdn't behav ; tha'd
ạlwas gĕt ĭntọ à rou, or stel sŭmthĭng, ănd
thĕn tha'd be shŭr tọ gĕt lĭkt.

Sĭlvĭà, tha sa thăt yu är vĕrў̃ old, ovĕr à
hŭndrĕd yers old—dọ yu no hou old yu är ?

Nŏt ĕxăctlў̃—căn't tĕl exăctlў̃ ; tha dĭdn't
uṣd tọ kep à rĕcŭrd ŏv the bĭrth ŏv nĭgĕrs ;
tha hardlў̃ kĕpt à rĕcŭrd ŏv the bĭrth ŏv hwit
chĭldrĕn ; nŭn bŭt the grănd foks kept à rĕcŭrd
ŏv the bĭrth ŏv thar chĭldrĕn—tha dĭd'nt no
mor kep the dat ŏv à yŭng nĭgĕr, thăn tha dĭd
ŏv à càlf or à colt ; the yŭng nĭgĕrs' wĕr born
ĭn the Fạl or ĭn the Sprĭng, ĭn the Sŭmĕr or ĭn
the Wĭntĕr; ĭn căbag tim, or hwĕn chĕrĭs wĕr
rip ; hwĕn tha wĕr plăntĭng corn, or hwĕn tha
wĕr hŭskĭng corn ; ănd thăt's ạl the wa tha
tạkt àbout à nĭgĕr's ag.

Bŭt, Sĭlvĭà, ĭs thĕr no wa tọ tĕl àprŏxĭmatlў̃
hwĕn yu wĕr born ?

Tọ be shur thĕr ĭs ; ănd thăt's hwạt maks
foks sa thăt I ăm à hŭndrĕd ănd fĭftĕn yers
old. Tha tĕl thĭs bў̃ the rĕcŭrd ŏv the bĭrth
ŏv Rĭchàrd Cŭmptŭn. Mў̃ mŭthĕr ănd mĕnў̃
ŭthĕr old foks, uṣd tọ tĕl me thăt, hwĕn mў̃

mŭthĕr wąs á slav tọ Rīehárd Cŭmptŭn, thĕr wąs born tọ hĭm á sŭn, họm tha cąld Rīeh-árd, áftĕr hĭs fąthĕr. Hwĕn thĭs sŭn Rīehárd wąs tụ dąs old, I wąs born; so thĕr ĭs bŭt tụ dąs dĭfĕrĕnç betwen the dat ŏv Rīehárd Cŭmptŭn's bĭrth ănd mȳ bĭrth.

In ăn old Bĭbl hwĭeh ĭs nou ĭn pŏsĕshŭn ŏv Mr. Rīehárd Gomo, họ lĭvs ner Rŏk Mĭls, ĭs the rĕcŭrd ŏv the Cŭmptŭn fămilȳ. Bȳ rĕfĕr-ĭng tọ thĭs rĕcŭrd tha tĕl họu old I ăm. Bŭt I dọ nŏt no họu old I ăm—I căn't red; bŭt I ĕxpĕct tha tĕl me rit. I no thăt I ăm oldĕr thăn ĕnȳbŏdȳ ĕls ăround her—oldĕr thăn thar parĕnts wĕr; ănd ĭn most casĕs, I nou thar grat-gránd parĕnts.

I remĕmbĕr thăt hwil we wĕr smąl ehĭldrĕn, I ănd Rīehárd Cŭmptŭn wĕr ábout ŏv á siz, ănd thăt we ụsd tọ pla togĕthĕr. Mȳ mŭthĕr ănd hĭs mŭthĕr ụsd tọ tĕl me thăt we both nŭrst the sam brĕst, ăltĕrnatlȳ, the sam da; ăs we wĕr so ner the sam ag, hwĕn hĭs mŭthĕr wĭsht tọ go áwă tọ vĭsĭt, or ŭpŏn bĭsnĕs, Rīeh-árd wąs lĕft ĭn the car ŏv mȳ mŭthĕr; ănd whil hĭs mŭthĕr wąs áwa, he ụsd tọ nŭrs mȳ mŭthĕr wĭth me. Wŭns, Mrs. Cŭmptŭn ănd wŭn ŏv the nabors wąs gŏn tọ the cĭtȳ á hol

wek; ănd hwil gŏn, Rĭehȧrd wąş lĕft ĭn ehȧrġ
ŏv mȳ mŭthĕr. Thĕn she uşd tǫ tak ŭş
both ŭpŏn hĕr lăp, ănd hwil he wąş nŭrsĭng
wŭn brĕst, I wąş nŭrsĭng the ŭthĕr. Tha uşd
tǫ sa thăt thĭs wąş the reşŏn Rĭehȧrd ănd I
gŏt ȧlŏng so wĕl tǫgĕthĕr. Aş lŏng ăş he lĭvd,
he ȧlwąş clamd tǫ be ȧbout mȳ aġ, ănd we ȧlwąş vĭsĭtĕd, ănd we uşd tǫ tąk ovĕr the cĭr-
cŭmstȧnç thăt we uşd tǫ be tǫgĕther hwĕn we
wĕr babĭş, ȧnd hwĕn we wĕr ehĭldrĕn, ănd
thĭt we hȧd ȧlwąş vĭsĭtĕd, ănd ȧlwąş ĭntĕndĕd
tǫ vĭsĭt.

A grat mĕnȳ old foks uşd tǫ tĕl me that tha
hăd sen me nŭrs mȳ mŭthĕr ăt the sam tim
thăt Rĭehȧrd Cŭmptŭn wąş nŭrsĭng hĕr, ănd
thăt he ănd I wĕr ȧbout the sam ĭn aġ. Aş
we lĭvd ăt ȧ tăvĕrn, I ĕxpĕt foks są ŭs mor,
ănd thăt mor foks notĭçt ŭş thăn wųd hăv dŭn
so, ĭn ȧ lĕs pŭblĭc plaç.

Tǫ vĕrifȳ the stătmĕnts ȧbŭv mad, rĕspĕctĭng Sĭlvĭȧ'ş aġ, I vĭsĭtĕd Mr. Gomo to cŏnsŭlt
the ȧnshĕnt rĕcŭrd ŏv the Cŭmptŭn fămĭlȳ. I
sǫn lĕrnĕd thăt Mrs. Gomo wąş ȧ neç ŏv Rĭehȧrd Cŭmptŭn; thăt she wąş the dątĕr ŏv Rĭehȧrd Cŭmptŭn'ş sĭstĕr Dĕborȧ, hǫ wąş born

Jăn. 5th, 1793. Thĭs lădў, Dĕborȧ Cŭmptŭn, hăd mărĭd Vănlĭeu, bȳ hom she hăd Mrs. Gomo. Aftĕr Vȧnlĭeu's dĕth, she mărĭd D. Dănbŭrў. Aftĕr Dănbŭrў's dĕth, she lĭvd wĭth hĕr datĕr, Mrs. Gomo, tọ họm she uṣd tọ tĕl that hĕr brŏthĕr Rĭehȧrd, ănd Sĭlvĭȧ Dŭboiṣ, wĕr ȧbout ŏv ăn aġ. Mrs. Gomo, now ăn ŏld ladў, ĭnformṣ me, that sĕvĕrȧl old foks uṣed tọ tĕl hĕr hwĕn ȧ gĭrl, that hĕr Uncl Rĭehȧrd ănd Sĭlvĭȧ Dubois, wĕr ȧbout ŏv the sam aġ; that tha hăd sen both Rĭehȧrd ȧnd Sĭlvĭȧ nŭrs the sam mŭthĕr ăt the sam tim; ănd that her Uncl Rĭehȧrd uṣd tọ tĕl that hĭṣ mŭthĕr uṣd tọ sa that he waṣ tụ daṣ oldĕr thăn Sĭlvĭȧ.

It hăpĕnĕd that the old Bĭbl ĭn the posseshŭn ŏv Mrs. Gomo, dĭd nŏt cŏntan ȧ fụl rĕcŭrd ŏv the Cŭmptŭn fămilў; that thĕ rĕcŭrd her mad datĕd no färthĕr băk thăn the bĭrth ŏv Dĕborȧ Cŭmptŭn, hwĭeh ŏccŭrd äṣ ȧbŭv statĕd, Jăn. 5th, 1793; bŭt. Mrs. Gomo ĭnfŏrmd me that the old Bibl, hăvĭng the anshĕnt recŭrd for hwĭeh I waṣ sĕrehĭng, waṣ ĭn pŏsĕsshŭn ŏv hĕr datĕr, Mrs. Jŏn Elbĕrtsŏn, lĭvĭng ȧbout tụ milṣ est ŏv Rŏk Mĭlṣ. Upŏn vĭsĭtĭng Mrs. Elbĕrtsŏn, ănd statĭng the pŭrpos ŏv mȳ vĭsĭt, she kĭndlў prŏduçt the old bǫk, ănd wĕlcŭmd me tǫ the hŏspitălitĭs ŏv hĕr cŭmfortåbl hom. In thĭs rĕcŭrd, I found, ámŭng ŭthĕrs, the fŏlo-wĭng statmĕnt : Rĭeh-árd Cŭmptŭn born Märeh 3d, A. D., 1768 ; Dĕborå Cŭmptŭn, born Jăn. 5th, A. D., 1793 ; Hĕnç, we lĕrn thăt, wĕr Rĭehárd Cŭmptŭn stĭl lĭvĭng, hĕ wǫd be ålmost 115 yers old. Thĕn, ĭf tradĭshŭn ĭs trǫ, ănd, ĭn thĭs căs ĭt ĭs cŏrŏb-ŏrated ĭn so mĕnў was thăt I cănnŏt doubt ĭt, Sĭlvĭå Dǫbois wĭl be 115 yers old ŭpŏn the 5th da ŏv Märeh, 1883.

Sĭlvĭå ĭs ĭn gǫd hĕlth, ănd ĭn gǫd cŏndĭshŭn ŏv mind. Hĕr mĕmorў ĭs ĕxçĕlĕnt ; ănd she ĭs ăs mueh ĭntĕrĕstĕd ĭn the áfars ŏv lĭf ăs ĭs the mŏst ŏv pĕpl ăt thĭrtў-fiv. She lǫks ăs ĭf she mit lĭv mĕnў yers yĕt.

Untǫ Sĭlvĭå hăv bĭn born sĭx ehĭldrĕn : Mŏsĕs, Judĭth, Chärlŏt, Dorcŭs, Elĭzábĕth ănd Raehĕl. Raehĕl lĭvs ĭn Prĭnçtŭn. Lĭzĭ ons, ănd resĭds ŭpŏn the lŏt dĕscrĭbd ĭn this ärtĭel. Wĭth hĕr, nou lĭvs hĕr agĕd mŭthĕr. She ĭs á lärg ănd stout womån, ănd lǫks ăs ĭf she mit lĭv tǫ be ăs old ăs hĕr mŭthĕr. She ĭs wĕl prŏpŏrshŭnd ănd vĕrў ăctĭv. It ĭs sĕd thăt ĭt ĭs nŏt esў tǫ find evĕn ámŭng the "bǫlĭs," á măn thăt ĭs á măteh for hĕr, ĭn á hănd tǫ hănd

cŏnflĭct, or ĭn à fĭst fit. Pĕrhăps she ĭs ăs
ner. lĭk her mŭthĕr, ĭn bĭld, prouĕs ănd ĕndur-
ánç, ăs à dątĕr căn be ; she sems mĭld, cŏmpla-
çĕnt ănd cŭrteŭs. Bŭt, rųmŭr ses thăt she hăs
takĕn pärt ĭn mĕnў à priz fit ; thăt she hăs
nĕvĕr bĭn pärticulár hwĕthĕr the champeŏn ho
wąs tǫ met hĕr wąs mal or femal ; ănd thăt
she hăs sĕldŭm, ĭf ĕvĕr, cŭm out ŏv thĕ cŏntĕst
sĕcŭnd bĕst. It ĭs ąlso told thăt she hăs sŭmtims gŏn à lŏng dĭstánç tǫ met the champeŏn
ho dard tǫ chălĕng hĕr, or tǫ prevok hĕr ir.

Lĭzĭ Dųbois ĭs fär famed ăs à fŏrtun tĕl-
lĕr. Tǫ her hĕr dĕscănt ŭpŏn the evĕnts ŏv
hĭs lif, mĕnў à yŭng fĕlo wĕnds hĭs wa tǫ the
hŭmbl hŭt ŏv thĭs sabl ladў, ănd, elated wĭth
the ĭnformashŭn gand, drŏps hĭs peç ŏv sĭlvĕr
ĭntǫ Lĭzĭ's hănd, hăsts áwa tǫ wătch secrĕtlў,
the ŭnfoldĭng ŏv ĕvĕrў mĭstĕrў. Nor ĭs hĕr
stŏck ŏv lor bărĕn ŏv wĭcherў. Frŏm áfár,
the vŏtcrĭs ŏv wĭchcráft go tǫ Lĭzĭ ĭn qwĕst
ŏv nŏlĕg rĕspĕctĭng stolĕn gǫds, ănd ŭthĕr
thĭngs thăt är sŭposd tǫ be non onlў tǫ thos
ho är ĭn cŏmŭnĭcashŭn wĭth the spĭrĭts ŏv the
nĕthĕr ábods.

Lĭzi ĭs ábout 78 yers ŏv ág ; bŭt she ĭs so

wĕl prĕsĕrvd thăt she wụd pàs for å negrĕs ŏv
40. Hĕr ehăncĕs tọ lĭv tọ be 120 yers old, är
vĕrÿ gọd.

Sĭlvĭă, yu hăv ăn ŭnusụalÿ strŏng fram, ănd
yu hăv lĭvd tọ ăn ĕxcẹdĭnglÿ grat aġ; yu mŭst
hăv bĭn vĕrÿ prŏpĕrlÿ fĕd in ehĭdhụd, or ĕls
thĕs thĭngs cụd nŏt be. Upŏn hwạt dĭd tha
uṣ tọ fed yu, thăt yu hăv grŏn so lärġ ănd so
strŏng?

Tha găv uṣ Indĭăn dŭmplĭngs, sămp, pŏraġ,
corn-brĕd, potatoṣ, pŏrk, bef, mŭsh ănd mĭlk,
ănd nĭgĕr bŭtĕr; ănd we dĭd'nt gĕt å bĕlÿ-fụl
ŏv theṣ, sŭmtimṣ—I'v ŏfĕn gŏn tọ bĕd hŭngrÿ,
bŭt, 'twạs no uṣ tọ cŏmplan;—yu hăd yur
maṣur ănd yu gŏt no mor. Thăt's the wa tha
fĕd yŭng nĭgĕrs, ĭn old timṣ, bŭt tha mad 'ĕm
gro.

Tĕl me hou the dŭmplĭngs, pŏraġ, corn-brĕd
ănd nĭgĕr bŭtĕr wĕr mad.

Tọ mak ĭndĭăn dŭmplĭngs, scạld the ĭndĭăn
mel, wŭrk ĭt ĭntọ å bạl, ănd thĕn boil ŭntĭl
dŭn, ĭn the lĭqŏr thăt met—pork or bef—hăṣ
bĭn boild ĭn. Theṣ wĕr etĕn wĭthout ĕnÿ dĭp,
bŭtĕr or sạç.

Tọ mak sămp pŏraġ: Boil ĕqwàl pärts ŏv

bef ănd pork togĕthĕr, ŭntĭl dŭn; remǫv the
met ănd stĭr intǫ the lĭqǫr ĭn hwĭeh thĕ met
wąs boild, cors ĭndĭán mel, ănd bȯil tĭl dŭn.

Corn-brĕd wąs mad bȳ mĭxĭṉg eqwȧl masurs
ŏv ĭndĭán mel ănd rȳ mel togĕthĕr, ănd bakĭṉg
ĭn ăn ovĕn.

Nĭgĕr bŭtĕr wąs mad bȳ mĭxĭṉg tǫ pärts ŏv
lärd wĭth wŭn pärt ŏv molásĕṡ.

Thĭs nĭgĕr bŭtĕr wąs hwąt we hăd tǫ ŭṡ on
our brĕd; ănd we dĭd wĕl ĭf we dĭd'nt hăv tǫ
sprĕd ĭt duçĕd thĭn. The brĕd wąs so härd
thăt ĭt nedĕd gresĭṉg; ănd thĭs wąs ąl thăt we
hăd tǫ gres ĭt wĭth—we hăd no gravȳ.

We uṡd tǫ hăv piṡ ŏcąṡyŭnȧlȳ. Sŭmtimṡ tha
wɛr mad out ŏv swet ăplṡ; sŭmtimṡ out ŏv
sour wŭns, wĭthout ɛnȳ shụgȧr ŏr molásɛṡ;
dĭd'nt fed nĭgɛrṡ shụgȧr ănd molásɛṡ mŭeh ĭn
thoṡ daṡ; the hwit foks dĭd'nt gɛt mŭeh ŏv
'ɛm—thar piṡ wɛr ąlmost ăṡ sour ăṡ ourṡ; ănd
thɛr wąs vɛrȳ lĭtl shụgȧr ĭn thar cŏfe, ănd the
shụgȧr thăt tha uṡd wąs ăṡ blăk ăṡ mȳ hid.

We nɛvɛr drănk cŏfe or te. Sŭmtimṡ we
gŏt sŭm çidȧr. The hwit foks onlȳ drănk te
ănd cŏfe ŏn Sŭnda, or hwɛn tha hăd cŭmpánȳ.

Tha u̱s̱d to̱ boil, or rost our potatos̱, wi̱th the skins ŏn, ánd then we̱ dĭd'nt tak the skĭns ŏf, we at 'ĕm skĭns ănd a̱l. And the hwit foks at thar's jŭst so ; bŭt tha hăd gravy̆, or bŭter, to̱ pu̱t ŏn thar's̱. The hwit foks dĭd'nt et hwet brĕd only̆ ŏn Sŭnda, or hwĕn tha hăd cŭmpány̆. Tha ăt ry̆ bre̱d ; tha dĭd'nt cŭltĭvat mŭch hwet, 'twu̱d'nt gro ; nĕvĕr hăd mor thăn enŭf to̱ mak pi-crŭst ănd caks̱, out ŏv. Tha at a̱ grat del ŏv mŭsh ănd sămp po̱rag̱, ănd ĭndĭán caks̱, ănd thes̱ wĕr go̱d enŭf ĭf yu hăd a̱ plĕnty̆ ŏv go̱d mĭlk ănd bŭtĕr, and gravy to̱ et wĭth 'ĕm.

I ĕxpĕct foks nou-á- das̱, thĭnk thăt thĭs was̱ hărd far, bŭt 'twas̱ go̱d enŭf—hwĕn we hăd enŭf ŏv ĭt ; bŭt sŭmtims̱ we dĭd'nt gĕt a̱ bĕly̆-ful—thăt wĕnt a̱ lĭtl härd. If the foks nou-á-das̱ wu̱d lĭv ăs̱ we u̱s̱d to̱, tha'd be ă go̱d del strŏngĕr, mor hĕlthy̆, ănd wu̱ld'nt di so so̱n. Tha et so mĕny̆ dantĭs̱ ; to̱ mŭch shu̱gár, to̱ mĕny̆ swet pu̱dĭngs̱ ănd pis̱, to̱ mŭch rĭch cak, and to̱ mŭch frĕsh brĕd ; ănd tha drĭnk to̱ mŭch cŏfe ănd te ; ănd tha dŏn't drĕs wa̱rm enŭf; thăt călĭco 'ant the thĭng for hĕlth. We u̱s̱d to̱ war wo̱lĕn ŭndĕr cloths̱, ănd our skĭrts wĕr a̱lwas̱ mad ŏv lĭndsy̆-wo̱lsy̆. Our stŏckĭngs̱ wĕr wo̱lĕn ănd our shos̱ wĕr mad ŏv go̱d thĭck lĕthĕr, so hĕvy̆ thăt yu cụd kĭk å măn's trip out wĭth 'ĕm.

Thĭs ĭs the wa we usd tọ drĕs, ănd ĭt wạs å gọd wa tọ. The old mästĕrs neu hou tọ tak car ŏv thar nĭgĕrs.

We hăd gọd bĕds tọ slep ĭn; the tĭks wĕr fĭld wĭth strạ, ănd we hăd plĕnty̆ ŏv wọlĕn blănkĕts, ănd cŭvĕrlĕts, ăs tha usd tọ cạl 'ĕm. The firs wer ạl mad ŏv wọd, ănd ŭsuály̆ tha wĕr bĭg. The fir plạçẹs ŭsuály̆ ĕxtĕndĕd ĕntirly̆ ácrŏst wŭn ĕnd ŏv the kĭtchĕn—15 tọ 20 fet wid, wĭth lárġ ston jäms thăt mad 'ĕm 3 or mor fet dep, providĕd wĭth å chĭmny̆ thăt 2 or 3 cụd clim ŭp ănd stănd ĭn, sid by̆ sid. In the băk pärt ŏv thĭs huġ fir-plạç å lärġ băk-lŏġ,—ăs mŭch ăs tụ or thre cụd căry̆—wạs plạçt, ănd ŭpŏn thĕ händirŭns ănŭthĕr lŏġ cạld å for-stĭk, ăs mŭch ăs å măn cụd cărẏ, wạs plaçt; ănd thĕn betwen thĭs băk-lŏġ ănd for-stĭk wạs pild smạlĕr wọd, ŭntĭl ĭt mad å fir thăt wụd scar thĕ yŭng foks ŏv thĭs gĕnĕrashŭn out ŏv thar wĭts. Thĭs bĭg fir nŏt only̆ wạrmd, bŭt ĭt ạlso lited thẹ rọm. As å rul, the nĭgĕrs hăd no ŭthĕr lit, ănd no ŭthẹr fir thăn thĭs—tha hăd tọ sta ĭn the kĭtchĕn—thĭs wạs thar pärt ŏv the hous, ănd her tha hăd gọd tims, tọ. The hwit foks wĕr ĭn ănŭther pärt ŏv the hous, hwar the fir-plaç wạs nŏt qwit so bĭg. Sŭmtims the hwit foks hăd stovs; ănd thĕn tha litĕd thar rọms wĭth tălo căndls; thĕr wạs no kĕrosĭn thĕn, nor ĕnў col, tha dĭd'nt no hou tọ us sŭeh thĭngs.

Thŭs ĕndĕd our cŏloquў wĭth Sĭlvĭă Dụbois. As the da wạs fär spĕnt, we găthĕrd our utĕn-sĭls, drŏpt ĭntọ the hănd ŏv our agĕd hostĕs ăn ĕxprĕshŭn ŏv our ehărĭtў towạrd hĕr, băd hĕr gọd-bў, mountĕd our sla ănd sĕt ŏf tọ vĭsĭt Rĭehȧrd Gomo, ăt Rŏk Mĭls, to ĕxămĭn the rĕcŭrds ŏv the Cŭmptŭn fămĭlў. Hwĕn the rĕcŭrds hăd bĭn ĕxămĭnd, the nit wạs fȧst cŭm-ĭṇg on, ănd we hastĕnd towạrd Rĭngos. We ȧrivd hom ȧftĕr the shads ŏv nit hăd fụlў supĕr-vĕnd, tĭrd ănd hŭngrў, bŭt delitĕd wĭth the ăcqwisĭshŭns ŏv the da. The agĕd ănd car-worn vĭsag ŏv Sĭlvĭă Dụbois, hĕr hŭmbl hŭt and sparç fŭrnitur, hĕr shrĭl, stĕrn voiç hĕr pĕrt replis, hĕr qwĭk ănsĕrs, hĕr eherfụl dĭspoĭshŭn ănd hĕr cŏntĕntmĕnt wĭth hĕr lŏt, hạs formd ȧ pĭctur ĭn our minds so ĭndĕlȧbl, thăt tim wĭl nĕvĕr cras ĭt.

APENDIX.

———

Elĕvĕn mŭnths hăv ĕlăpst sĭnç the ritĭng ŏv the preçedĭng pagĕs, ănd stĭl Sĭlvĭă Dubois lĭvs—hal, hărtў, wĭtў, ănd ăs piŭs ăs ĕvĕr The flăsh ŏv hĕr ўe (eye) stĭl ĭs lik á glem ŏv á fălchŭn. Hĕr gat ĭs firm, hĕr voiç cler, hĕr herĭng ăcut, hĕr visўŭn ĕxçĕlĕnt. She ets wĕl, drĭnks wĕl, ănd smŏks bĕtĕr. Hĕr mĕmorў ĭs ĕxçĕlĕnt, ănd she taks ăs mŭch ĭntĕrĕst ĭn pásĭng evĕnts, ăs wŭd wŭn ŏv fŏrtў yers. She ĕnjoўs á jok ăs wĕl ăs ĕvĕr ; ănd tĕls wŭn wĭth ĕxçedĭng graç. Hĕr láf ĭs ăs ĭndĭkatĭv ŏv mĕrimĕnt ăs thăt ŏv á wĕnch ŏv aten. Inded, Sĭlvĭă ĭs áliv yĕt.

Sĭlvĭă's god spĭrĭts do mŭch towards prŏlŏngĭng hĕr das. Hĕr mătĕr–ŏf–făct wa ŏv vuĭng lif, prevĕnts wŭrў, ănd keps the măshenĕrў ŏv hĕr sўstĕm frŏm frĭcshŭn. Thăt hwĭch wars out the măshenĕrў ŏv the hŭmán fram mor thăn ĕnў ŭthĕr wŭn thĭng (I hăd álmost

sĕd mor thăn al els cŏmbind) ĭş wŭrў. Frŏm
thĭs Sĭlvĭă ĭş ĕvĕr fre ; she hăş thăt fĭrm rĕli-
ănç ŭpŏn Prŏvidĕnç thăt ĕntirlў prĕvĕnts ĕnў
ánxietў ábout the futur. To find wŭn bĕtĕr
botŭmd ŭpŏn the Cālvănĭstĭc fath, ĭş nŏt eşў ;
she sĕş she gru ŭp ámŏng the Old Scol Prĕs-
bўtereáns, thăt she sa thar waş wĕr god ănd
thăt she ádŭptĕd thĕm—thăt ĭş, thoş ŏv thar
waş thăt sut hĕr ; she sĕş : If wŭn wĭl onlў do
rit, Prŏvidĕnç wĭl provid for hĭm. 'Tant no
uş to wŭrў—ĭt onlў maks thĭngş wŭrs ; lĕt cŭm
hwàt wĭl, yu'v gŏt to bar ĭt—'tant no uş to
flĭneh. Prŏvidĕnç noş bĕst—He sĕndş to yu
hwatĕvĕr He wants yu to hăv, ănd yu'v gŏt to
tak ĭt, ănd mak the bĕst ŏv ĭt. I'v alwaş gŏt
álŏng sŭmhou, ănd I alwaўs wĭl—bŭt sŭmtimş
ĭts prĕtў dămd hărd slĕdĭng, I tĕl yu.

Sĭlvĭă nĕvĕr fĭdgĕts. Hwĕn she sĭts, hĕr
hăndş rĕst ĭn hĕr lăp, ănd she ĭş ăş moshŭnlĕs
ăş á stătu. Hwĕn she stăndş, she¦ ĭş ăş fĭrm
ăş á tre. Hwĕn she waks, hĕr gat iş prĕcis ănd
ădroit. Hwil takĭng, she gĕstĭculats nŏt á lĭtl ;
bŭt ĭn the manuvĕrĭng ŏv hĕr hăndş, thĕr ĭş
mŭeh graç ănd märkt proprietў ; she ĭş a härtў
láfĕr, bŭt hĕr láf ĭş ágreàbl—ănd not vĕrў ăf-
ricănĭc—ĕntirlў fre frŏm thăt labĭál Gĭne-negro

làf—wạ, wạ, wạ, wạ! or thắt pălatál làf so pe-
culïär tọ the negro: yạ, yạ, yạ, yạ! In the ăct
ŏv làfĭng, hĕr hol fram ĭs ĭn moshŭn, so mŭeh
so, thăt wŭn mit thĭnk she'd shak the solş ŏf
frŏm hĕr shụş.

Wĭth ạl hĕr vivăçĭtў, she shoş declin. Durĭng the làst yer, she hăş gron old răpĭdlў—hăş
becŭm emàsheatĕd ănd sŭmhwạt boud. Färthĕr, hĕr mind shoş declin, ănd hĕr cŏnvĕrsashŭn ĭndicats that she ĭş vĕrġĭng towàrd the
end ŏv lif; she tạks mŭeh ŏv dĕth, ănd ŏv di-
ĭng, ănd semş wĭlĭng tọ di. In the cors ŏv
cŏnvĕrsashŭn, she remärkt: "Nŭn ŏv ŭs hăv à
les ŏv lif; bŭt, I no I ăm old, ănd ăcordĭng tọ
the wa ĭt hăş bĭn wĭth ĕvĕrў bŏdў ĕls, I se I
mŭst di; I ma di vĕrў sŭdĕnlў—hwĕn nŭn är
ĕxpĕctĭng ĭt—sŭeh old foks sŭmtimş di vĕrў
sŭdĕnlў, bŭt, thĕrş no tĕlĭng àbout thăt.

Upŏn the fĭrst ŏv Novĕmbĕr làst, I cạld ăt
the hŭmbl mănshŭn ĭn hwĭeh Sĭlvĭă reşidş, tọ
ĭnqwir àftĕr hĕr hĕlth, hĕr wạnts, &c., &c. It
wạş evĕnĭng, ănd the shadş ŏv nit hăd wĕl ni
prevĕntĕd me frŏm fŏloĭng mў wạ; so, tọ mak
mătĕrs shụr, I wạş ĕscortĕd ovĕr the rọckў,
wĭndĭng pàth, bў à gid. Aftĕr sĕvĕrăl stŭm-
blş, ănd serătehĕş bў cĕdàr bŭshĕş, ĭn the dĭs-

tánç áperd á fant lit. Tọ thĭs, I sạ our gid wạṣ
ámĭṉg. It wạṣ the lămp thăt ĭlụmĭnats the
hŭt ŏv our hcroĭn; sọn we ărĭvd ăt the dor
wạṣ wĕlcŭmd ĭn, ĕntĕrd ănd stătĕd the rẹṣŭn
ŏv our crănd. The old lădy̆ săt ĭn hĕr ăcŭstŭmd plaç—ĭn the nĭeh bctwen the stov ănd
the wĕst wạl. Bcsid hĕr, I plaçt á prŏfĕrd ehar,
ănd bẹgăn cŏnvĕrsashŭn. She dĭstĭnctly̆ rẹ-
mĕmbĕrd my̆ vĭsĭt ŭpŏn the 27th ŏv Jănuary̆,
1883, ănd mŭeh thăt we tạkt ábout,—fạltĕd
me for nŏt hăvĭṉg cŭm tọ se hĕr sọnĕr, ănd ĭnqwird áftĕr the wĕlfar ŏv thoṣ họ wĕr wĭth me
durĭṉg my̆ lást vĭsĭt.

Upŏn ĭnqwiry̆, she ĭnfŏrmd me thăt she hăd
ĕnjŏy̆d gọd hĕlth—thăt she wạṣ strŏṉg ănd stĭl
cụd wạk á lŏṉg wa—thăt she hăd jŭst rcturnd
frŏm Härlĭṉġĕn—á dĭstánç ŏv 4½ mils. Tọ
be cĕrtán ăṣ tŏ the mănĕr ŏv retŭrnĭṉg frŏm
Härlĭṉġĕn, I ăskt hĕr:

Họ brŏt yu frŏm Härlĭṉġĕn?

Tọ thĭs, ĭn hĕr pĕculiár sty̆l, she replid: Brŏt
my̆sĕlf—nobŏdy̆ brŏt me!

Hwạt! dĭd yu wạk hom frŏm Härlĭṉġĕn thĭs
áftĕrnọn?

Tọ be shụr I dĭd; hou ĕls wọd I gĕt her!

Hwạt! à womán 116 yers old, wạk for ănd à háf mils ĭn ăn áftĕrnon?

Yĕs; thĕrs no ŭthĕr wa—I hăd tọ wạk.

Hou lŏng wĕr yu ŭpŏn the wa?

About tụ ours, I gĕs—we cam slo—hăd à gọd del tọ cărў—ănd I căn't wạk făst ĕnў mor.

Ar yu nŏt vĕrў tird?

No; I 'ant mŭch tird—I'm à lĭtl tird, tọ be shụr—ănd à lĭtl hŭngrў.

Hĕr dạtĕr (wĭth họm Sĭlvĭå lĭvs) semd tọ be găthĕrĭng hĕr wĭntĕr stor; ănd ĭn the lĭtl hŭt wĕr mor peçĕs ŏv fŭrnĭtur ănd bŏxĕs, thăn I hăd sen befor. A tăbl, à bărĕl or tụ, ănd à pil ŏv chĕs-bŏxĕs, wĕr croudĕd ĭn the băk pärt ŏv the rọm, ănd the spaç ĭn the lŏft semd vĕrў fụl. Inded, the lĭtl hous semd so fụl that thĕr wạs härdlў sĭtĭng rọm or stăndĭng rọm.

Elĭzàbĕth, ăs uṣuál, wạs lăvĭsh wĭth àpŏlogў. Hĕr hous wạs nŏt ĭn ordĕr,—ĭt nedĕd reparĭng —she'd hăd à cärpĕntĕr tọ veu ĭt tọ se hwạt cụd be dŭn; mămў's drĕs wạs old ănd răgĕd, and nedĕd wạshĭng; the fir wạs pọr—she'd nŏt yĕt gŏt hĕr wĭntĕr wọd, ănd hĕr stov hăd álmost gĭvĕn out—ănd I no nŏt hwạt thĕr wás for hwĭch she dĭd nŏt ăpŏlogiz.

Tọ mak ărangmĕnts for the Fotogrȧf ŏv our heroin, ŭpŏn the 20th ŏv Novĕmbĕr, I ȧgĕn cạld ăt hĕr dạtĕr's hom.   I found Sĩlvĭȧ ĭn hĕr ȧcŭstŭmd nĭeh,—wĭth hĕr hĕd ănd faç vĕrȳ mŭeh swolĕn, ănd vĕrȳ mŭeh mŭfld wĭth răgs ănd poltĭçĕs.   She hăd sŭferd ȧ sever qwĭnzȳ, ănd hăd nŏt yĕt fụlȳ recŭvĕrd hĕr hĕlth.   She wạs febl, ănd nedĕd sŭportĭng tretmĕnt.   Acordĩngly, I prĕscrĭbd for hĕr, ănd ădvĭzd hĕr dạtĕr hou tọ mănaġ hĕr poltĭçĕs, &c., &c. Hwil I wạs fĩxĩng hĕr mĕdiçĭn, Sĩlvĭȧ remärkt: I dĭdn't uṣd tọ gĕt qwĭnzȳ, nor ĕnȳ ŭthĕr kĭnd ŏv sor throt ; bŭt nou I'm old, ănd mȳ teth är out, ănd the wĭnd blọs rit doun mȳ throt, ănd I tak cọld.   Hwȳ! sŭmtims ĭt blọs cler doun tọ mȳ stŭmáç, ănd fŭrthĕr tọ ; hwi! ĭt blọs cler thrụ me.   Hwĕn I hăd teth, ĭt dĭd'nt uṣd tọ dọ so.

Arangmĕnts wĕr mad wĭth Sĩlvĭȧ tọ sĭt for hĕr fotogrȧf ăṣ sọn ăṣ she wạs wĕl enŭf to rid tọ the Artĭst's Gălerȳ.   Upŏn tĕlĭng hĕr thăt ȧ cărĭag wụd be rĕdȳ tọ tak hĕr ăt ĕnȳ tim, she replid :

I wạnt yu tọ ĭnform me ĭn tim for me tọ fĭx mȳsĕlf, ănd gĕt ŏn sŭm decĕnt clọs—thĕm foks ăt Lămbĕrtvĭl är ȧ proud sĕt—ănd I don't wạnt

tọ go doun thar lọkĭng jŭst ĕnў hou; I wạnt
tọ lọk prĕtў snĭpshŭs.

I replid :

I se, Sĭlvĭă, yu är sŭmhwạt proud ĭn yur
old das.

I ạlwas wạs proud,—ănd likt tọ ăper deçĕnt;
ănd I ạlwas dĭd ăper deçĕnt, wĕn I cụd; bŭt I
nĕvĕr drĕst beyŏnd mў mens—I wŭd'nt dọ
thăt!

At 10 o'clŏk, ŭpŏn the 30th ŏv Novĕmbĕr,
Sĭlvĭă săt for hĕr Fotogrăf. Altho wĕl ni 116
yers old, thĭs wạs hĕr fĭrst ĕxperĭĕnç ĭn lọkĭng
ĭntọ the ärtĭst's cămeră. Bŭt, the frŏntĭçpeç
ŏy thĭs vŏlum, gĭvs sŭm ideă ŏv the graçfụlnĕs
ŏv hĕr mănĕr ăt thes ădvănct yers. The pĭctur
shos thăt she wạs ả lĭtl tird. Thĭs wĭl be ĕx-
pĕctĕd bў ĕvĕrў wŭn, hwĕn ĭnformd thăt the
old ladў hăd rod ảbout nin mils betwen the tim
ŏv brĕkfăstĭng ănd thăt ŏv ĕntĕrĭng ĭntọ the
Artĭst's Gălerў. It ĭs nŏt liklў thăt so old ả
wọmản hăs ĕvĕr befor sĕt for ả fotogrăf; ănd
ĭt ĭs nŏt liklў thăt so old ả wŭn wĭl ĕvĕr pre-
sĕnt hĕr faç tọ the ạrtĭst's cămeră.

Imĕdĭatlў ăftĕr takĭng the nĕgătĭv for Sĭlvĭă's
pĭctur, the ärtĭst ădjŭstĕd the cămeră tọ the

faç ŏv Elĭzabeth, the yŭngĕst dạtĕr ănd cŏn-
stánt cŏmpănўŭn ŏv our heroin.   Thŭs á wǫmán ĭn the 78th yer ŏy hĕr aġ, ănd hĕr mŭthĕr
ĭn the 116th yer ŏv aġ, wĕr fotográft ŏn the
sam da.

GLENINGS.

About 21 yers ȧgo, the prăctĭç ŏv mĕdiçĭn brŏt me ĭnto ăcqwántánç wĭth mĕnў ŏv the mŏst agĕd pepl lĭvĭng ĭn the sŭthĕrn pärt ŏv Hŭntĕrdŏn ănd Sŏmĕrsĕt Countĭs, ănd the nŏrthĕrn pärt ŏv Merçĕr. Sĭnç thăt tim, ĭt hăs bĭn mў fortun to mantan ăn ăcqwantánç wĭth nerlў ạl the old foks for mĕnў mĭls ȧround. As I hăv ạlwas hăd ăn er for hĭstorў, ănd ĕs-peshălў ȧ dep ĭntĕrĕst ĭn ạl thăt relats to the hĭstorў ŏv mў nativ countў, ănd ŏv the pepl ho dwel her, I hăv ĕvĕr lĭstĕnd to, ănd ŏfĕn mad nots ŏv, the storĭs thăt the agĕd hăv told me. Hĕnç, I hăv slolў ăcumulatĕd ȧ stor ŏv făcts, sŭch ăs ĕvĕrў lŭvĕr ŏv hĭstorў cănŏt wĕl forgĕt —ĕvĕn ĭf he wạntĕd to.

Ov thes făcts, sŭm relat to the farĕst fazĕs ŏv lif—to heroĭc patrĭŏtĭzm, to hi-sold filăn-thropў, to ŭntirĭng devoshŭn to the Crĭstyȧn cạs, to fĭlyȧl ăfĕcshŭn ănd the lik; sŭm, to the

därkĕst. dreryĕst fazĕs̬ ŏv hŭmán-lif,—tọ sens̬
ŏv rĕvĕlrў̆, ăcts ŏv debäehĕrў̆, tọ sqwálĭd pŏv-
ĕrtў̆, tọ ȧbjĕct degĕneraçў̆, ănd tọ hanŭs crims̬.
Bŭt făcts är făcts; ănd, ĭt häs̬ takĕn ceh ănd
al ŏv thes̬, ănd thousánds̬ that är yĕt ŭntold
tọ form the livs̬ ŏv the çĭtizĕns̬ ŏv our countў̆
—the dọĭngs̬ ŏv the pepl ȧmọng họm we lĭv;
ănd no hĭstorў̆ ŏv our countў̆ căn be complet,
nor ŏv mŭch vălu ăs̬ ȧ rĕcord ŏv the livs̬ ŏv ȧ
pepl thăt dŭs̬ nŏt crŏnicl, ăt the sam tim, the
dọĭngs̬ ŏv the grat ănd the smạl, the rĭeh ănd
the pọr, the proud ănd the hŭmbl, the ĕxạltĕd
ănd the ăbjĕct, the vĭrtuŭs ănd the vĭçyŭs,
the frŭgȧl ănd the sqwạlĭd. Tọ ŏfĕn, hwạt ĭs̬
cạld hĭstorў̆, ĭs̬ bŭt the rĕcŭrds̬ ŏv the farĕst
făcts ŏv ȧ sĭngl famŭs ĭndĭvĭduȧl, or ŏv ȧ fav-
ord fĕw, hwĭeh lọk wĕl ŭpŏn papĕr ănd är ples-
ĭng tŏ the er, bŭt hwĭeh only rĕprespĕnt the sĭn-
tĭlashŭns̬ ŏv soçietў̆, or ŏv sŭm favŭrd ĭndĭvid-
uȧl, ĕntĭrlў̆ ignorĭng the dọĭngs̬ ŏv the másĕs̬,
ănd shŭnĭng wĭth dĭsdan, the deds̬, the pashĕnts
ănd the sŭfĕrĭngs̬ ŏv the pọr. Tọ ŏfĕn we
forgĕt thăt ĭt taks the pĕsĕnt ăs̬ wĕl ăs̬ the prest
ănd the prĕsĭdĕnt, tọ mak soçietў̆, tọ fŏrm the
Cŏnstĭtuȧnçў̆ ŏv ȧ Stat. Tọ ŏfĕn we forgĕt
thăt the degĕnerat, ănd the abjĕct är ĭndĭspĕn-

çibl pärts to soçietў,—that tha håv rits ănd privĕlags—ănd thăt tha är bŭt the countĕrparts ŏv the bĕst ŏv the cĭtĭzĕns ŏv à cŏmŏnwĕlth.

On thĭs ŏcashŭn, ĭt ĭs mў bĭznĕs to recŏrd the ăcts ănd saĭngs ŏv wŭn ho hăs nŏt bĕn ĭllŭstrĭŭs for fĭlănthropĭc deds. But, à stŭdў ŏv thĭs rĕcord—-ŏv thes ăcts ănd saĭngs—-ĭs wŭrthў, ănd wĭl wĕl repa ĕnў wŭn ho wĭshĕs to no the resŭlts ŏv à lif ŏv dĭsolŭtnĕs; ho wĭshĕs to se hwat ŭnbrĭdld păshŭns led to; ho wĭshĕs to no hou ăbjĕct ănd sqwålĭd à pĕrson căn be, ănd yĕt lĭv nŏt fär frŏm the farĕst fazĕs ŏv cĭvĭlĭzd lif.

Thăt mў redĕrs ma the bĕtĕr cŏmprehĕnd the lif ŏv the heroin ŏv thĭs tal, I wĭl gĭv à bref skĕteh ŏv ăn anshĕnt mountĭn tăvĕrn, wŭns famŭs for ĭlfam. Thĭs hous, tradĭshŭn sĕs, stod ŭpŏn the north sid ŏv the rod thăt ĕxtĕnds wĕstwård frŏm the Rŏck Mĭls, ner ĭts intĕrsĕcshŭn wĭth the rod thăt ĕxtĕnds frŏm Wĕrtsvĭl to Hopwĕl. It was the prŏpĕrtў ŏv à manŭmĭtĕd negro, ănd was cald Pŭt's Tăvĕrn—àftĕrwårds, Pŭt's Old Tăvĕrn; à prŏpĕrtў thăt Sĭlvĭă Dubois ĭnhĕrĭtĕd frŏm hĕr grăndfáthĕr, Hărў Cŭmptŭn.

The foundĕr ŏv thĭs hous, ănd for mĕnў yers

ĭts prŏprĭetŭr, waṣ the cărăctĕr ho fīgurṣ ĭn the
cōloquy̆, ĭn thĭs bok, aṣ Hăry̆ Cŭmptŭn, the
fīfĕr, ŏv not ĭn the ärmy̆ ŏv the Rĕvoluṣhŭn,
Hăry̆ waṣ à slav to Gĕnĕràl Rufŭs Pŭtnám, ho
sold hĭm to Căptĭn Ry̆ner Staṭs, ho sold hĭm
to Rĭchárd Cŭmptŭn, frŏm hom he bŏt hĭṣ
tim ănd becam fre. Aṣ Gĕnĕràl Rufŭs Pŭtnám waṣ hĭṣ fīrst mästĕr, ănd mor dĭstĭngwĭsht
thăn ethĕr ŏv the ŭthĕr tu mästĕrs, Hăry̆ waṣ
ŏfen cald áfter hĭs fīrst mästĕr, Hăry̆ Pŭtnám;
ĭnded, thĭs nám he prefĕrd. Acordĭngly̆, hwĕn
he becam the proprietor ŏv à hotĕl, ănd à măn
ŏv not aṣ à mountĭn tăvĕrn kepĕr, for short,
tha cald hĭm Hăry̆ Pŭt; ănd the hous thăt he
kĕpt, waṣ usuály̆ cald Pŭt's Tăvĕrn.

Hăry̆ Pŭtnám's hous, altho fär famd, ănd
mŭch freqwĕntĕd, espĕshăly̆ by̆ sportĭng cărăctĕrṣ, waṣ nĕvĕr liçĕnst. In ĕrly̆ timṣ, the sĕlĭng
ŏv hwĭsky̆ ănd ŭthĕr ĭntŏxĭcatĭng lĭqwĕrs aṣ à
bĕverag, waṣ aloud to almost ĕvĕry̆ wŭn—ŭnlĕs, by̆ so doĭng, the vendĕr becam vĕry̆ ŏfen-
çĭv. In the plaç, ĭn hwĭch Hăry̆'s hous waṣ
bĭlt, evĕn ăn ĕxtravĭgànç ĭn the sal ŏv lĭqwĕr,
or ĭn the dĕmŏnstraṣhŭnṣ cŏnseqwĕnt ŭpŏn the
us ŏv ĭt, waṣ lĕs likly̆ to be cŏmpland ŏv,
thăn to be ĕncŭragd. Cŏnseqwĕntly̆, ĭn peç

ănd prŏspĕrĭtў, he mănagd hĭṣ bị̆ṣnĕs, ăcumŭ-
latĕd wĕlth, ănd becam rĕnound. Hĭṣ hous,
fär removĕd frŏm the gaz ŏv the cŭlturd, ănd
the piŭs, becam the sen ŏv cŏk-fĭts, fŏx-
chasĕṣ, hŭslị̆ng machĕs, priz-fits, &c., &c. Inded, Pŭt's Tävĕrn becam famŭs ăṣ a plaç ŏv
rẹ̆ṣort for al sŭch ăṣ ĭndŭlgd ĭn sŭch gamṣ, or
likt to be prẹ̆ṣent hwĕr sŭch thị̆ngs trănspird.
It wạṣ the çĕntĕr for the dị̆solụt. Frŏm afär,
renound gamstĕrs cam,—ănd trădĭshŭn sẹ̆ṣ,
mĕnў wĕr the poundṣ, shĭlị̆ngs ănd pĕnç tha
cärĭd ŏf wĭth thĕm; ănd mĕnў wĕr the yŭng
mĕn ănd yŭng. wĭmĕn ruĭnd ĭn thăt hous.

At Put's Hous, cŭlŭr wạṣ bŭt lĭtl regärdĕd.
Blăks ănd hwits, alik, pärtọk ĭn the pástimṣ,
or the bị̆ṣnĕs, ŏv the ŏcashŭn. Thăt the blaks
wĕr regärdĕd eqwäl wĭth the hwits, thĕr ma be
sŭm dout; bŭt thăt the blăks wĕr ăṣ gọd ăṣ
the hwits, thĕr ị̆s no qwĕstyŭn. Bŭt be theṣ
thị̆ngs ăṣ tha ma, tha pretĕndĕd to ăsoshĭat
ŭpŏn tĕrmṣ ŏv ĕqwälitў,—to mŭch so for the
wĕl beị̆ng ŏv thĕr pŏstĕrĭtў.

Twĕntў yerṣ àgo I wạṣ fisĭshŭn to sĕvĕräl
old gamstĕrs, the mălädaṣ ŏv họm wĕr ĭncŭrd
bў freqwĕntị̆ng thĭs cĕlebratĕd hous ŏv ĭlfam,
ănd the cŏnseqwĕnt ĭntĕrcors wĭth sŭch ăṣ

cŏngregatĕd thar. Altho the mĭshăps ledĭng tọ dĭsēs ŏcŭrd durĭng boy-họd, or ĕrlўّ mănhọd, the mâteres morbi wĕr nĕvĕr erădicatĕd, ănd thes old ŏfĕndĕrs ŏv Natŭr's lạs, ăs tha grụ oldĕr, cŏnstăntlўّ nedĕd the car ŏv à mĕdĭcàl ădvisọr. Altho tha wĕr wŏnt tọ cŭrs the da tha lĕrnd tọ fŏĕnd, ănd deplord the sham ănd mĭserў hwĭch thar ŏfĕnçẹs hăd brŏt thĕm, yĕt ŏfĕn, hwil I wạs ĕngagd ĭn prĕparĭng medĭçĭn for thĕm, tha usd tọ delit ĭn tĕlĭng me ŏv the grănd old tims tha usd tọ hăv ĭn thar yŭng das, ăt Pŭt's old tăvĕrn. Nŏt wŭn ŏv thēs numĕrŭs bĭts ŏv hĭstŏrў ĭs fĭt tọ be recordĕd ĭn this nărătĭv ; ĕvĕrў wŭn ŏv thĕm wạs rĕvoltĭng tọ pepl ŏv cŭltur ; mŏst ŏv thĕm wụd shŏk the mŏdĕstў ŏv à Hŏtĕntŏt, ănd mĕnў ŏv thĕm wụd blănch the chek ănd chĭl the blọd ŏv the mŏst dĭsolụt. Tha wĕr sens pĕrpetratĕd bўّ intĕlĕctuàl, bŭt lud mĕn, ŏv the băsĕst‾pàshŭns, fĭrd bўّ hwĭskў ănd hilărĭtў, ĭn ăn ătmŏsfer ĕntirlў fre frŏm decĕnsў or sham. Thŭs lĕt lọs, ĭn cŭmpánўّ wĭth ther pĕrs, thar pàshŭns wŭrkt out sŭch thĭngs ăs cụd be dŭn onlўّ bўّ the most darĭng, the most lŭstfụl, ănd the most wạntŭn. Tọ thos họ no onlўّ à frăgmĕnt ŏv the hĭstorўّ ŏv this ănshĕnt hous, ĭt ĭs nŏt à wŭndĕr thăt

thĕr är so mĕnÿ shads̱ ŏv cŭlŭr ĭn the pŏpula-
shŭn ŏv the naburhọd ŏv çedär sŭmĭt, nŏr thăt
ĭn thos̱ ŏv litĕr shads̱, thĕr ĭs̱ so mŭch tĕndĕncÿ
tọ viç ănd crim.

Hărÿ Pŭt hăd ăn instĭnctĭv desir tọ be fre.
Beĭṉg ĭndŭstĭrŭs, frụgȧl ănd hŏnorạbl, he man-
aġd tọ bȳ hĭs̱ tim ŏv hĭs̱ mästĕr, Rĭehȧrd
Cŭmptŭn.   Chärcol beĭṉg mŭch ĭn demănd ĭn
thos̱ tims̱, he tŭrnd hĭs̱ ătĕnshŭn tọ the bŭrn-
ĭng ŏv colpĭts, ănd ăt the bĭs̱nĕs, ăcumulatĕd
ȧ lĭtl mŭnÿ.   Wĭth hĭs̱ ĕrnĭṉgs he pŭrehast ȧ
sit ănd erĕctĕd ȧ hous.   Hĭs̱ soshȧl qwȧlĭtĭs̱,
ănd the sŭplÿ ŏv lĭqwŭr ạlwas̱ on hănd, mad
hĭs̱ hous ȧ pŏpulȧr plaç ŏv resort.   Sọn he
found ĭt nĕçĕsarÿ tọ ĕnlärġ—so rapĭdlÿ dĭd hĭs̱
patrŏnaġ ĭncres ; ănd, fĭnȧlÿ, he found ĭt nĕçĕsarÿ tọ rebĭld.

The neu hous, tradĭshŭn sĕs̱, was̱ sŭmhwạt
pretĕnshŭs.   It cŏnsĭstĕd ŏv for lärġ rọms̱ ŭpŏn
the fĭrst flor, ănd ȧ hȧlf storÿ, sụtȧblÿ dividĕd
ĭntọ rọms̱, ȧbŭv.   Alŏṉg the ĕntir frŭnt was̱ ȧ
poreh ; ănd the wĭndos̱ ănd dors̱ wĕr ămpl.
Ner bÿ stọd the shĕds̱ ănd ŭthĕr nĕçĕsarÿ out-
bŭldĭṉgs ; the hol sŭroundĕd bȳ ȧ vĭrġĭn fŏrĕst
thăt ĕxtĕndĕd for mils ĭn ĕvĕrÿ dirĕcshŭn.

It ĭs̱ härdlÿ tọ be sŭposd, thăt Hărÿ Pŭt, ȧ

slav, ho's hi spĭrĭt prŏmptĕd hĭm to mak the săcrĭficĕs̱ nĕcĕsȧrў̄ to pŭrehas̱ hĭs̱ frĕdŭm, hăd ȧ vĭshŭs tĕndȧnçў̄. It ĭs̱ es̱ĭĕr to belev thăt he was̱ ăn ĭndŭstrĭŭs, ez̄ў̄-goĭn̲g, flĕxibl, fär-seĭn̲g negro, ho, ŭnscold ĭn ethĭks, ănd frĕshlў̄ lĭbĕrȧtĕd frŏm bŏndaġ, hăd nŏt ȧ jŭst ăprĕshĕashŭn ŏv fredŭm ănd mŏrȧlĭtў̄ ; ănd, wĭthal, ȧ strŏn̲g gred for gan, ănd ȧ dcsir to be pŏpŭlȧr. Thŭs, cŏnstĭtŭtĕd, he becam ȧ fĭt tol for sŭeh ăs̱ desird tŏ frĕqwĕnt ȧ hous so fär removd frŏm the gaz ŏv the la̱-ȧbidĭn̲g ănd the piŭs, thăt, hwil thar, thĕr păshŭn̲s̱ cud be ŭnbrĭdld, thar ăcts ŭnsen bў̄ the vĭrtuŭs, ănd thar deds̱ ŭn-non, ĕxçĕpt to the vasĕst ŏv mĕn.

The ġĕsts thăt vĭsĭtĕd Pŭt's Hous wĕr nŏt al frŏm the mountĭn, nŏr yĕt frŏm the ȧdjaçĕnt vălĭs̱. Fär frŏm ĭt,—frŏm Trĕntŭn tha căm, ănd frŏm Prĭnçtŭn, ănd Neu Brŭns̱wĭç, ănd Neu York, ănd Fĭlȧdĕlfĭȧ, ănd evĕn frŏm cĭtĭs̱ farthĕr ȧwa. The neus̱ ŏv ȧ cŏk-fĭt, ăn old gamstĕr ses̱, us̱uȧlў̄ sprĕd thru ȧ cŏmŭnĭtў̄ ănd reeht the ers̱ ŏv gămblĕrs, ĭn oldĕn tims̱, făstĕr thăn the stĭnk ŏv ȧ skŭnk trăvĕrsĕs̱ the ar ŏv ȧ vălў̄. The sam old wĭt ŭs̱d to sa, the er ŏv ȧ gamstĕr ĭs̱ ăs̱ sharp to her the report ŏv ȧ cŏk-fit, aṣ the noz ŏv a vŭltur ĭṣ tọ sĕnt a dĕd hors.

So, hwĕnĕvĕr the ar ŏv the mountĭn becam polutĕd wĭth the cŏncŏcshŭn ŏv a cŏk-fit, ĕvĕrȳ gamstĕr that snĭft the ar for a hŭndrĕd milṣ around wĭnded the gam, ănd, wĭth hĭṣ wĕneh or hĭṣ drăb, sĕt out for the mountĭn. Aṣ a cŏnseqwĕnç, a spekld host ăsĕmbld. The negro ŏv the mountĭn waṣ thar; ănd thar tọ, waṣ the negro ŏv the valĭṣ round about. The mountĭn bandĭt waṣ thar; ănd thar, tọ, wĕr thĕ bandĭtĭ ŏv the ădjaçĕnt vălĭṣ, ănd ŏv the nerĕr cĭtĭṣ. And thar, tọ, waṣ ĕvĕrȳ gămblĕr họ dwĕlt wĭthĭn a radĭus ŏv mĕnȳ a mil, họ cụd wạk or rid, that cụd posĭblȳ lev hom. The nĕgrĕs ĭn răgṣ, ănd the drăb ĭn brŏcad, ănd ĭn sătĭn; the negro wĭth hĭṣ păeht cot, the cĭtȳ băndĭt ĭn hĭṣ bevĕr sụt; the farmĕr gamstĕr ĭn hĭṣ lĭnsȳ-wọlsȳ, the mecănĭc ĭn satĭnĕt, drĭnk-ĭng ănd tạkĭng, làfĭng ănd shoutĭng, ĭntĕr-mĭngld ăṣ thọ ĕvĕrȳ elĕmĕnt ŏv dĕstĭncshŭn hăd bĭn remọvd, ănd the bĭṣnĕs ŏv lif waṣ onlȳ hilărĭtȳ.

I recàl a statmĕnt mad mĕnȳ yerṣ àgo, bȳ a vĕrȳ wŭrthȳ pashĕnt, respĕçtĭng a cŏk-fit that he wĭtnĕst ăt thĭs plaç, that ŏcŭrd ĭn hĭs boy-họd. The storȳ—or thặt pặrt ŏv ĭt hwĭeh I vĕntur tọ tĕl—rŭng thŭs : Hwĕn àboṳt 18 yerṣ old, I wạṣ sĕnt bȳ mȳ fàthĕr tọ se à cĕrtĭn mặn respĕctĭng à cĕrtĭn bĭṣnĕs. Hwĕn I àrivd at hĭṣ hoṳs, I wạṣ ĭnformd thặt he wạṣ nŏt ặt hom —thặt he hặd gŏn tọ Pŭt's Old Tặvĕrn tọ ặtĕnd à cŏk-fĭt. Acordĭnglȳ I dĭrĕctĕd mȳ wa thĭthĕrwàrd ; ặnd, hwĕn ner the hoṳs, I sạ à grat cŏncors ŏv pepl—ŏv ạl cŭlŭrṣ, ŏv ạl sĭzĕṣ, ặnd ŏv both sĕx. Tha wĕr ĭn the wọd, à lĭtl wa frŏm the hoṳs. Sŭm wĕr wĕl drĕst, sŭm wĕr sŭpĕrblȳ drĕst, sŭm wĕr bặdlȳ drĕst, ặnd sŭm wĕr härdlȳ drĕst ặt äl. Tha wĕr ĭntĭmatlȳ mĭxt—the răgĕd ặnd the dặndȳ. Her à wĕneh wĭth härdlȳ enŭf pặehĕṣ tọ kep the flĭṣ ŏf, stụd tạkĭng tọ à mặn drĕst ĭn cŏstlȳ brŏd-clŏth ; thăr à thĭk lĭpt negro, răgĕd ặnd dĭrtȳ, ặnd drŭnk, stụd tạkĭng wĭth wĭmĕn drĕst ĭn brŏcad, ặnd dĕkt wĭth the mŏst gạdȳ juelṣ. Her à grụp, boĭstĕrŭs ĭn makĭng bĕts, thar à bŭneh hĭlặrĭŭs wĭth fŭn ặnd rŭm ; yŏndĕr à rĭng förmd ăroṳnd tụ bụlĭṣ—wŭn à hwĭt mặn, the ŭthĕr blăk—fĭtĭng for no ŭthĕr reṣŭn thặn tọ se hwĭeh cụd hwĭp. Hwil, ĭn thĭs grụp ặnd ĭn thặt, wĕr hwit mĕn ặnd negroṣ, hwit wĭmĕn ặnd wĕnehĕs, wĭth scrặteht façĕṣ ặnd swolĕn ȳs̱ (eyes),—the resŭlts ŏv cŏmbăts thặt hăd gron out ŏv jĕlŭsў, hwĭskў, or the ĭntrĭg̱s ŏv shrụd mĕn họ likt tọ se fits.

The wọd wặs̱ vocȧl wĭth negro lȧf—yặ, yặ, yặ, yặ—ănd wặ, wặ, wặ, wặ; ănd wĭth shouts ŏv mĭrth ănd merĭmĕnt, ŏv ĭndeçĕnt sŏng̱s, ănd ŏv boistrŭs profănĭtў. A mor ȧpạlĭng̱ ănd ȧ mor dĭsgŭstĭng̱ sen, I nĕvĕr wĭtnĕst. I wặs̱ ŭpŏn ȧ hors̱; I dĭd nŏt dĭsmount. I ĭnqwird for, ănd found, the măn I wặs̱ sĕnt tọ se, trănsăctĕd, mȳ bĭs̱nĕs, rand mȳ hors̱ towärd the rod, ănd lĕft the wọd ĭn ŭtĕr dĭsgŭst.

Ov ạl the ĭnçĭdĕnts respĕctĭng̱ Put's Hous, thặt hăv cŭm tọ mȳ ers̱, the ȧbŭv ĭs̱ the mildĕst. Bŭt, the ȧbŭv ĭs̱ onlў ȧ pärt ŏv the storў; the rĕst ĭs̱ tọ därk tọ be told.

Thặt the hous wặs̱ bĕtĕr kĕpt ăftĕr ĭt dĕçĕndĕd ĭntọ the hănds̱ ŏv our heroin; or thặt the gĕsts thặt freqwĕntĕd ĭt wer ŏv ȧ hiĕr ordĕr, ĭs̱ mŭch tọ be doutĕd. Houĕvĕr, ĭts pŏpŭlărĭtў wand, ănd ĭts patrŏns̱ wĕr thos̱ ŏv lĕs̱ not. As̱ the demănd for tĭmbĕr ĭncrĕst, the wọd ŭpŏn the sid ănd the tŏp ŏv the mountĭn wặs̱ cŭt ȧwa; the sun shon ĭn ŭpon plaçĕs thặt hĭthĕrtọ wĕr därk, the lănd ĭn plaçĕs wặs̱ tĭld, çĭvĭlizashŭn ănd vĭrtu ĭncroeht ŭpŏn the ĕnvirŏns ŏv the sen ŏv the dĭsolṵt; Pŭt's Tăvẽrn becam ȧ thĭng ŏv ŏprobrĭŭm, ănd ĭn the yer 1840, ĭt wạ̱s bŭrnd tọ ăshĕs. Sŭch ĭs̱ the hĭstorў ŏv the hoṵs thăt wạs the ȧrenȧ, tradĭshŭn sĕs̱, ŏv the vilĕst dedṣ thăt wẽr ĕvẽr pẽrpetratĕd ĭn Hŭn- tẽrdŭn Coṵntў.

Sĭlvĭȧ mŭch cŏmpland ŏv the lŏs ŏv prŏp- ĕrtў ĭncŭrd bȳ the cŏnflăgrashŭn. Al thăt she hăd wạ̱s ĭn thĭs bĭldĭng; bĕds, chars̱, bọks, culĭnarў ăpȧratŭs, ănd hwạ̱tĕvẽr els ĭs̱ nĕsĕsarў tọ ăn outfĭt tọ kep ȧ moṵntĭn tăvẽrn. The cŏnflăgrashŭn ŏcŭrd durĭng hẽr ăbsĕnç. She stats thăt she ĭs̱ sătĭsfid thăt the hoṵs wạ̱s plŭndẽrd befor ĭt wạ̱s fird. In ĕvidĕnç ŏv thĭs̱, she stats thăt sevĕrȧl ärtĭkls̱ ŏv fŭrnitur ănd sĕvĕrȧl bọks,—wŭn ȧ bibl cŏntanĭng the fămilў rĕcŭrd, wẽr found scătĕrd ovẽr the moṵntĭn,— sŭm ĭn wŭn hoṵs, sŭm ĭn ănŭthẽr. Bŭt, ĭt sems, she wạ̱s nĕvẽr abl tọ rĕclam wŭn ŏv thĕs̱ thĭngs̱.

In Sĭlvĭȧ's da, Put's Tăvẽrn wạ̱s regärdĕd onlў ăs̱ ạ cak ănd ber hoṵs. Bŭt, thăt ŭthẽr drĭnks cṵd ŏfĕn bĕ gŏt thar, thẽr sems tọ be ăn abŭndȧnç ŏv ĕvidĕnç. Inded, on wŭn ŏca- shŭn, ĭt ĭs̱ sĕd, the hoṵs wạ̱s vĭsĭtĕd bȳ ăn ŏfĭcĕr ŏv the la̱, ănd the proprietŭr, fre ŏv charġ, ĕnjoyd a̱ rid to̱ the county set.

In hĕr da̱, Sĭlvĭa̱ wa̱s sŭmhwa̱t famŭs ă̱s a̱ bredĕr ŏv hŏgs̱. For thĭs bĭṣnĕs, the grat un-fēn̠c̣t mountĭn forĕst, wa̱s vĕry̆ favŭrabl. Hĕr hĕrd wa̱s ŏfĕn vĕry̆ larġ, ănd hĕr stŏck vĕry̆ notĕd. Ofĕn, to̱ ĭmpro̱v hĭ̱s bred, a̱ farmĕr wŭd go a̱ lŏ̱ng wa to̱ Sĭlvĭa̱'s hĕrd, to̱ bȳ a̱ hŏg. Nor dĭd he ĕxpĕct to̱ pŭrchas hĕr stŏk ăt a̱ lo fĭgur. She wĕl neu the vălu ŏv hŏgs̱, ănd a̱l-wa̱s̱ ġŏt a̱ far prĭc̣.

Aftĕr the bŭrnĭ̱ng ŏv Put's Tăvĕrn, I am told, tha̱t Sĭlvĭa̱ erĕctĕd ănŭ̱thĕr hous, ănd dwĕlt ŭpŏn the lănd tha̱t she hăd ĭnhĕrĭtĕd. Thĭs hous, ĭt ĭ̱s sĕd, wa̱s bĭlt ŏv c̣edärs̱. The ärcitĕctur wa̱s prĭmatĭv. The pols̱ ŏv hwĭch ĭt wa̱s mad, wĕr cŭt about ă̱s lŏ̱ng ă̱s a̱ ral, ănd ăranġd sŭmhwa̱t aftĕr the pătĕrn fŏlod ĭn bĭld-ĭ̱ng the fram ŏv a̱ wĭgwa̱m. Thes̱ pols̱ wĕr cŭvĕrd wĭth c̣edär brŭsh, ănd the lik, ăranġd sŭm-hwa̱t aftĕr the mănĕr ŏv fĭxĭ̱ng stra̱ ĭn thăch-ĭ̱ng a̱ rŭf.

Hwa̱t the fŭrnĭtur ŏv thĭs hous wa̱s, I hăv fald to̱ lĕrn. Bŭt, tha̱t ĭt wa̱s ampl, ănd tha̱t the ĕdifíç wa̱s̱ spashŭs, ănd cŭmfortábl, thĕr căṇ be no do̱ut. Nor căn ĭt be do̱utĕd thăt Sĭlvĭá wă̱s̱ ĕvĕr sĕlfĭsh, or ĭnhŏspĭtábl. Evĕn hĕr so̱w ănd pĭgs̱, ĭt ĭs̱ sĕd, shard wĭth hĕr the cŭmforts ŏv hĕr mănshŭn. Nor dĭd she cŏm-pĕl hĕr chĭckĕns to go to̱ ăn o̱ut-bĭldĭng, or á tre, to̱ ro̱st; bŭt, cŏnsĭdĕrat ănd cŏnsĕrvatĭv, she mad eeh wŭn fel ăt hom beneth hĕr hospĭt-ábl ro̱f.

Thŭs ăt peç wĭth best ănd fo̱ul, Sĭlvĭá, for á hwil, spĕnt hĕr da̱s̱. Bŭt, pĕrpĕtuál ănd ŭn-sŭled hăpĭnĕs hă̱s̱ nŏt bĭn bĕqwetht to̱ ĕnỹ mortál. Durĭ̱ng hĕr ăbsĕnç, sŭm vil ĭnçĕndu-arỹ fird hĕr dŏmicĭl, ănd Sĭlvĭá ágĕn wa̱s̱ hous-lĕs. Advánçt ĭn yeṟs̱, pĕnỹlĕs ănd dĭsmad, she ăçĕptĕd ăn ĭnvitashŭn to̱ abid wĭth hĕr da̱tĕr, ănd wĭth hĕr da̱tĕr she stĭl lĭvs̱.

OUR LAST VISIT.

———

Excĕptĭng the pagĕs rĭtn ŭndĕr thĭs hĕd. the mătĕr ŏv thĭs bǫk ĭs nou ĭn tȳp, rĕdў for the prĕs, ănd, bŭt for the prĭntĭng ŏv the pagĕs thăt I ăm nou ritĭng, Dec. 21st, 1883, the lást form ŏv thĭs bǫk wŭd go tǫ prĕs tǫ-da. Bŭt, çĕrtĭn çĭrcŭmstánçĕs sem tǫ wärĕnt á dela ŭntĭl I căn pĕn á feu pagĕs, ănd mȳ prĭntĕr căn pụt thĕm ĭn tȳp. Thes çĭrcŭmstánçĕs är ăs fŏlos :

Upŏn the nintĕnth ŏv Deçĕmbĕr, ŏcŭrd á sever storm, ănd durĭng ĭt, á sno fĕl tǫ the dĕpth ŏv sĕven ĭnehes. Tǫ ĕvĕrў wŭn ĭt semd thăt wĭntĕr hăd begŭn wĭth ĕxtrem vĭgŏr, ănd the thŏtfụl begăn tǫ mĕditat respĕctĭng the prĕpärashŭns tha hăd mad for the blĕk das ănd the frĭgĭd nits, ŏv thes trȳĭng wĭntĕr mŭnths. Our thŏts wĕr nŏt ĕntirlў cŏnfind tǫ our on cŏndĭshŭn, nor tǫ the prĕpárashŭns thăt we hăd mad for ourselvs álon. Amŭng the dĕstitut thăt ŏcŭrd tǫ our mind, wąs thăt agĕd ladў, the heroin ŏv thĭs vŏlum, Sĭlvĭă Dųbois, hŏ dwĕls wĭth hĕr fathfųl dątĕr Lĭzĭ, ĭn thăt Lĭtl Old Hŭt ner the tŏp ŏv the mountĭn. Tǫ vĭsĭt hĕr, tǫ ĭncŭraġ hĕr, ănd tǫ lĕrn hĕr neds, wąs qwĭklў detĕrmĭnd ŭpŏn, ănd the mornĭng ŏv the 20th ŏv Dec., 1883, wąs the tim ăpoĭntĕd tǫ pa our respĕcts tǫ hĕr aġĕd ladўshĭp.

The slaĭng wąs gǫd, the är sălubrĭŭs, ănd the senĕrў ĭnvitĭng. Altho the skў wąs ovĕr-căst, the da wąs delitfųl. It mŭeh reṣĕmbld thos qwiĕt, cloudў das thăt l uṣd tǫ se so ŏfĕn fŏlo à hĕvў sno-stŏrm ĭn Northĕrn Neu Yŏrk ănd ĭn Cănàda.

Nŏt wilĭng tǫ ĕnjoy the slaĭng àlon, nor the tret ŏv vĭsĭtĭng the hom ŏv thes aġĕd moun-tĭners, on mў wa, àbout 9 ĭn the mornĭng, I cąld ŭpŏn tu ŏv mў pashĕnts, Mrs. Rebĕcà Prąl ănd Mĭs Elizà Prąl, hǫm I ĭnvitĕd tǫ shar wĭth me, the evĕnts ŏv the da. Sǫn we wĕr ăs-çĕndĭng the slop ŏv the mountĭn. The prŏs-pĕct wąs delitfųl—à eherfųl wĭntĕr sen. Hi ŭp the hĭl, ŭpŏn à favŭràbl spŏt, we stŏpt tǫ yu. The sno-clăd plan beneth ŭs strĕteht àwa so gĕntlў thăt we cųd detĕct nethĕr rĭdġ nor mĕdo, nethĕr the cors ŏv the rods, nor the meănder-ĭng strems. The vĭlaġĕs thăt wĕr bŭt à feu mils áwa cud härdlў be distinguisht ; hwil thos hwïch wĕr bŭt lïtl färther ŏf, cud nŏt be dĕscrid—so cŏmpletlў wĕr äl things cuvĕrd wïth the neu–falĕn sno.   Towärd the northest, the plan semd intermïnâbl—streeht áwa wïthout hïl or val, ŭntïl the snoў ĕxpánc semd boundĕd bў the estĕrn skў.   Bŭt, ovĕr áganst ŭs, 15 mils áwa, ros ŭp the gracful form ŏv Lŏng Rïdġ, hwïch lïfts ïts gracful crĕsts ănd ïts bold sŭmïts to relev the veu ănd butïfў the lăndscap.

Son we reeht the crĕst ŏv Cedär Sŭmït. The senerў her, was espĕshálў dĕlitful.   The cedärs cuvĕrd wïth sno, semd things ŏv ärt ; hwil the hug round rŏks, wïth snoў băks, lŏkt lik the pïcturs ŏv houses ïn Arctïc sens. Thru the windïng wa we wĕndĕd our cors, amïd á fŏrĕst mostlў ŏv cedär, ŭntïl, ăt wŭnc, á mountïn vïstá căm to veu, ănd we lŏkt estwärd, fär out ovĕr á dĕlitful plan that streehĕs áwa ŭntïl ït ïs boundĕd bў the se. Bŭt son the vïstá was pást ; ănd ágĕn we wound áround hug rŏks ănd thru thïkĕts ŏv cedärs, ŭntïl—Thar ! Hwat ïs thăt? Thăt sqwalïd hŭt bïlt ŏv lŏgs, ănd rŭft wïth bords—wïndolĕs ănd chïmnўlĕs, ănd ïs fást yeldïng to deca ?

Thăt! Hwȳ, thăt's the mănshŭn,—the hom ŏv Līzĭ Dubois. Thăt's the hous yu'v longd to se.

We dĭsmountĕd frŏm the sla; bŭt, er we reeht the hous, Jo, the fathful dŏg, gav ă feu shrĭl bärks, ănd out căm the hostĕs to se hwạt wạs dĭstŭrbĭng the qwiĕt ŏv thår secludĕd hom. She mĕt ŭs wĭth à smil, ănd băd ŭs go ĭn. We ĕntĕrd, wĕr setĕd ner à vĕrȳ wạrm stov, found Sĭlvĭă ĭn hĕr ăcŭstŭmd plaç—betwen the stov ănd the wĕst wạl, begăn to ehat, ănd the tim påst plĕsĕntlȳ. Dirĕctlȳ, we ĭnqwird åftĕr the hĕlth, ŏv our host ănd hĕr agĕd mŭthĕr, ănd åftĕr ther sŭplis for the wĭntĕr. We wĕr ĭnformd thăt tha wer dĕstitut; —thăt tha wĕr ĭn wạnt ŏv mĕnȳ thĭngs—bŭt ĕspĕshălȳ, tha wĕr ĭn wănt ŏv wọd. Tha hăd ĕmployd sŭm hănds to cŭt thar wĭntĕr wọd—bŭt so fär, tha hăd fald to find tems to hạl ĭt hom. Bŭt, hwil tạkĭng, sŭm wŭn drov ŭp wĭth à lod ŏv wọd; ănd thĕn thĕr wạs grat rejoiçĭng; the old wọmăn ĕxclamd: Thănk hĕvĕn! I'm so glăd—nou we wĭl be abl to kep wạrm.

Sĭlvĭă hăd qwit regand hĕr hĕlth, wạs vĕrȳ cherful, ănd mŭeh ĭnclind to tạk; she ĭnqwird åftĕr the hĕlth ŏv mĕnȳ ŏv hĕr old ăcqwantånçĕs̱, ănd ĭn a̱l respĕcts s̱hu̱ thăt s̱he wa̱s̱ a̱liv to̱ the a̱fars̱ ŏv the da; s̱he ta̱kĕd ŏv the cŭmĭng holida̱s̱, ănd told ŭs hwa̱t go̱d tims̱ tha us̱d to̱ hăv durĭng Crĭstmás ănd Neu Yer; hou mĕnȳ pärtĭs̱ s̱he us̱d to̱ ătĕnd, hou tha us̱d to̱ dáno̱, &c., &c.

I remärkt: Dĭd I ŭndĕrstănd yu to̱ sa thăt yu us̱d to̱ dáno̱ ŏn Crĭstmás?

She replid: To̱ be s̱hur, we dĭd! Hwȳ! the old slavs̱ no mor neu the menĭng ŏv Crĭstmás, thăn the hŏgs̱ ĭn the pĕn! Tha onlȳ neu thăt ĭt wa̱s̱ a̱ hŏlida, ănd thăt tha wĕr tŭrnd lo̱s̱ for sŭm fŭn, ănd, ŏv cors, tha hăd ĭt; to̱ be s̱hu̱r tha dáno̱t. In thos̱ das̱ tha cu̱d dáno̱, to̱.

I sĕd: Thĕn yu thĭnk tha căn't dáno̱ now-à-das̱?

She replid: No; nŏt à bĭt; tha thĭnk tha căn; tha stŏmp, ănd jŭmp, ănd hŏp, ănd rŭn, ănd lik enŭf tŭrn hels̱ ovĕr hĕd; ănd tha ca̱l ĭt dáno̱ĭng; bŭt ĭt ĭs̱'nt dáno̱ĭng; tha don't no hou to̱ dáno̱; tha'v ġŏt no stĕps—tha don't no ĕnȳ stĕps.

Hwa̱t stĕps dĭd yu lik bĕst hwĕn yu us̱d to̱ dáno̱?

Wĕl; I likt the elĕvĕn tims̱, the twĕlv tims̱, ănd the thĭrten tims̱; thes̱ wĕr the bĕst stĕps for me; thes wĕr the stĕps thăt mȳ grăndfäthĕr, Hărȳ Cŭmptŭn, uṣd to̤ lik, ănd a̤l ŭthĕr go̤d dánçĕrṣ.

Wa̤ṣ Hărȳ Cŭmptŭn á go̤d dánçĕr?

Wĕl he wa̤ṣ! He wa̤ṣ cŏnsĭdĕrd the bĕst dánçĕr on the mountìn, or thăt hăṣ ĕvĕr bĭn o̤n thĭs mountĭn, or ĕnȳhwĕr ĭn thes pärts; I hăv sen hĭm hwĕn he wa̤ṣ old, dánç ăt Prĭnçtun; ănd ĕvĕrȳ bŏdȳ ho̤ sa̤ hĭm, sĕd he wa̤ṣ the bĕst dánçĕr tha ĕvĕr sa̤.

Wa̤ṣ Hărȳ Cŭmptŭn á lärġ măn?

No; he wa̤ṣ short, bŭt vĕrȳ stoŭt, ănd vĕrȳ strŏng; he wa̤ṣ cŏnsĭdĕrd the strŏngĕst măn o̤n the mountĭn; ănd tha uṣd to̤ sa thăt he wa̤ṣ the strŏngĕst negro that ĕvĕr lĭvd; ănd he wa̤ṣ vĕrȳ áctĭv; he cṳd pṳt ĕnȳ măn ŭpŏn the ground—hwit or blăk.

Sĭlvĭá, do̤ yu thĭnk yu cṳd dánç yĕt?

Yĕs; I cṳd dánç yĕt—onlȳ had á gṳd fĭdl—1 lik muṣĭc. A go̤d fĭdl a̤lwa̤ṣ stärts the ne-gro,—ĕvĕn ĭf he'ṣ old.

Wĕl! do̤ yu thĭnk yu'l dánç thĭs Crĭstmás?

Gĕs nŏt; gĕs I'd bĕtĕr thĭnk ábout sŭm-thĭng ĕls; foks ŏv mȳ aġ hăd bĕtĕr thĭnk ábout dȳĭng. Bŭt I lik to̤ se 'ĕm dánç—ĭt lo̤ks go̤d.

In the cors ŏv cŏnvĕrsashŭn, Sĭlvĭă ădvĕrtĕd tọ the dĭficŭltў she hăd hăd wĭth cĕrtĭn foks họ trid tọ sĕl hĕr lănd frŏm hĕr. Hĕr ӯs (eyes) sọn begăn tọ spạrkl, hĕr voiç grụ loud, ănd hĕr wŭrds mor bŭlkў ănd ȧ lĭtl sŭlfŭrŭs; she sọn coind sŭm prĕtў hărd ĕpithĕts, ănd uṣd thĕm wĭth no lĭtl forç.

I ȧskt hĕr: Iṣ the ġĕntlmȧn họ trid tọ sĕl yur lănd frŭm yu, lĭvĭng yĕt?

Tŭrnĭng hĕr faç towạrd me, ĭn ȧ vĕrў pŏsĭtĭv manĕr, she replid: Heṣ no gĕntlmȧn!—heṣ ȧ dămd răskl!

I sĕd: Wĕl, ĭṣ he lĭvĭng?

She replid: I don't no wĕthĕr the dĕvĭl hăṣ sĕnt for hĭm yĕt or not; ĭf he han't yĕt, he wĭl sŭm ŏv theṣ daṣ. He pretĕndṣ he'ṣ so dămd gọd; bŭt he'l nĕvĕr gĕt tọ hĕvĕn. Hwĕn he berĭd hĭṣ făthĕr, he wăntĕd tọ sho hĭṣ pĭety, ănd he hăd cŭt ŭpŏn the ornȧmĕnt (mŏnumĕnt, I sŭpoṣ) thăt he plaçt ŭpŏn hĭṣ grȧv, ȧ hănd, wĭth wŭn fĭngĕr pointĭng towạrdṣ hĕvĕn.— Thăt lọkṣ prĕtў wĕl; bŭt he ŏt tọ hăv hăd ȧ bŏtl ŏv hwĭskў ĕngravd jŭst ȧbŭv the ĕnd ŏv the fĭngĕr; thăt wụd lọk bĕtĕr; wụd be mor signĭfĭcȧnt —spĕshȧlў tọ thoṣ ŏv uṣ họ neu hĭm.

Hwȳ! wạs hĭs fäthĕr á bằd mằn, tọ?

No; hĭs fäthĕr wạs nŏt á bằd mằn; bŭt he dĭd lik á drằm ŏv hwĭskȳ most dĕspĕrat wĕl; ănd he cụd tak sŭeh á sokĕr, tọ.

Relȳ, hĭs fäthĕr wạs á gọd mằn,—wạs vĕrȳ gọd tọ the pọr—ănd we ạl likt hĭm. He wạs ằs mŭeh tọ be likt for hĭs gọdnĕs, ằs hĭs sŏn ĭs tọ be dĭspiṣd for hĭs bằdnĕs. The trŭbl ĭs, hwĕn the old mằn did, he tọk ạl thĕ gọdnĕs ŏv the fằmilȳ wĭth hĭm; hwạt ĭs lĕft behind ĭs nŭthĭng bŭt dằmd trằsh. Hĭs sŏn ĭs wŭrs thằn the dĕvĭl hĭmsĕlf, ănd wĭl ehet ĕnȳbŏdȳ he cằn.

Hwil tạkĭng, I hĕrd the voịçĕs ŏv ehĭkĕns. Tha semd tọ be dĭrĕctlȳ behind the ehar ŏv wŭn ŏv our pärtȳ. Tọ lĕt mȳ compằnyŭns se hou mountĭners car for thar poltrȳ, I sĕd: Don't I her sŭm ehĭkĕns?

"Yĕs—I gĕs yu dọ," replid Lĭzĭ. "We hằv tọ fĕteh our ehĭkĕns ĭn the hous ặt nit, tọ kep thĕm frŏm thevṣ. Tha stel ĕvĕrȳthĭng ŭp her, hwĕn tha cằn. So I jŭst pụt mȳ ehĭkĕns ĭn thĭs bŏx, ănd brĭng thĕm ĭn. Aṣ ĭt ĭs snoȳ to-da, I hằv nŏt pụt thĕm out; tha är nịç wŭns—yu cằn se 'ĕm." So saĭng, she razd the lĭd ŏv á lärg bŏx, ănd thar stọd the bĭrds ằs slek ằs dŭvṣ, ănd ằs dọçĭl ằs ehĭldrĕn.

Sĭlvĭa—do yu ĕvĕr ătĕnd ehŭreh?

Yĕs; sŭmtims. Hwĕn I was yung, I usd to go to ehŭreh vĕrў ŏfĕn; bŭt, nou I don't go vĕrў ofĕn. Thĕr ĭs no ehŭreh ner ŭs; ănd I căn't wak so fär ĕnў mor. I usd to wak ă god was to metĭng—to Pĕnĭngtŭn, to Prĭnctŭn, to Hopwĕl, ănd to Härlĭngĕn, ănd to cămp-metĭng; bŭt, I căn't wak so fär ĕnў mor. We usd to hăv metĭng ner bў, ănd thĕn I alwas wĕnt. Bŭt, the hwit trăsh brok our metĭng ŭp; ănd now I don't her preehĭng ĕnў mor—bŭt I'd lik to.

Dĭd yu sa yu usd to go to cămp-metĭng?

Yĕs; I alwas wĕnt to cămp-metĭng—spĕsh-álў hwĕn I was yŭng. Thăt was the bĕst kind ŏv metĭng for me—I likt thăt. I'd wak ten mils to á cămp-metĭng—fŭrthĕr to.

Tha usd to hăv grat tims at cămp-metĭngs. Tha'd tŭrn out frŏm ĕvĕrўhwar—both blăks ănd hwits. I'v sen 2,000 foks ăt wŭn metĭng. Thĕr was á cămp-metĭng ábout sĕvĕntў-fiv yers ágo, ábout four mils belo Trĕntŭn, ner á plac cáld Crŏswĭks; ănd I ănd sŭm mor ŏv our cŭlŭr, wĕnt doun; we wakt doun. Thăt was the bĭgĕst cămp-metĭng I ĕver ătĕndĕd, ănd the nicĕst wŭn, to. The cămp-ground was á mil lŏng—ănd tha hăd sŭch gọd ordĕr; thĕr wạs nobŏdў drŭnk, ănd thĕr wĕr no fits, ănd ther wạs no noĭs ŏv ĕnў kind, ĕxcĕpt hwạt the metĭn' foks mad—ănd tha hăd a bĭg tim—the bĭgĕst kind ŏv a tim; tha hŏlĕrd ănd shouted, tĭl yu'd thĭnk the dĕvĭl wạs ĭn 'ĕm. I nĕvĕr hĕrd sŭch shoutĭng—yu cụd her 'ĕm tọ Trĕn-tŭn; thĕr wĕr for pulpĭts—a gọd wa apärt—ănd for preehĕrs wĕr prĕchĭng al the tim. And tha hŏlĕrd, ănd the foks hŏlĕrd—gọd Gŏd, hou tha hŏlĕrd; I nĕvĕr sạ sŭch a tim—I gĕs no-bŏdў dĭd. I wĕnt tŏ sta al the wek, bŭt ĭn about thre das, I gŏt a bĕlўfụl ŏv ĭt, ănd mor tọ—ănd then I stärtĕd hom. And hwĕn I gŏt hom I gĕs I wạs glăd—I gĕs no nĭgĕr wạs ĕvĕr so glăd tọ gĕt hom. I gŏt enŭf cămp metĭng ĭn thos thre das, tọ làst a yer; bŭt the nĕxt yer I hĕrd ŏv anŭthĕr cămp-metĭng, ănd I wạntĕd tọ go jŭst ăs băd ăs ĕvĕr.

Dĭd yu sa the hwĭt foks dĭstŭrbd yur metĭng?

Yĕs; tha brọk ĭt ŭp. We usd tọ hăv a gọd metĭng ovĕr her, ner the Rŏk Mĭls; bŭt thĭs hwĭt träsh around her cụdn't behav.; tha'd cŭm into the metĭng-hous ănd tak rit out ĭn met-ĭng, ănd cal eeh ŭthĕr's nams—ănd dọ ĕnў-thĭng tọ dĭstŭrb us. And hwĕn qwạrtĕrlў metĭng cam, the hwit trăsh frŏm al ovĕr cam, ănd fĭld the hous ănd the spaç áround the hous, ănd behavd so bădlў, ănd mad so mŭch nois out ŏv dors, thăt we cud'nt hăv metĭng ĕnў mor.

Wĕl, Sĭlvĭă, thĭs ĭs á härd storў. It's á dis-graç to the mor respĕctábl hwit pepl ŏv the nabŭrhod, thăt tha hăv nŏt protĕctĕd the cŭlŭrd church. Cĕrtĭnlў, thĕr ĭs mŭch ned ŏv á church jŭst her; ĭnded, I no ŏv no plaç, hwar wŭn ĭs mor nedĕd. The pepl ŏv thĭs mountĭn, cĕrtĭnlў ned preching to; ănd ĭf the cŭlŭrd pepl trў to hăv á church her, thĕr ŏt to be re-spĕctábl hwit pepl enŭf to ĕnforç the la, ănd se thăt thar metĭngs är nŏt dĭstŭrbd. Thĭs mătĕr mŭst be lokt áftĕr; wĕ'l se ĭf thĭs church căn't be reorgánĭzd.

Hwĕn the tim árivd for ŭs to dra our vĭsĭt to á clos, we băd Sĭlvĭă ádu, ănd procedĕd towárd the sla. The päths wĕr nŏt shŭvld, ănd ĭn Lĭzĭ's ópĭnyŭn, thĕr was sŭm dangĕr thăt the ladĭs' ĭn wakĭng to the sla, wud gĕt thar shos snoў, and ăs á cŏnsĕqwĕnç, befor tha árĭvd hom, wud sŭfĕr cold fet. To ŏbvĭat thĭs dĭfĭcŭltў, the kind womán tok á bord frŏm the sĭd ŏv the hous, ĕxtĕndĕd ĭt frŏm the dor-sĭl to the sla, ănd thŭs secŭrd ŭs ágĕnst the ĕfĕcts ŏv the sno.

What is Said of the Book:

"The American Educator," Lockport, Ill.

We recommend this work very strongly as a help to all students of orthoepy, and as a great assistance to teachers in preparing lessons upon phonics. It contains excellent drills for the vocal organs, and is thorough in every department of the study.

" The Normal Teacher," Danville, Indiana.

Those who are pursuing this study, will find much in this book to interest them.

M. K. Reading, M. D., Nokesville, Va.

Any one can see that this book has grown up out of school room work. I like it for its arrangement, and for its excellent Hygienic and Physiologic teachings.

C. P. Hoffman, Professor of Music in the Bordentown Female College, Bordentown, N. J.

C. W. LARISON—*Dear Sir* : I have looked through your book quite carefully, a few times, and my general impression of the work is, that it is in a high degree logical, novel, and withal, practical. The diagrams of the elements of the language—vowels and consonants—are striking and entirely natural ; and, I confess to having perused this department with genuine pleasure. * * * The calisthenic maneuvers are the very best for the purpose. * * * I have a hearty good opinion of the book, and its practical adaptedness to the end aimed at.

R. F. Y. Pierce, Principal Reading Academy, Flemington, N. J.

DR. C. W. LARISON—*My Dear Sir :* I have carefully examined your " Elements of Orthoepy," and am greatly pleased with it. I am sure it will supply a long felt want, and trust that it may find a place in every school room.

" Journal of Education,"—New England and National.

This little manual was compiled by the author as a text book. The author has invented diagrams, suggested by the action of a tuning-fork in striking la, which shows the outlines of the vocal organs in representing the proper sounds. By the intelligent study of his diagrams, many things that seem obscure are made plain in the science and art of orthoepy. It is a manual that will be of great practical service to teachers.

THE TENTING SCHOOL.

The book entitled THE TENTING SCHOOL, describes :

1st. The outfit of the school, the carry-all and its arrangement, the tents and how to use them, the tent furniture and how to use it, the culinary apparatus, the instruments for geographic, geologic, botanic, zoologic, perspective and photographic work while in the field.

2nd. The party while working in the field and making excursions and tours.

3rd. An excursion to Pickle's Mountain and the work done by the teachers and students while upon the excursion.

4th. A tour of Central New Jersey, requiring eight days.

5th. In Appendix A, the cost of the tour and of the expenditure of the tourists, in an itemized bill.

6th. Appendix B is An Essay by Jennie Dilts, one of the students, entitled "Our Sail on Barnegat Bay," during the tour of Central N. J., read at the 7th anniversary of the Academy of Science and Art, at Ringos, N. J., July 12th, 1882.

7th. Appendix C, is An Essay, entitled "The Villages by the Sea," by Mary Rudebock.   This essay was also read at the 7th anniversary of the Academy, July 12th, 1882.

In printing the book, the type made expressly for printing the author's work on Orthoepy has been used. Hence, every vowel, and every consonant that needs one, has a diacritical mark to show just what sound it is intended to represent. In the orthography and utterance of the scientific and artistic terms, these diacritic marks are very valuable, showing at once, without consulting a Dictionary, just how each word should be pronounced.

The book is very fully illustrated by wood cuts, showing the form of apparatus and instruments, and of buildings, geographic areas, maps and the like, geologic sections, etc., etc.

The work is neatly and substantially bound in cloth, and will be sent prepaid to any address, on the receipt of price, $1.00.

Liberal discount to the trade.

Opinions of the Press and Teachers respecting "The Tenting School."

" Lambertville Record," *1883.*

THE TENTING SCHOOL is not a dry scientific work, alone interesting to teachers and schools. It will well repay any one to read it. It contains a great deal of useful information given in an entertaining way, with some spicy bits of description of characters met with, with excellent descriptions of scenery and popular explanations of scientific facts. Here and there are scraps of "word painting" that are unusually fine.

"Democratic Advertiser," July 28th, 1883.

After describing the necessary equipments for a tenting party, the author takes his readers on a tour through Central New Jersey, and by his very easy manner, conveys to their minds much instruction in the geography, geology, botany and zoology of that part of the State. He adopts the diary style, thus enabling his readers, in fancy, to travel with him over the route. Having descriptive power of a high order, he clothes his thoughts in glowing words that cannot fail to wake responsive throbs in the breast of every appreciative reader.

"Hopewell Herald, Aug. 1st, 1883.

The author of this book is an untiring investigator in all matters pertaining to the Natural Sciences. His zeal in the cause of education is well known, and his method of combining field practice and observation with the daily duties of the class-room, is attracting attention among other educators and scientific men.

" The School Bulletin," Syracuse, N. Y., Aug. 1883.

This book is unique. * * * We predict that any one who takes it up will read it through and think his time well spent.

" The Blairstown Press," Aug. 29th, 1883.

To teachers, a work of this kind must be very valuable.

WORKS PUBLISHED

BY

C. W. LARISON, AT RINGOES, N. J.

These Works are Printed in Phonic Orthography.

ANY BOOK SENT PREPAID ON RECEIPT OF PRICE.

DESCRIPTIVE CIRCULARS SENT UPON APPLICATION.

ELEMENTS OF ORTHOEPY.

The ELEMENTS OF ORTHOEPY was prepared
to be used as a text book in the Academy of
Science and Art, at Ringos, N. J.   A few volumes were sent to the editors of leading jour-
nals of education, and to such distinguished
teachers as are eminent for scholarship in the
field of English literature.   The reception of
the book has been so cordial, and the criticisms
upon its plan and the matter it contains has
been so favorable, that I have concluded to
place it in the market.

The work, though brief, covers the whole
field of Orthoepy.   To accomplish brevity and
at the same time perspicuity, the scientific
method is followed in every part.   The author
first deals with Phonics, the elementary sounds

of the language; then with Syllabication—the coalescing of the sounds into syllables; then with Articulation—the joining of the syllables into euphonic words; and then with Accent.

Under each heading, after the principles have been discussed, are enough examples to afford ample practice for the learner. And to afford scope in drilling upon difficult combinations of words, following the text is a collection of phrases and sentences that are difficult of utterance. In this collection of phrases, nearly all the orthoepical difficulties of our language are met and the ways in which they are to be overcome pointed out.

To facilitate the study of Orthoepy, the work begins with an introduction discussing Utterance and the Hygiene of the Vocal Apparatus, Calisthenic Maneuvers, Phonic Laughter, etc. This part of the book is especially valuable.

PRICE,   –   –   – $ .60

Sent pre-paid, by mail, to any teacher, on receipt of the price.

C. W. LARISON,

Publisher and Bookseller,

RINGOS, N. J.

" The Teacher," Philadelphia, Pa., Sept. 1883.

We commend the book to the careful notice of Principals of Academies, Seminaries, etc. It is descriptive of a highly interesting feature in school life, which would be followed to advantage in many of our schools, and which would prove an element of popularity with patrons and pupils.

———

" The Educationist," Topeka, Kansas, Sept. 1883.

The work gives some very interesting and somewhat humorous descriptions of places and people, as Long Branch and others.

———

From the Principal of The Female Institute, Lewisburg, Pa., Sept. 1st, 1883.

None will read this book, without a desire to accompany the author on one of these tenting tours.

KATHERINE B. LARISON.

———

From Lizzie M. Reading, Teacher of Cedar Grove School, Princeton, N. J., Sept. 3d, 1883.

THE TENTING SCHOOL is an invaluable work to the excursionist and naturalist.

THE
FONIC SPELLER AND SYLABATER.

This little volume has been prepared as an aid in teaching beginners to spell and pronounce fonically. It has been compiled and printed with much care and pains.

In arrangement, it is progressive. Thus:

1st.–The Fonic Alphabet is arranged by the side of key words, or words in which the exact pronunciation, or utterance, of each character used in the fonic spelling, is properly and distinctly sounded, thus enabling one to see at a glance just what sound is to be given to each individual character.

The Fonic Alphabet consists of the letters of the "English alphabet" modified by the affixing of suitable diacritic marks. In the main, the diacritic marks are the same as those used in Webster's Dictionary.

2d.—The spelling and syllabating exercises begin with the simplest sounds and the shortest words, homophonously arranged; then gradually the more difficult sounds and harder words are introduced; then words of two syllables, of three, four, five, six, seven and eight syllables homophonously arranged so far as respects the first syllable, thus leading the learner by degrees from the alphabet through the simplest combination of fons or sounds, to the most complex combinations and to the largest and most difficult words.

In this way, the child is taught, successfully, the science and the art of spelling and syllabating, and soon learns to master the most formidable words.

3d.—The reading exercises are carefully graded so that the pupil passes inductively from easy words of one syllable, to more difficult words.

Where properly used, the book cannot fail to greatly aid the beginner in acquiring a knowledge of the spelling and reading of our language.

The book will be sent by mail to any address, on receipt of the price, $0.25.

Liberal discount to the trade.